Eclipse of Empires

Eclipse of Empires

World History in Nineteenth-Century U.S. Literature and Culture

Patricia Jane Roylance

THE UNIVERSITY OF ALABAMA PRESS
Tuscaloosa

The University of Alabama Press
Tuscaloosa, Alabama 35487-0380

Manufactured in the United States of America

Typeface: Garamond

Cover photograph: "A Chart of History," by J. E. Worcester. From Worcester, Joseph Emerson, *Elements of History, Ancient and Modern.* Boston: W. J. Reynolds, 1850. Photograph by David Paul Broda of the Syracuse University Photo & Imaging Center, with assistance from William T. La Moy, Bird Library Special Collections Librarian.
Cover design: Todd Lape/Lape Designs

∞

The paper on which this book is printed meets the minimum requirements of American National Standard for Information Sciences—Permanence of Paper for Printed Library Materials, ANSI Z39.48-1984.

Library of Congress Cataloging-in-Publication Data

Roylance, Patricia Jane.
Eclipse of empires : world history in nineteenth-century U.S. literature and culture / Patricia Jane Roylance.
pages cm
Includes bibliographical references and index.
ISBN 978-0-8173-1382-1 (trade cloth : alk. paper) — ISBN 978-0-8173-8703-7 (e book)
1. American literature—19th century—History and criticism. 2. Imperialism in literature. 3. World history in literature. I. Title.
PS217.I47R69 2013
810.9'358—dc23

2013006460

The image appearing in the conclusion is a one-sheet for the film *Apocalypto*. Courtesy of Icon Entertainment, 2006.

For my family

Contents

Acknowledgments ix

Introduction 1

1. American Principles and Italian Things: Cooper's Political Gleanings in Italy 20
2. Calculating the Consequences: Property Fears in Prescott's *Conquest of Peru* 45
3. Inquisition: Religious Tolerance and Motley's *Rise of the Dutch Republic* 74
4. The Vanishing Dutchman: Ethnicity in Irving's *A History of New York* 96
5. Northmen and Native Americans: Longfellow's Resistance to Eclipse 119

Conclusion 148

Notes 163

Bibliography 203

Index 219

Acknowledgments

A version of the fourth chapter of this book has previously been published as "Northmen and Native Americans: The Politics of Landscape in the Age of Longfellow," *New England Quarterly* 80.3 (2007): 435–58. I thank the *New England Quarterly* for permission to republish it here.

Financial support for this project has been provided by the Stanford Humanities Center Theodore H. and Frances K. Geballe Dissertation Fellowship; the Stanford University English Department Tomas Killefer Dissertation Fellowship; the Friends of the Longfellow House Stanley Paterson Fellowship; and the American Antiquarian Society Jay and Deborah Last Fellowship. The Syracuse University College of Arts and Sciences awarded me a vital research leave to work on the book. I owe a debt of gratitude to the intellectual communities at the American Antiquarian Society (AAS) and the Longfellow House National Historic Site, especially Anita Israel, Georgia B. Barnhill, Paul J. Erickson, Lauren B. Hewes, Elizabeth Watts Pope, Laura E. Wasowicz, and the fall 2008 AAS research fellows.

This book bears the marks of the shrewd and perceptive guidance provided to me in the early stages of the project by Gavin Jones, Albert Gelpi, and the late Jay Fliegelman. Todd Dapremont, Joel Burges, Dawn Coleman, and Christopher Phillips gave me encouragement and intelligent advice during the project's formative period.

My colleagues in the Syracuse University English Department have been an exceptional source of intellectual and moral support, especially the members of the faculty writing group: Jeanne Britton, Manan Desai, Carol Fadda-Conrey, Mike Goode, Roger Hallas, Christopher Hanson, Rory Loughnane, Erin Mackie, Kevin Morrison, Stephanie Shirilan, Linda Shires, Vincent Stephens, and Monika Wadman. Amy Lang has been a generous and committed mentor. Susan Edmunds's wise advice has been invaluable, but her friendship has mattered even more to me.

Eric Wertheimer and the other anonymous reviewer for the University of Alabama Press made this a much better book than it would otherwise have been, and I am indebted to them for their rigorous and thoughtful feedback. My experience of working with the University of Alabama Press has been consistently rewarding. I thank Dan Waterman for his professionalism and his belief in this project. Robin DuBlanc's skillful and careful copyediting respected my prose but improved it.

Debora Burgard and Dennis McKillop have helped me to realize how much joy my work brings me. Mary Brinig, Karen Gross, Crisi Benford, Jessica Straley, and Sinead Mac Namara have put up with a lot and kept me (mostly) sane.

This book is in honor of Robert D. Frandsen and his family. It is dedicated to David, Margaret, Stephen, Michael, Brian, and Christina Roylance, with my deepest love and gratitude for their support.

Eclipse of Empires

Introduction

People in the United States must understand world history. So argues Emma Willard, nineteenth-century U.S. writer and educator, in her 1857 world history textbook, *Universal History in Perspective*: "Universal history, as a science, is . . . at this moment, particularly important to the citizens of our republic." According to Willard, the urgent importance of world historical knowledge for U.S. Americans springs from the fact that the United States' future is precarious and uncertain. She writes that "[i]f, as we believe, they are wrong, who teach that it is the inevitable destiny of our republic to fall into anarchy and thence pass to despotism; no less do they err, who treat with levity every suggestion that such is our danger." Given this danger, the past "might teach our posterity what we as good citizens must desire them to know—the virtues which exalt nations, and the vices which destroy them—that so they may practise the one, and avoid the other." As Willard wrote earlier, in an 1849 textbook, the U.S. republic, "if it stands, must remain by avoiding the rocks, upon which all former republics have foundered. History must make them known."[1]

I argue in this book that a series of popular nineteenth-century U.S. representations of world history embody the philosophy that Willard articulates here. Texts by James Fenimore Cooper, William Hickling Prescott, John Lothrop Motley, Washington Irving, and Henry Wadsworth Longfellow re-create pivotal moments in the histories of Venice, Peru, Spain, the Netherlands, and the Ojibway, in what I call "narratives of imperial eclipse." These stories depict the surpassing of a great civilization by an emerging power: for example, Incan Peru being conquered by Spain, the Ojibway ceding dominance to the French, and Venice being replaced by New York as a global commercial force.

Narratives of imperial eclipse all share certain key features. They capture moments in world history when the trajectories of two great states, one on the rise and one in decline, intersected. They work against the monumental conceptual backdrop of the rise and fall of empires, but they humanize this monumental pattern by representing the declining empire in detail, giving the reader an opportunity to become familiar with and invested in its culture, not immune to the pathos of its status as a now-lost world. Two elements of imperial eclipse narratives are particularly important in facilitating readers' engrossment into the world of the declining empire: their length and their incorporation of substantial historical research. These texts provide sustained depictions, generally multiple volumes in length, that give the reader time to become absorbed in the culture being represented and affected when it is threatened by eclipse from an outside force. The authors of these narratives furthermore used considerable historical research—often original, archival research—to inform their depictions, which adds realism and depth to their representations of empires in decline, and helps to facilitate reader engrossment into the imperial lost worlds.[2]

Extensive contemplation of eclipsed empires becomes a springboard for nationalist self-scrutiny when the present starts to resemble the past. In the case of each eclipsed empire, as represented by the authors examined in this book, the eclipse by an outside force had been preceded and in fact enabled by the internal weakening of the waning empire, plagued by political, economic, or social problems. These international histories thereby became a source of intranational concern for their authors, once they began to recognize parallels between internal problems faced by the fallen empires and corresponding problems within the United States of the nineteenth century. These parallels are sometimes acknowledged in the text itself and sometimes addressed only in other writings by the author (or even in reviews of the book, in the case of John Lothrop Motley). Precisely because the narratives attribute the empires' downfall to some extent to these problems, the appearance in U.S. society of social and political malfunctions also experienced by the Venetians, Peruvians, Spanish, Dutch, and Ojibway caused these authors justifiable concern.

This book does not present a comprehensive survey of all nineteenth-century world history writing, or even all imperial eclipse narratives; the richness of this body of writing deserves much additional inquiry, to which I hope this study will be a contribution. Nonetheless, the texts that I discuss do constitute a coherent intellectual set because they present a reasonably complete picture of imperial decline in the early modern period, when great states declined in rapid succession. In the early modern era, each empire that eclipsed another seemed doomed to be quickly eclipsed in turn, as when Spain conquered Peru in the sixteenth century but soon thereafter started to lose its control over the Netherlands, which would transform in the seventeenth century from a Spanish colony to a global power before suffering an eclipse of its own. Taken as a whole, then, the corpus of texts discussed in this book offers a meditation not only on the downfall of each individual civilization whose history is represented, but also on the overall instability of early modern empires. If the United States did not want to fall prey to the imperial domino effect that had governed the dynamics of Western power in the period just before its national ascendance, it had to study the causes of early modern imperial decline and attempt to avoid the mistakes made by previous civilizations, as Emma Willard advocated.

The United States in the early to mid-nineteenth century—my primary focus in this book—did not precisely fit our modern definition of an "empire," but this term still figured frequently in that era's nationalist debates. The idea of a U.S. empire delighted those who celebrated the greatness of the nation's manifest destiny and terrified those who understood that empires often emerged from the ruins of democratic republics. I use the term *empire* in this book in the sense that Samuel Whelpley describes in his discussion of the Roman empire in an 1806 world history textbook: "The word *Empire* is here used in its popular sense, to represent merely government, or dominion, without reference to its form."[3] In the nineteenth century, "empire" implied broadly any great state or civilization, a fuzziness that allowed the discourse of empire to encompass the United States as well as early modern empires that varied widely in organization and extent, from a small city-state like Venice to a global empire like Spain.[4]

Narratives of early modern imperial eclipse illustrated the panoply of problems that had fatally undermined previous empires, and authors were unsettled to discover these problems breeding unchecked in their own beloved nation. In this context, the conditional mood of Willard's prediction takes on more significance: the United States, "*if* it stands, must remain by avoiding the rocks, upon which all former republics have foundered." Despite the ideology of triumphant national exceptionalism prevalent in much nineteenth-century U.S. discourse, the world's grim imperial track record did not reassure the authors of imperial eclipse narratives about their nation's prospects.

International/Intranational

Interest in world history as a topic soared to great heights in the first half of the nineteenth century, one manifestation of what George Callcott has characterized as "the remarkable rise of historical consciousness in the United States" during this period.[5] Authors of books on world history tended to give narrative shape to the vast amount of information involved in their subject by tracking the rise and fall of empires.[6] This focus entailed not only enormous inherent drama but also crucially important lessons for U.S. Americans to learn. In studying how empires, once strong and secure, succumbed to internal weaknesses and external threats, U.S. politicians could plot their course more wisely, and the U.S. public could choose leaders most likely to steer the ship of state aright. I argue in this book that well before George Santayana observed that those who cannot remember the past are condemned to repeat it, some people in the United States were operating under that assumption, studying world history in an effort to avoid the mistakes of past empires.

This agenda resulted in a tendency toward morbid anxiety in a certain strain of U.S. world historical thinking. Rufus Choate—a prominent Massachusetts Whig, who therefore came from the same cultural milieu that produced many of the authors discussed in this book—advocated in 1845 for a peculiar kind of national deathwatch: "By what means a State with just that quantity of liberty which belongs to the States of America . . . may be preserved through a full life-time of enjoyment and glory, what kind of death it shall die, by what diagnostics the approach of that death may be known, by what conjuration it is for a space to be charmed away, through what succession of decay and decadence it shall at length go down to the tomb of nations—these things are the largest, pertaining to the things of this world, that can be pondered by the mind of man."[7] He supports his point with reference to the fall of ancient Greece: world history provided a comparative context by means of which the current patient's state could be assessed. Careful study of the world's failed empires would yield the necessary diagnostics—the characteristic symptoms of national disease that forecast irreversible decline.

In this mindset, contemplation of episodes in world history could function as an indirect method of national self-examination. Although I will focus in this book primarily on the particular significance that early modern history had for U.S. writers, narratives of early modern imperial eclipse were riffs on depictions of imperial decline in the classical world. One such depiction, Robert Montgomery Bird's 1831 play *The Gladiator*, a tragedy about the slave revolt led by Spartacus in 73 B.C.E., nicely illustrates the national meaning that world history could be made to hold. One month before Edwin Forrest produced the play at the Park Theatre in New York, Nat Turner and other escaped slaves murdered nearly sixty white people in Virginia.[8] The violence of the gladiators turning on their audience, with Spartacus shouting, "Ho, slaves, arise! it is your hour to kill! / Kill and spare not—For wrath and liberty," would have had awful contemporary resonance for many theatergoers (198). Whether one interprets the play as supporting the right of slaves to their freedom or drawing an implicit contrast between noble white revolution and violent black revolt, theatergoers at the time clearly could recognize the modern domestic significance of ancient Roman history.[9]

If Spartacus could be Nat Turner, then Rome could be the United States, and Bird's play suggests what a disaster that would be. Roman forces do eventually subdue the rebellion and kill Spartacus, but the play makes clear that this constitutes only a temporary victory. Spartacus curses Rome in a speech that serves as a reminder to the audience of the coming downfall of the Roman empire: "May the gods, / Who have seen Rome fill the earth with wo and death, / Bring worse than wo and death on Rome; light up / The fires of civil war and anarchy, / Curse her with kings, imperial torturers; / And while these rend her bowels, bring the hosts / Of Northern savages, to slay, and feed / Upon her festering fatness" (238).[10] Spartacus's curse foreshadows the time when Rome—stretched too thin from the extent of its conquests, its social fabric weakened by systemic inequities like slavery—will be overrun by barbarian hordes from the north.

The Gladiator thus offers a glimpse into the anatomy of a doomed empire. The hopeless heroism of Spartacus plays itself out against the backdrop of a larger story—the unraveling of Rome, whose victory over the slaves indicates not its immense power but rather its growing tyranny, which will eventually destroy everything that had made republican Rome great. Those attentive to the lesson could find serious cause for concern in the ample parallels between Roman and U.S. slavery and their shared susceptibility to slave revolt.

I argue in this book that for Bird and other historically minded nineteenth-century U.S. writers, international history became a crucial context for thinking about intranational troubles—divisive conflicts within the nation's borders that fragmented its society. Stories about the deterioration of once-powerful empires like Rome proved viscerally compelling because they heightened anxiety about intranational problems then plaguing the United States, given the downfall of civilizations previously plagued by those same problems.

An analysis of these kinds of stories therefore demands a simultaneously internationalist and intranationalist perspective—in other words, an attention to the cultural connections between the United States and other countries as well as an attention to the multiple, often antagonistic cultures (of race, class, and so on) within the United States.[11] This dual perspective has significant implications given the history of its constituent angles of vision within American studies. A vocal contingent of transnationalist theorists has attempted to distinguish transnationalism from U.S. multiculturalism as a critical preoccupation, identifying a philosophical and methodological split between the two focuses.[12] However, this book shows the internationalist and intranationalist modes to be highly complementary, and indeed inextricable, forms of analysis, especially for writers of eclipse narratives who treat international history as intranational prognosis.

As signaled by my embrace of the terms *international* and *intranational* (which reinforce the nation-state as an organizing principle, unlike alternatives such as *transnational* and *subnational*), I seek in this book to account for the status of the nation in certain nineteenth-century U.S. engagements with the rest of the world.[13] I investigate U.S. materials and phenomena informed by global critiques and concerns and fueled by an archive revealing the rich interpretive contexts provided by often-unexpected international sources.[14] "The aim," as Thomas Bender writes, "is to contextualize the nation" and thereby "thicken" its history.[15] Using the national lens makes sense for understanding the relationship that the authors discussed in this book adopted toward the wider world. When James Fenimore Cooper and John Lothrop Motley traveled in Italy and the Netherlands, when William Hickling Prescott solicited and received research material from archives in Spain and Mexico, and when Henry Wadsworth Longfellow learned Swedish and translated Swedish poetry, they did so self-consciously as Americans. Their transnationalism was conducted within a nationalist framework and they experienced transnationalism as national subjects.

A sensitive reckoning of the subject position from which people participate in transnationalism should always be a priority. As David Damrosch has written, "For any given observer, even a genuinely global perspective remains a perspective *from somewhere*."[16] This grounded subjectivity can serve as a tool for complicating our map of the political thrust of transnationalist activities and imaginaries, which are generally represented as undermining national borders for purposes either nefarious ("globalization") or utopian ("postnationalism"/"planetarity").[17] In contrast, the materials in this book indicate that an investment in the nation fueled a certain segment of nineteenth-century U.S. transnationalism; this particular kind of transnationalism worked to support and help steer the nation, rather than to destabilize its borders.

Analyzing a nationalist internationalism that concerned itself with intranational issues requires a conceptual model able to account for and move fluidly among these multiple frameworks. John Carlos Rowe has proposed restructuring the field of American studies around Mary Louise Pratt's concept of the "contact zone," which he argues can accommodate both multicultural and transnational materials and emphases.[18] I agree with Rowe's assessment of the intellectual flexibility of the "contact zone" idea. Furthermore, although the "contact zone" has generally been interpreted as a spatial and geographic term—an actual region "where disparate cultures meet, clash, and grapple with each other"—it is important to remember that in Pratt's articulation, the contact zone has a temporal as well as a spatial dimension. It refers to "the space in which peoples geographically and historically separated come into contact with each other. . . . It invokes the space and time where subjects previously separated by geography and history are co-present."[19]

In this book, I am working with a spatiotemporal form of the contact zone: a domain in which both times and spaces "meet, clash, and grapple with each other." This kind of contact zone does not require proximity to constitute a borderland.

Thus, the typical association of a contact zone with the area at the edge between two adjoining territories, where their two cultures interpenetrate, does not apply. In contact zones that connect nonadjoining spaces, the mechanism of contact will be different: not in bodily form but rather through the mediation of text, cultures from noncontiguous spaces and nonsuccessive times can come together in a shared imaginative realm.[20] This kind of contact zone can infiltrate the very heart of an empire. Via mediation, contact has the potential to touch the center as well as the edges of a culture, wherever a connection opens up between one time and space and another.

Wai Chee Dimock has proposed in her theory of "deep time" that when an individual reads texts from far-flung times and places, and feels that those texts speak to his or her present moment, the fabric of time is reconfigured. Time, she writes, functions as "a continuum that, at any given moment, can be cut in any way. These 'cuts'—their lengths, their angles of incision, the folds being gathered together as a result—are generated . . . under the shaping hand of particular events. As these events resonate with the past, drawing it into the orbit of the present, . . . events otherwise far apart can find themselves suddenly side-by-side." These cuts and gathers produce "temporal hybrid[s]," "adjacencies between what was and what will be."[21] They are idiosyncratic, determined by an individual's particular constellation of interests and imaginative encounters with the past. Analyzing them therefore requires careful attention to subjectivity.

"World history" as it emerges in this book, constructed around and by various spatiotemporal contact zones created from the fabric of deep time, parallels David Damrosch's definition of "world literature." According to Damrosch, "world literature" describes not a corpus of texts but a mode of textual circulation. Literary works "become world literature by being received *into* the space of a foreign culture, a space defined in many ways by the host culture's national tradition and the present needs of its own writers. . . . [It] is thus always as much about the host culture's values and needs as it is about a work's source culture." World literature operates "on two planes at once: present in our world, it also brings us into a world very different from ours, and its particular power comes from our doubled experience of both registers together."[22] The dynamic that Damrosch sees in the circulation of foreign texts, I see in the circulation of foreign histories that are taken up and written about by U.S. writers. The "world history" of this book's subtitle doesn't refer to a particular set of content, namely the events that have happened in the world over time. Rather, "world history" for me signifies the movement of individual histories beyond their original temporal and spatial setting, and the kinds of histories that so move, becoming "worlded" in the process.

For a history to evoke the doubled register of being both "present in our world" and a conduit into "a world very different from ours," it has to originate in a setting that seems foreign to the culture into which it circulates. Although the assessment of a setting's degree of foreignness will always be subjective and therefore difficult to define, the writers that I discuss in this book came from roughly the same cultural milieu, and their perception of foreignness had some shared elements. Most prominently, for the purposes of my selection criteria, ethno-racial identity seems to have played a significant role in these authors' sense of the foreign. I have thus excluded the numerous nineteenth-century U.S. representations of colonial Virginia and New England history, in which British settlement activities slip too easily into a teleological proto-national narrative, co-opted as stories of the United States' emergence as a nation. On the other hand, I treat places that would become New York (Irving) and the upper Midwest (Longfellow) as foreign territory, because both Irving and Longfellow represent these areas as controlled by groups clearly alien to their own English-speaking Anglo-American U.S. culture: the Dutch, the Ojibway, and the French. Interposing these groups between the land and Anglo-U.S. possession disrupts the kind of immediate U.S. identification that often characterized nineteenth-century attitudes toward British colonial efforts and the territories on which they focused.[23]

The foreignness of a given history arises less from anything inherent in the history than from the nature of an author's representation of it. Any history could lose its feeling of foreignness if an author purposefully domesticated it. For example, David Ramsay's 1819 *Universal History Americanised* contains a three-volume history of the United States followed by a history of the world in which the account "of foreign countries is more or less expanded, in proportion to" a given country's "connexion with the United States, or as furnishing useful and practical information to its citizens, or as the paternal soil of their ancestors."[24] The depth and type of coverage that Ramsay devotes to any given place or people derives directly from his sense of its correspondence to the United States.[25] *Universal History Americanised* approaches foreign times and spaces with an unabashed eye toward intellectual colonization; it literally annexes—Americanizes—world history, transforming the entire world into an extension of Americanness.[26]

In contrast, authors of imperial eclipse narratives generally did not attempt to fully Americanize the world historical other (in part because many of them aspired to and achieved an international readership). They worked in a middle ground between, as David Damrosch puts it, "extremes of assimilation and discontinuity" in which other cultures either "reflect a consciousness *just like ours*, or they are unutterably alien, curiosities whose foreignness finally tells us nothing and can only reinforce our sense of a separate identity."[27] Authors of imperial eclipse narratives preserved a sense of the foreignness of their subjects, in part through the extent of their research, generally visible in their texts and conveying the message that these histories cannot be casually understood. For authors who engage in serious historical inquiry, "the past is a foreign country," in David Lowenthal's formulation.[28] Distanced from the nineteenth-century United States along the dimensions of both space and time, these authors' eclipsed empires are clearly foreign lands. Nonetheless, they also contain disturbing analogues to nineteenth-century U.S. problems. These analogues open up spatiotemporal contact zones between the here and now and the there and then.

In this book, I document the circulation of various episodes of global history into nineteenth-century U.S. culture and consider what significance these episodes had for the authors who acted as the agents of that circulation. I explore the U.S. phenomena that recolored each episode's meaning in its new cultural setting and the spatiotemporal adjacencies each episode struck up between the foreign and the familiar. For the U.S. Americans who wrote about them, these world histories operated in both the international and intranational registers. They originated in situations radically dissimilar and yet eerily, uncomfortably similar to the United States in the nineteenth century, and that doubleness gave them their particular imaginative power.

International

The symbolic importance of ancient Greece and Rome for the early U.S. republic—evidenced by works such as Bird's *Gladiator*—is well-trodden critical territory, so this book will primarily explore international ground other than the classical world.[29] As the nineteenth century progressed, historical writers turned with increasing frequency to more recent history, which stimulated fresh and thought-provoking insights into the nature of modern empires, their failings and their fates. However similar ancient Greece and Rome seemed to the U.S. republic, the United States existed in the modern world, and its rules would determine U.S. destiny.

Emma Willard begins her discussion of modern history by saying that "[a]t the commencement of this period in history, we find the nations entering upon a new order of things." She notes that "[i]t has been said that nations are like individuals, and therefore must have their growth, maturity, and decay": a standard articulation of the rise and fall of empires concept.[30] But Willard argues that despite the fact that every empire of the ancient world eventually declined,[31] nations "are unlike individuals, because there is no physical necessity for their decline . . . their prosperity or decay will be according to their own conduct, and [God's] Providential appointment."[32] She holds out the possibility that in the "new order of things" governing the modern world, empires would not have to fail.

Despite this effort to identify a distinct historical logic governing modernity, a noteworthy number of great states did in fact fail during the early modern period, from roughly the fifteenth century to the eighteenth century. Although a sense of potential national exceptionalism encouraged U.S. Americans like Willard to hope that the United States would not succumb to this pattern, the country would have to function differently than these other states had in order to follow a different course: its "conduct" had to be better and wiser. This would require a deep understanding of the histories of these other states in order to perform the necessary diagnostics of their declines and thereby craft a moral and political regimen for the United States to follow.

María DeGuzmán has argued that the Spanish empire has traditionally served as an alter ego for the U.S. empire, with U.S. writers alternately embracing and disavowing the history of Spanish colonization in the Americas as they constructed a U.S. imperial identity.[33] But Spain was not the only country that served this purpose in U.S. culture; many other early modern states did as well. Therefore, unlike scholars who explore the way that one particular place inspired U.S. cultural production, I have chosen in this book to examine a broad range of nations and civilizations that both individually and collectively functioned to facilitate national self-understanding in the U.S. authors who wrote about them, by representing a dismal track record of modern imperial durability.[34]

The precarious blend of identification and disassociation that DeGuzmán identifies in representations of Spain also characterizes my authors' attitudes toward commercial and cultural powerhouses like the Italian city-states and the Netherlands, whose dominance waned as the early modern period progressed; their attitudes toward the Incas, the Aztecs, and more northerly indigenous peoples, whose civilizations declined with the incursions of Spanish and French colonization; and their attitudes toward the Spanish and French empires themselves. Some of these great states rose and fell with startling speed: the Netherlands began its revolt from Spain in the fifteenth century but didn't win full recognition of its independence until 1648, and in 1664, the British takeover of the Netherlands' New World territory already spelled the beginning of the end of the Dutch "golden age." Early modern states toppled in rapid succession: Peru fell to the Spanish, Spain was weakened by the Dutch revolt, New Netherland fell to the British, the British empire eventually suffered humiliating defeat in the U.S. Revolutionary War. Similarly, the Ojibway yielded to the French, the French holdings in the Americas were lost to the British, some of which the British then lost to the United States. Halting this pattern (because of course the United States would be the next logical domino to fall) would require understanding how powerful empires could lose momentum or be superseded even when seemingly in their prime.

The importance of early modern history for the United States can be gauged in part by the extensive coverage that it received in pedagogical literature: U.S. Americans lavished historiographical attention on the early modern period. George Callcott, in his assessment of space allotted to particular subjects in history textbooks popular from 1800 to 1860, observes that the years 1400–1800 occupied 34 percent of the total space, more than any other subject; the runner-up, ancient Greece and Rome, occupied only 26 percent.[35] These figures, I would argue, suggest two important conclusions: first, that educators felt that the early modern period deserved substantial coverage, and second, that they could not render concise accounts of this period because it wasn't fully and comfortably understood.

Textbooks had the history of Greece and Rome down pat: the topics to be covered, the analysis explaining the reasons for their rise and fall, the significance of the subject for their readers—all standardized almost to the point of formula. The spectacle of their downfall for nineteenth-century readers had been rendered tame by a conventionalized rhetoric of obsolescence, which mourned the decay of Greece and Rome with what amounted to a pleasant melancholy. In contrast, more recent history had not been so fully domesticated. Textbooks that marched efficiently through the rise and fall of Assyria, Babylon, Persia, Greece, Macedon, and Rome faltered at the medieval period, digressing into discourses on chivalry and feudalism before moving into ungainly accounts of the events of the early modern era. The key turning points of this era had not been satisfactorily identified; its causes and effects had not been convincingly determined. Understanding the early modern era required further research and thought by scholars before textbook writers could provide an effective digest of it.

The authors treated in this book helped to produce the needed new scholarship on the great civilizations of the early modern era. William Hickling Prescott (Spain, Peru, and Mexico), John Lothrop Motley (the Netherlands), Washington Irving (New Netherland), and Francis Parkman (New France) all did groundbreaking archival work to flesh out the history of this period. Even historical novels and poems like James Fenimore Cooper's on Venice and Henry Wadsworth Longfellow's on the Ojibway relied on and helped to disseminate substantial historical scholarship on these civilizations. These authors as a group took the lead in the United States in attempting to study and understand the significance of the great early modern empires.

With these efforts, they embodied a shift in the discipline of history, which changed over the course of the nineteenth century, only gradually becoming identifiable as a discrete discipline with specialized methods and target audiences.[36] The authors that I discuss are transitional figures. On the one hand, they incorporated intensive, often archival historical research into their works at a time before the discipline of history, with its more rigorous evidentiary standards, existed in its modern form. On the other hand, these authors reflect the less disciplinarily compartmentalized culture of letters that operated in the first half of the nineteenth century, which did not draw strict distinctions between literary writers and historians: narratives of imperial eclipse appeared in a variety of genres—drama, poetry, satire, and fiction as well as historiographical nonfiction.[37]

David Levin points out in his 1959 *History as Romantic Art* (an important intellectual precursor to my study) that the Romantic historians such as Prescott, Motley, and Parkman understood themselves as men of letters, participants in a literary culture that extended beyond historiography as such.[38] Nonetheless, Levin stops short of placing these historians' work in dialogue with extended readings of work by nonhistorians. Different insights result when placing Prescott, Motley, and Parkman into dialogue with Cooper, Irving, and Longfellow, as I do, than when placing them into dialogue with George Bancroft, as Levin does. Levin's inclusion of Bancroft, author of the influential *History of the United States*, obscures the particular creative energy and challenging questions that world history provoked in the other historians. Bancroft's more triumphalist Democratic political viewpoint also contributes to Levin's conclusion that the Romantic historians felt confident in the United States' status as the highest point of human progress. However, reading Prescott, Motley, and Parkman in the context of Cooper, Irving, and Longfellow—writers whose more skeptical politics matched the historians' apprehensive conservative viewpoint better than Bancroft's did—reveals the doubt about the nation that lurked in their representations of world history. The United States had apparently not progressed far enough beyond the failed empires of the early modern era to avoid facing reincarnated versions of their problems.

The nature of imperial eclipse authors' careers—engaged with the evolving evidentiary protocols of the historical discipline but not quarantined within an insular intellectual community of professional historians—enabled a particularly combustible marriage of international and intranational thinking. Their in-depth research, which necessitated an extended and fine-grained intellectual encounter with their historical subjects, gave them the exposure necessary to alert them to similarities between their historical subjects and their own culture, creating a spatiotemporal contact zone that allowed them to see the intranational in the international. In contrast to David Ramsay's comparatively shallowly researched *Universal History Americanised*, for example, their consciousness of U.S. analogues to world historical phenomena seems to have sprung in large part from their close scrutiny of past empires rather than inspiring that scrutiny in the first place: authors of imperial eclipse narratives apparently did not turn to world history for the purpose of producing either an encomium to or a jeremiad on U.S. society.[39]

Furthermore, though, writing what they understood as popular texts for a popular audience heightened the stakes of parallels between world history and U.S. culture. Attention to the readerly demands of their audiences required that these writers produce dramatic, striking narratives, which would engage readers and draw them into imperial cultures about to be eclipsed, so that the moment when those cultures were eclipsed would have maximum emotional impact. Apprised of parallels between the contemporary United States and early modern empires by their intensive and prolonged historical research, they produced dramatic, sensationalized depictions of imperial failure that therefore cast the U.S. situation in the most anxiety-producing terms: a perfect storm of international erudition and national apprehension.

Intranational

The array of different empires treated in imperial eclipse narratives corresponded to a matching array of social problems facing the United States in the nineteenth century. World historical knowledge sensitized authors to the great variety of internal weaknesses undermining the soundness of the United States in the nineteenth century. Over the course of this book, intranational tensions surrounding race, ethnicity, religion, politics, economics, class, urbanization, and regional and sectional divisions will all come into play. Furthermore, though, the intranational valences of imperial eclipse narratives arise not only from their subject matter but also from the social identities of the authors that produced them.

This book does not often raise gender as an explicit intranational problem, but the lack of female representation among authors of imperial eclipse narratives indicates that issues of gender in fact underlie the whole genre. Women had less reliable access to advanced historical education than men did, but Nina Baym has shown that they nonetheless managed to produce significant quantities of historiography in the period from 1800 to 1860.[40] Women's world history writing most commonly took the form of textbooks, pedagogy being a more socially acceptable type of women's work than substantial research-based scholarship.[41]

Textbooks do differ in their overall effect from narratives of imperial eclipse, in that textbooks provide universal histories—histories of the whole world—rather than in-depth looks at particular historical moments. The surveys of information required by the textbook form usually preclude sustained analysis of particular cultures. On the whole, then, they do not give the reader the opportunity to engage very deeply with empires brought down by societal problems also afflicting the United States—a key element of eclipse narratives' effect. Textbooks therefore cannot produce the same level or type of nationalist anxiety that narratives of imperial eclipse do, both individually (in providing an intimate anatomy of a particular doomed empire) and collectively (in tracing the domino effect of failing empires in the early modern period). However, women textbook writers certainly argued that the nation's current course was cause for concern and that the study of world history offered crucial lessons for the concerned U.S. citizen, articulating a world historical philosophy that the male writers of imperial eclipse narratives shared.

Although they operate differently as a literary genre, then, textbooks can be useful as a gloss on narratives of imperial eclipse, because textbook writers typically provided pedagogical rationales for the importance of their subjects and thereby made explicit a warning that often remained implicit in the works of imperial eclipse authors. Due to the inherent didacticism of textbook literature, with its correspondingly more dictatorial narrative voice, writers such as Emma Willard could advocate more unambiguously than the male eclipse narrative writers usually did for the importance of historical literacy in the United States. In the process, textbook writers helpfully spelled out the underlying cultural values that also drove imperial eclipse narratives.

For example, Elizabeth Palmer Peabody, a Transcendentalist educator, publisher, and textbook writer (and sister-in-law to Nathaniel Hawthorne), lauded history in her textbook *First Steps to the Study of History* as a "source of practical wisdom," a way to "deliver the mind from the thralldom of the present, and to prepare it to comprehend the future"—a constant refrain in world history writings.[42] History's value lay in its ability to expand a person's narrow individual perspective. Peabody wrote that world history and the study of other cultures provided "the surest means of destroying dogmatism, and making the mind genuinely modest and free from slavery to its own peculiarities": "Youth who are made acquainted with [primary sources narrating the histories of other countries], grow up as it were in many ages, and many countries, and have a chance to escape the influences of the present age, to which many surrender themselves to perish with it; and to feel the influences of the great relations of humanity, before they are circumscribed to those of any party, or even any single country."[43] This statement celebrates the soul-enlarging possibilities of cosmopolitanism, but it also associates the present with perishing, if the "slavery" of dogmatism and party peculiarity cannot be escaped.

Similarly, Susanna Rowson, author of the novel *Charlotte Temple*, concludes her late-career world history textbook with a meditation on the United States, writing that a "bountiful Providence sheds abundantly every blessing of life upon this highly favored land. . . . May the piety, gratitude, unanimity and christian spirit of its inhabitants, to the giver of all good, be such as not to forfeit a continuation of these inestimable blessings."[44] Instead of wishing simply for the continuation of God's blessings upon the country, Rowson frames her hope awkwardly in the negative—a wish that U.S. Americans will avoid forfeiting those blessings. The task of prolonging national good fortune falls to the inhabitants of the United States, and Rowson raises the prospect of their failure as the final note of her history. Ominous endings such as this, ranging from the equivocal to the apocalyptic, frequently appear in world history books that conclude with a history of the United States.[45] They reflect the nationalist anxiety that frequently seems to have accompanied U.S. writers' world historical reflections.

Due to the wide readership that textbooks as a genre enjoyed, and the formative moments at which people read and absorbed their lessons, the imperial discourses found in world history textbooks had the potential to be extremely influential. They helped to cement the rise and fall of empires pattern as the predominant framework for understanding world history, and they worked to make this pattern relevant to the trajectory of the United States. Women world history writers, though generally prevented from producing "higher" forms of historiography by gendered inequities in education and culturally sanctioned forms of intellectual labor, nonetheless proved deft commentators in their textbooks on the significance of world historical knowledge for the nineteenth-century United States. They had a role in shaping the cultural milieu out of which the male historiographers emerged and into which their imperial eclipse narratives entered.

Beyond their gender, though, authors of imperial eclipse narratives shared some other key determinative intranational identities. They were white: the barriers that discouraged white women from producing research-based historical scholarship operated even more strongly on women and men of color. They tended to be wealthy or from wealthy backgrounds: the time and resources required to conduct extensive archival research and produce truly original historiography did not come cheap. In accordance with their financial privilege and class status, these authors tended to affiliate politically with the party of money: the Federalists and later the Whigs.[46] James Fenimore Cooper, the exception to this rule, voted as a Democrat but his socioeconomic beliefs grew increasingly conservative as his career proceeded. These writers' conservatism—the desire to conserve the political, economic, and social status quo—predisposed them to interpret national change as threatening.[47] For them, the nineteenth century's many innovations to the nation's political and economic system and social structures usually meant declension rather than progress. Their historical knowledge reinforced their apprehensive interpretations of change, given the panoply of fallen world empires that had undergone what they believed were similar innovations.

Regional identity also played an important role in predisposing authors toward the production of imperial eclipse narratives. Writers of these narratives hailed disproportionately from New England, a trend that conformed to New England's overall dominance in the production of historiography during this period.[48] As a region, New England identified itself with history more strongly than did its main rival, New York, as the titles of two recent studies—*The Athens of America: Boston, 1825–1845* and *Young America: The Flowering of Democracy in New York City*—make clear.[49] (The Philadelphia of Robert Montgomery Bird also trended anti-Democratic and also billed itself as the Athens of America.) In *Young America*, Edward Widmer writes of New York's obsession with the concepts of youth and newness, and its literary and political rivalry with Whiggish New England; the project of the New York literati who clustered around the *Democratic Review* "involved taking control of American culture from Boston, from the Whigs, and from old conservatives everywhere."[50] This intranational competition, concretizing around the opposing historical ideologies that characterized the intellectual cultures of the two regions, helped to shape the imperial eclipse narratives produced by New England writers.

The two New York writers discussed in this book, Washington Irving and James Fenimore Cooper, do complicate this schematic regional breakdown. Significantly, though, the Irving and Cooper texts that I consider both fall chronologically in the first third of the century, when New York had not yet fully acquired the character that Widmer analyzes. Irving and Cooper were both associated with the Knickerbockers, generally a more conservative and historically oriented group than the *Democratic Review* crowd that began to dominate New York literary life as the nineteenth century progressed.[51]

During the twentieth century, this same *Democratic Review* circle, which included Hawthorne, Melville, and Whitman, began to dominate the national literary canon to the exclusion of many of the New England writers. Both regions had sought in the nineteenth century to articulate visions for the nation and for the role of time and history in national identity, but the New York form of nationalist discourse began to take over twentieth-century critics' accounts of nineteenth-century U.S. literary culture.[52] For instance, R. W. B. Lewis's *The American Adam* takes the ideology of newness, with its strong regional inflection, as an archetypally "American" mythology. Lewis forces historically oriented writers awkwardly into his thesis: citing the *Democratic Review* and the *Literary World* (another Democratic New York magazine) to introduce the interest in history evinced mainly in New England, he argues that historians such as William Hickling Prescott practiced a "scrupulous setting-off of the past from the present; the investigation of the past in its intact, reassuring pastness."[53] While Prescott and the other writers of imperial eclipse narratives may well have wished that the present could be scrupulously set off from the past—that the United States would not repeat the mistakes of former empires—this book argues that the past for them constantly breached the boundaries of its "intact, reassuring pastness," meeting the present in spatiotemporal contact zones and encroaching on their attempts to determine the meaning of their own nation.

When twentieth-century critics rebranded nineteenth-century U.S. literary culture as primarily focused on youth and an isolationist Americanness (that is, cultural independence, long touted as the central preoccupation of antebellum U.S. writers), the vibrant nineteenth-century tradition of historiography, especially the world history writing, became less visible. Writers such as Longfellow, Irving, and Prescott, and even to a certain extent Cooper, lost the place in the literary canon that they had held in their own day. These writers unquestionably had the public ear to a degree unmatched by Melville, Whitman, and Hawthorne.[54] Although an extended study of the cultural reception of imperial eclipse narratives is beyond the scope of this book, the large readerships that imperial eclipse authors commanded do suggest that they were tapping into and influencing widely shared cultural preoccupations with their world history writing. I therefore approach the analysis of their narratives as a series of authorial case studies that demonstrates the prominence in the nineteenth-century United States of a world history discourse steeped in the international but with serious ramifications for the intranational.

As interesting as world history for its own sake can be, narratives of imperial eclipse could not have engaged their writers and readers deeply without contemporary resonance and relevance. These narratives raised all the vexed social and political questions of the day: what antidemocratic values were animating U.S. politicians? what obstacles to economic progress were looming? how steep would the cost of ending slavery be? how seriously committed to religious tolerance were U.S. Americans when push came to shove? how could the nation accommodate stubbornly distinct ethnic identities in its midst? what claims did Native Americans actually have to their land? World history provided unsettling precedents for all these issues. Internationalism, it seemed, *was* intranationalism, writ (spatially and temporally) large.

With the exception of Irving's *A History of New York*, I handle the primary texts in approximate chronological order. But another organizing logic is intellectually more central to the book's argument: the chapters catalogue the falling dominoes of early modern empires in order. Although Cooper, the subject of the first chapter, writes about eighteenth-century Venice, long after the city-state's medieval heyday, Venice's decline actually began in the 1400s, with events like Columbus's discovery of the lucrative New World.[55] The Peruvians fell to the Spanish in the 1530s (a story told by Prescott, subject of the second chapter); Spain began to lose its hold over the Netherlands in the 1570s (Motley—third chapter); New Amsterdam was taken over by the British in 1664 (Irving—fourth chapter); Hiawatha's Ojibway yielded to the French sometime in the mid-seventeenth century (Longfellow—fifth chapter); and the French ceded their New World territories to the British in 1763 at the conclusion of the Seven Years' War (Parkman—conclusion). Together, then, the texts discussed in this book form a survey of the instability of empire in the early modern period and the implications of that instability for the United States.

In chapter 1, I set out the basic terms on which the rest of the book will build through an analysis of two novels by James Fenimore Cooper that explore the ascending and descending phases in the rise and fall of empires pattern: *The Water-Witch* (1830), in which Cooper complacently depicts the eighteenth-century eclipse of Venice by New York as a global power; and *The Bravo* (1831), in which he re-creates the tyrannical dying days of formerly republican Venice, noticing in the process the disturbing resemblance between U.S. congressional misconduct and the machinations of Venetian senators. As he made clear in other writings from this period, he grew ever less sanguine about the state of the nation, given increasing evidence in the United States of the same oligarchic despotism that signaled the collapse and eclipse of Venice. But Cooper's obvious desire for an elite social aristocracy gave his political opponents a rebuttal to his concern about oligarchy among U.S. Whig politicians.

Chapter 2 deepens the picture of the imperial eclipse narrative that emerges in Cooper's work by moving out of Europe and into the Americas and by taking up a more complex intranational concern: the status of U.S. property rights. In William Hickling Prescott's 1847 *History of the Conquest of Peru*, preconquest Incan Peru and postconquest conquistadorial Peru (both eventually eclipsed by centralized Spanish imperial power) raise the specter of threats to the U.S. system of personal property from communist and abolitionist movements, growing in popularity during the 1840s. The proto-communist institutions of Incan society and the destabilizing efforts to end native slavery in the conquistadorial period taught Prescott to fear similar property initiatives in his own society.

With chapter 3, I begin to complicate the basic schematic of imperial eclipse narratives as modeled by Cooper's and Prescott's works. John Lothrop Motley's 1856 history of the Dutch revolt from Spain, *The Rise of the Dutch Republic*, presents a variation on the imperial eclipse theme. Motley equates U.S. religious tolerance with Dutch freedom of worship, thereby attempting to associate the United States with the winning side in the Netherlands' eclipse of Spain. But Motley's reviewers once again forecast doom, likening the religious fanaticism of Philip II and the Inquisition to the anti-Catholicism of the recently created Know-Nothing Party in the United States.

Chapter 4 continues to explore variations of the imperial eclipse model. It analyzes the ethnic politics of Washington Irving's 1809 *A History of New York*, which alienates and anachronizes the nineteenth-century Dutch communities of New York and New Jersey by associating them with the bumbling seventeenth-century New Netherland colony, a foreign land despite its eventual territorial incorporation into the United States. Through his depiction of a community that qualifies as both foreign and domestic, Irving complicates the line between the international and the intranational.

With Irving, the international world relocates to home territory, and chapter 5 continues this line of investigation by examining "native" ground. I contend that Henry Wadsworth Longfellow resists the total eclipse of the Ojibway in his 1855 *The Song of Hiawatha* by incorporating Ojibway terms and stories into his poem and by depicting the land as permanently marked by their occupation, although some of his reviewers sidestepped this politically inconvenient message by attributing the poem's tales to Longfellow's supposed plagiarism of the Finnish epic *Kalevala*. The move to displace Native American culture with Scandinavia mirrored contemporary enthusiasm for the idea that Vikings had once settled New England, a spurious theory that distracted attention from the pressing land claims of the region's real first inhabitants and that thereby facilitated the suspect narrative that Native Americans had been completely eclipsed by Europeans.

The conclusion begins with Francis Parkman's seven-volume chronicle of colonial North America (1865–92). His account of France and Britain's contest for territorial control conforms to the pattern of imperial eclipse narratives and brings the domino effect of empires ever closer to the United States. It illustrates the nationalist anxiety that went hand in hand with nineteenth-century U.S. representations of world history.[56] The second half of the conclusion demonstrates that this anxiety did not end with the nineteenth century. Today, we can see the same dynamic operating in contemporary representations of world history. I jump forward in time to explore the current appeal of eclipse narratives as evidenced by Mel Gibson's 2006 film *Apocalypto*, which obviously references contemporary U.S. problems in its depiction of the cultural unraveling of the Maya just before the arrival of the Spanish. Nineteenth-century U.S. Americans believed the United States to be a nation on the rise; many twenty-first-century U.S. Americans suspect that the United States might be a nation on the decline (to be eclipsed by China? by the economic momentum of the BRIC countries—Brazil, Russia, India, China?). In both historical moments, self-consciousness about the United States' position in the world has inspired an engagement with other moments in world history that might illuminate the current state and possible fate of the nation.

1

American Principles and Italian Things

Cooper's Political Gleanings in Italy

James Fenimore Cooper provides a useful place to begin, because in his representations of early modern Italian history, he explicitly discusses where the United States fits into the historical model that seemed to govern the imperial trajectory of the great Italian city-states. In the other narratives of imperial eclipse examined in this book, authors merely hint at the position of the United States within the pattern of imperial rise and fall, by analogy to previous instances of imperial eclipse involving other empires. In contrast, Cooper locates the United States within the pattern, depicting it as having eclipsed Italy in its ascent to a position of global prominence but in danger of triggering its own decline by repeating the mistakes that Italy made in the early modern era.

Inspired by his 1828–30 trip to Italy and his sojourns in Florence, Rome, and Venice, Cooper wrote two novels in the early 1830s that dealt with Italy: *The Water-Witch* (1830) and *The Bravo* (1831). In *The Water-Witch*, a primarily comic novel about the maritime smuggling culture operating near New York City in the early eighteenth century, Cooper explicitly argues that the United States had surpassed the Italian city-states in commercial power, if not yet in cultural achievement. In *The Bravo*, a darkly gothic romance set in Venice and detailing the corruption that riddled the city-state's supposed republicanism, Cooper sets out to applaud the superior merits of U.S. republicanism but discovers disturbing resemblances between trends in the U.S. political scene and the oligarchic tyranny of pseudo-republican Venice.[1]

Both stories take place in the early eighteenth century, both discuss the relationship between the United States and Italy, and both rely on the idea of cyclical history—the inescapable rise and fall of empires. Taken together, *The Water-Witch* and *The Bravo* explore the full imperial cycle: ascendance, then decline and eclipse by another imperial power engaged in its own ascent. *The Water-Witch* focuses on the ascendance portion of the cycle; as John Lothrop Motley would later do in his *Rise of the Dutch Republic*, Cooper uses *The Water-Witch* to articulate a sense of pride in the rise of the United States. But with *The Bravo*, Cooper confronts the flipside of the imperial cycle. He produces an archetypal narrative of imperial eclipse, in which Venice's decline raises the specter of a possible U.S. decline, resulting from some of the same political malfunctions.

To understand what allowed Cooper to yoke the United States to Venice's fate in this way, we will first briefly examine his theory of the nation-state as articulated in the 1834 pamphlet *A Letter to His Countrymen*. Cooper posits a distinction between "American principles" and "American things" that allows him to relocate Americanness to foreign settings. This move opens the floodgates of national relevance; international scenes and situations suddenly become rife with intranational meaning. Unfortunately, *The Bravo* provides Cooper with an opportunity to discover more similarities between Venice and the United States than he would have liked. Cooper's stated motive in the novel is to glorify U.S. republicanism by painting a picture of its inverse—oligarchical Venetian tyranny. However, his project falters when his depiction of Venice starts to resemble certain problematic aspects of nineteenth-century U.S. political culture. Cooper feared that the Whig Party in the United States had ambitions to become a permanent governing aristocracy, and precisely this kind of aristocratic class had exploited and ultimately doomed Venice.

Ironically, given Cooper's repugnance for and fear of political aristocracy, he believed in the cultural importance of a gentry class, landowners whose refined way of life could temper the crass mercantilism of U.S. society. His critics, who responded very negatively to *The Bravo*, lambasted him for his aristocratic attitudes, seemingly so starkly at odds with his vociferous advocacy of popular rights, republicanism, and the Democratic Party. Cooper seemed intent on promoting a U.S. version of the class that had derailed republican Venice and propelled it into decline and eclipse.

Cooper's discussions of Italy in *The Bravo* and *The Water-Witch* show him wrestling with the relevance of Italy to U.S. national identity. Although *The Water-Witch* affords him the opportunity to celebrate the New World's eclipse of the Old World, *The Bravo* forces him to dwell on the example of a failed republic, supposedly to affirm a different future for the United States but in actuality showing him the likelihood of a similar U.S. fate. In presenting such a clear example of the rise and fall of empires, Italy provokes Cooper to speculate on his own country's position within this historical cycle. The United States had by the nineteenth century eclipsed Italy as a commercial and political power, but disturbing parallels between the United States and Venice suggested that one day in turn the United States would also be eclipsed.

Principles and Things

Cooper espoused a particular theory of national identity that encouraged him to understand international history as a prompt to conduct an intranational self-examination. By the early 1830s, he had gained an international reputation, which reflected well both on him and on the United States, as "a literary pioneer who proved that American materials are suitable for historical romance."[2] This fact was much touted by his contemporary reviewers and continues to be a critical commonplace even today. Cooper's most famous works, the five novels of the Leatherstocking Tales, all furnished with Indians, frontiersmen, and wilderness settings, cemented his reputation as an artist specializing in novelistic treatments of "American materials."

But Cooper chafed against the restrictions that this notion of his artistic program imposed. He clarified his own understanding of Americanness in *A Letter to His Countrymen*, where he writes of his willingness "to substitute American *principles* for American *things*" in his work.[3] He cared less about superficial signifiers of Americanness like frontier settings than he did about the ideals that his novels promoted. He thus embraced extranational settings such as Venice if they provided apt occasions for discussing fundamental American principles like republicanism. While the external furniture of *The Bravo*'s narrative may be Venetian, he argues that the novel needs to be interpreted—along with the other books in the "European trilogy," *The Heidenmauer* (1832) and *The Headsman* (1833)—as a tale "in which American opinion should be brought to bear on European facts" (12).[4] Furthermore, Cooper's prioritizing of "principle" over "thing" suggests that setting should not be the primary classifying tool used to parse Cooper's oeuvre. Grouping *The Bravo* with *The Water-Witch*, set in North America but dealing with many of the same principles that *The Bravo* engages, makes as much sense as grouping it with *The Heidenmauer* and *The Headsman* because they feature European settings.[5]

In creating a distinction between "American principles" and "American things," Cooper posits an ability to separate national principles and core identity from national trappings. America as concept and America as geographically bounded, bureaucratically delineated state do not always completely overlap. With this idea, he dissolves the "nation-state" into its two constitutive terms and focuses on the ideal nation and its values, whether or not they coincide with the physical territory of the United States. The itinerancy of the nation as a concept facilitates the creation of spatiotemporal contact zones between the nineteenth-century United States and other times and places where American principles might be found in operation.

In Cooper's philosophy, the essential elements of Americanness can be separated out from its incidental elements and applied to, or brought to bear on, the incidentals of another situation entirely. He called this reapplication for the purposes of comparison "gleaning." In visiting other countries, he wrote that he "endeavored to glean some general inferences from the comparisons that naturally suggested themselves" (14).[6] For him this constituted an especially effective method of national self-reflection. Venice allowed him to glean "some general inferences" about the history of republicanism. Its government claimed to be republican but actually ruled tyrannically, and in *The Bravo* Cooper holds this form of government up to the standard of ideal American republicanism and finds it wanting—a flattering message for U.S. Americans.

However, Cooper's strategy of distinguishing between American principles and American things did not always work to the United States' advantage. We will see how his argument concerning Venice's relevance to the U.S. situation allowed the emergence of both positive and negative national meanings. If American principles could operate independently of American things, then presumably other countries' principles could operate outside of their borders; Venetian principles might be at work in the United States even as American principles had manifested themselves in Venetian history—a dangerous possibility given pseudo-republican Venice's degeneration into tyranny and eventual downfall.[7]

Although Cooper theorizes conceptual distance between principles and things so that he can locate American principles in Europe as well as the United States, he implies that no essential connection binds together the principle and thing, which has repercussions beyond what he perhaps intends. As soon as the integral relationship between principle and thing is severed, doubt emerges about the true character of the thing, which may in practice be entirely bereft of a genuine American spirit. Fourth of July orations certainly qualify as American things, but do they always express the core principles that (should) characterize the nation in its ideal form? As Cooper assessed a U.S. society that allowed its attitudes to be shaped by foreign opinion and a U.S. government that sacrificed real republicanism to promote the interests of the wealthy few, he began to suspect the un-Americanness of many American things.

American Ascendance

The Water-Witch and *The Bravo* embody the schizophrenic mixture of self-congratulation and self-doubt that characterized nineteenth-century U.S. nationalist discourse. *The Water-Witch* reflects a triumphalist view of the rise of the United States as a global power, displacing Europe, and specifically Italy, as the primary locus of commercial energy. In contrast, *The Bravo* reflects an apprehensive view of the political problems faced by the United States that could precipitate its decline, as the same problems had done to Venice earlier in the cycle of imperial rise and fall. As in the culture at large, Cooper's rhetoric of nationalist self-congratulation and self-doubt existed side by side, in novels written in close succession. *The Water-Witch* and *The Bravo* can be productively interpreted as a pair, not only because recent evidence suggests that Cooper may have contemplated making *The Bravo* a sequel to *The Water-Witch* but also because the novels explore the ascending and descending slopes in the arc of imperial rise and fall.[8]

Both novels seek to plot the United States' position within this arc by means of a comparison with Italy. One attraction of the imperial eclipse narrative lay in the fact that it made cultural trajectories especially visible. Recognizing the signs of decline from within an empire may be difficult—a blindness that many of these narratives thematize—but when one empire eclipses another, their respective trajectories become more obvious. The temporal setting of both *The Water-Witch* and *The Bravo* works to capitalize on the clarifying effect of eclipse. Both stories take place in the early eighteenth century, a particularly useful moment to compare Italy and what would become the United States.

The Water-Witch, set in and around Hudson Bay, New York, depicts the city of New York as it existed in the early eighteenth century: a small pioneer town, bustling but crude. The book offers a running comparison between the commercial promise of New York at that time and the cultural achievements of Naples, coming to a head in a prolonged meditation on the competing merits of the Naples and New York bays. This comparison calls attention to New York's emergent global position. It may not yet possess the cultural refinement that Naples has acquired over the centuries of Italy's global prominence, but its commercial vigor points to the importance that it would soon assume.

The Bravo can be read as part of the same historical portrait. Also set in the early eighteenth century, it takes place in Venice, at a time when its power was fast declining, a contrapuntal note to New York's ascendance in *The Water-Witch*. However, when *The Bravo*'s story takes place, "Though the glory of Venice had departed, the trade of the city was not then at its present low ebb," Cooper writes.[9] The eclipse of Venice and Italy more generally by New York would not have been so forcefully emphasized if the novels had been set in Cooper's own day. In the nineteenth century, New York was the commercial center of the energetic, young United States, a country coming to preeminence among the world's nations. In contrast, Venice, once the marketplace of the Mediterranean and the political and artistic leader of the world, was in 1830 an Austrian colony, obsolete in the realms of politics, art, and trade.[10] So in order to make the trajectory that the two cities—and their respective countries—followed more clear, the novels instead depict a time when New York still had little claim to status and the republic of Venice still ruled itself, decaying inexorably from internal corruption and declining trade status but as yet proudly ignoring its degeneration. Taken together, then, *The Water-Witch* and *The Bravo* nicely encapsulate the idea of the contrasting courses of the United States and Italy, the one just beginning to eclipse the other (though *The Bravo* will also raise doubts about how long the United States will remain on the upswing).

In both of these novels, but especially clearly in *The Water-Witch*, Cooper explains the opposing national trajectories of Italy and the United States by means of the underlying historical logic that governs human history and propels empires into the pattern of rise and fall: cyclical history. The concept of cyclical history maintained that time moves cyclically and that civilizations, like human beings, move organically through a pattern of birth, growth, maturity, decline, and death. Popularized in the United States by Constantin-François Volney's musings on the ruins of the Syrian and Egyptian empires in his 1791 *Les ruines; ou, Méditations sur les révolutions des empires* as well as by Edward Gibbon's *The History of the Decline and Fall of the Roman Empire* (1776–88) and Marquis de Condorcet's *Esquisse d'un tableau historique des progrès de l'esprit humain* (1795), cyclical history helped to explain the seemingly inevitable decline of human societies, and had widespread intellectual appeal.[11] On the other hand, as we saw with Emma Willard, some thought that perhaps modern history might operate according to a different logic than the one that had shaped ancient history. Cooper attempted in *The Bravo* to articulate a loophole, an exception for modern republicanism that would exempt the United States from the cyclical pattern. However, this pattern clearly shaped his general understanding of world history.

Cooper foregrounds the centrality of cyclical history in *The Water-Witch* right from the outset. Just a few paragraphs into the novel, he writes: "It would seem that, as nature has given its periods to the stages of animal life, it has also set limits to all moral and political ascendency. While the City of the Medici [Florence] is receding from its crumbling walls, like the human form shrinking into 'the lean and slippered pantaloon,' the Queen of the Adriatic [Venice] is sleeping on her muddy isles, and Rome itself is only to be traced by fallen temples and buried columns, the youthful vigor of America is fast covering the wilds of the West with the happiest fruits of human industry."[12] From Cooper's perspective, the United States has eclipsed Italy as a vital global force. The "lean and slippered pantaloon" quotation comes from Shakespeare's *As You Like It*, in which the character Jaques outlines the seven ages of man: infant, child, lover, soldier, justice, old age, and imminent death. The speech ends, famously, with the verse, "Sans teeth, sans eyes, sans taste, sans everything." The "lean and slippered pantaloon" makes an appearance in the sixth age—old age—when a man's "shrunk shank" causes him to don the costume of the elderly. This allusion strengthens Cooper's analogy between "the stages of animal life" and the stages of moral and political life. Just as an individual inevitably reaches old age, so, too, do formerly vital civilizations, like the city-states of Italy. They are "receding," "shrinking," "sleeping" and "fallen"—so different from the rapidly expanding United States, "fast covering the wilds of the West." It is typical of the novel's tone that Cooper represents Italy as in the second-to-last age—not gone, not dead, not "sans everything," but slowly and quietly slipping away. This penultimate stage offers a poignant contrast to the "ascendency" of the United States but does not obtrude tragically as a dead civilization.

Although the novel, with its New World setting, focuses more sustained attention on the "youthful vigor of America" than on Old World decline, Cooper repeatedly associates Italy with obsolescence in *The Water-Witch*. The novel's story revolves around a smuggling ship, the *Water-Witch*, whose daring captain, the Skimmer of the Seas, flouts the British ban on the importation of European goods into the colonies. A woman from the ship, Eudora, in disguise as a male sailor named Seadrift, facilitates the sale of contraband materials, most notably luxurious Italian-made fabrics. Her exchanges with a customer, Alida, serve as an opportunity for comment on the fading fortunes of Italy. Tuscan satins occasion the description of Tuscany as "a country where nature exhibits its extremes, and one whose merchants were Princes"—note the past tense in the characterization of Tuscan power (104). Although Cooper would reserve his grimmest assessments of Venetian decline for *The Bravo*, Eudora explains to Alida during their perusal of some Venetian velvets that "commerce is like the favor which attends the rich, and the Queen of the Adriatic is already far on the decline. . . . The outer India passage has changed the current of prosperity, which ever rushes in the widest and newest track" (106). Venice, once perfectly positioned to capitalize on overland trade routes between Europe and Asia, has been sidelined by the discovery of more convenient sea routes.

Eudora widens the applicability of Venice's commercial displacement, remarking, "Nations might learn a moral by studying the sleepy canals and instructive magnificence of that fallen town" (106–7). Cooper then touches on a theme that will emerge with greater prominence in *The Bravo*: the inability of eclipsed empires to face their own dwindling power. Venice apparently cannot recognize the moral that it presents to the world, because "pride fattens on its own lazy recollections, to the last!" (107). As Eudora observes later in the novel, "It is ever the common fault of old communities to overvalue themselves, and to under-value new actors in the great drama of nations, as men long successful disregard the efforts of new aspirants for favor" (265).

However, Cooper does not dwell obsessively on this kind of imperial tragic irony in *The Water-Witch*, and Italy's obsolescence is offset by the cultural refinement that comes with civilizational maturity. In her comparison between the Naples and New York bays, Eudora equates Naples with the past and New York with the future, but the storied landscape and beauty of the Bay of Naples outstrip the primarily prospective grandeur of New York Bay.[13] To account for her familiarity with the Bay of Naples, Eudora explains, "Many years of early life did I pass on the noble coasts of that romantic region"; she can access the place only as a "memory" that induces "melancholy," and she seems to be "lost in images of the past" as she reminisces (261, 262). The biographical device of locating Eudora's experience with the Bay of Naples in her lost youth allows Cooper to associate Italy with pastness, fitting for what he sees as its historical trajectory but actually in direct contradiction to Cooper's own experience of the bay, which he could see from his windows when he wrote this passage, in the house that he had rented on the cliffs of Sorrento. Cooper gestures to this reality when he has Eudora say, "Though many years are gone . . . I can recall the beauties of that scene as vividly as if they still stood before the eye" (262). Cooper transforms his present into Eudora's past in order to yoke Italy to the idea of nostalgia.

But even though he thus makes a concerted effort to render Italy obsolete, Cooper devotes several pages to a rapturous description of the bay's landscape, which "teems with the recollections of three thousand years," a depth of historical richness with which the New York Bay cannot even begin to compete. Eudora judges the Bay of Naples the more elegantly beautiful bay, with finer and more glorious air than can be found in New York. She attributes New York's foggier atmosphere to vaporous exhalations from the area's forests. These forests constitute an untapped resource, an indication of New York's commercial promise, but their vapors interfere with the aesthetics of the bay. Eudora speculates, "When there shall be less exhalation from your forests," presumably because more of their wood has been harvested, New York's air may rival Italy's (266). Commercial potential exists in inverse relation to aesthetic charm. Similarly, even though Venice's heyday has passed, it retains some of the cultural fruits of its former preeminence. Eudora remarks of a beautiful necklace made in Venice, "The hand of Venetian could alone form these delicate and nearly insensible links" (104). As evidenced by the skill of the necklace's craftsmanship, Italy has achieved a state of cultural refinement that continues to be a source of pleasure even as its political and economic power wanes.

Cooper undoubtedly possessed a great fondness for Italian culture, as evidenced by statements such as these and the accounts in his letters and journals of the idyllic summer he spent in Sorrento, living in what had been Torquato Tasso's villa.[14] But the beauties of Italy—its rich fabrics and storied ruins—function primarily to inspire pathos in that they are relics of former glory, not indicators of cultural vibrancy in the present. However great his respect for Italian culture may be, Cooper portrays Italy as having been eclipsed by the "youthful vigor of America" (much as Cooper has symbolically replaced Tasso as a productive artist). Eudora's ultimate assessment of the two bays locates imperial momentum in New York: "The one [the Bay of Naples] is poetic, indolent, and full of graceful but glorious beauty; more pregnant of enjoyment than usefulness. The other, one day, will be the mart of the world" (265). Italy's poetry and beauty, though enjoyable, are by-products of its economic inertia—indolence and lack of usefulness.

Cooper has Eudora phrase her sense of American dominance in prospective terms; New York will "one day" be the mart of the world. However, Cooper clearly believed that by the nineteenth century, the United States had made great strides toward achieving its potential. He argues in the original 1830 preface to *The Water-Witch* that "America has preceded, rather than followed Europe, in that march of improvement which is rendering the present era so remarkable" (3). The United States has assumed the position of the world's moral leader, leaving Italy and the rest of Europe behind, a key context in which Cooper encourages his readers to interpret the novel.

Cooper also foregrounds American ascendance at the start of the novel proper. Directly after his articulation of the cyclical history philosophy, he proceeds to elaborate not on images of Italy's decline but on the rapid progress of the United States as exhibited by the rapid growth of Manhattan: "By the Manhattanese, who is familiar with the forest of masts, the miles of wharves, the countless villas, the hundred churches, the castles, the smoking and busy vessels that crowd his bay, the daily increase and the general movement of his native town, the picture we are about to sketch will scarcely be recognized. He who shall come a generation later, will probably smile, that subject of admiration should have been found in the existing condition of the City. And yet we shall attempt to carry the recollections of the reader but a century back in the brief history of his country" (10). The town of Manhattan has progressed so much in just over a century that Cooper's contemporaries would hardly recognize the tiny pioneer town; Cooper later makes a similar comment about the humble origins of the "noble street that now runs for a league through the centre of the island," Broadway (25). The scope and scale of the city in the early nineteenth century—emphasized with the descriptors "forest," "miles," "countless," and the like—are made more remarkable by the pace of its "daily increase." Only a relatively "brief" period, a single century, has been required to achieve this extraordinary development. Furthermore, the growth seems exponential: in only one generation, a future Manhattaner will be amused by the thought that the town of 1830 elicited such admiration.

The character of the Dutch merchant Myndert Van Beverout, Alida's uncle, embodies the dynamism of this vigorous development. Trade is the engine that drives New York's growth, and Van Beverout devotes himself wholeheartedly to trade and profit. As a representative of American ascendance, Van Beverout has no patience for reminiscences about the glories of Italy. In both instances when Eudora proffers her wares to Alida and amuses her with meditations on Italy, Van Beverout enters the scene and disrupts the nostalgia. In the first case, he judges Eudora's fabrics as "the cast off finery of our ancestors. . . . Here are stuffs of an age that is past" (115). Italy, and Europe in general, has been eclipsed, relegated to obsolescence. Van Beverout argues this in part to drive down the price of the goods, an indication of the obsessiveness with which he pursues profit, but it also reflects his future-oriented perspective. The melancholy fate of fallen empires does not concern him; he seeks only to capitalize on the developing commercial power of the American colonies.

This attitude seems in some ways unappealingly crass. After Eudora's sensibility-laden exploration of the comparative fineness of the air in the Naples and New York bays, Van Beverout enters the room uttering his own meteorological ruminations, which Cooper describes as unconsciously "apposite" to Eudora and Alida's conversation: "'Gales and climates!' exclaimed the merchant." But atmospheric beauty plays no role in his thoughts, in which weather matters only to the extent that it affects the speed of shipping. Storms mean "too much precious time wasted between markets" (268). If Van Beverout symbolizes American ascendance, then Cooper suggests that the great growth of the United States might as yet be attended by some cultural lack, especially in comparison with the refinement that Italy had attained as a result of its period of global preeminence. Cooper ideally would want this gaucherie to be tempered by infusions of European elegance, but in *The Water-Witch*, colonial callowness serves mainly as comic relief, an amusing side effect of emergent commercial drives, and one that should disappear as the country matures and continues on its path of ascent, fueled by the economic energies that Van Beverout embodies.

The Water-Witch remains a generally lighthearted novel throughout. Thomas Philbrick characterizes it as "a flight from the pressures and restrictions of reality."[15] Its representation of cyclical history highlights that idea's advantages for the nation on the rise while de-emphasizing the inescapable manifestations of decay in the nation on the decline. Its tone prompts James Grossman to remark, "Nations in their decline, living off the accumulations of past energies, were happier, he [Cooper] learned, than nations busily accumulating in the present."[16]

However, this sense of lazy Italy's "happiness" derives from the novel's significant idealization of Italian decline, to which it refers only briefly while stressing the cultural refinements that linger after power itself has departed. Cooper emphasizes the aesthetic pleasure produced by the Bay of Naples, unmarred by the crudities of commercial vigor, "more pregnant of enjoyment than of usefulness." He does not dwell on the ramifications of the bay's lack of usefulness for Neapolitan society. He includes only one mention of the lazzaroni, the beggars so great in number and abject in condition that U.S. tourists constantly mentioned them in their accounts of Naples: Eudora speaks of a "Paris gourmand" wishing to "enjoy the bounties of a low latitude" and therefore relishing a fig "that a Lazzarone of Naples would cast into his bay" (261). Cooper depicts the Italian beggar actually spurning food rather than serving as an illustration of the rampant poverty and degradation of southern Italy in the era of its decline. The novel's comments about Italy stay mostly within a gently nostalgic mode and highlight luxury goods like velvets and satins. The rich cultural products of Italy enter New York Bay without the attendant social problems.

A similar evasion can be discerned in Cooper's handling of the characters most closely associated with Italy—the Skimmer of the Seas, captain of the *Water-Witch*, and Eudora, who not only spent her youth in Italy but is actually likened to it. At one point, as she blushes, Cooper writes that on her face "colour went and came like lights changing in an Italian sky" (414). This description occurs just before the end of the novel, linking Eudora's fate closely with the idea of Italy itself. The Skimmer and Eudora, whose romanticized marine banditry will become obsolete once the U.S. Revolutionary War ends the British ban on foreign goods, have no clear future usefulness (and so share the predicament of Natty Bumppo in the Leatherstocking Tales). Like the Italian culture with which they are associated, their glory days will soon be done.

But Cooper does not force his readers to confront the Skimmer and Eudora's imminent extinction. At the end of the novel, they sail off into the sunset and are never seen again, frozen in time, while the U.S. characters proceed with their lives. Cooper narratively halts the decline of Italy even as he allows the ascendance of the United States to proceed. In *The Water-Witch*, Italy's decline functions primarily to highlight American ascendance by offering a contrast to it. The upward trajectory of the United States becomes visible in the action of overtaking Italy. The clarifying effect of this imperial eclipse serves its self-congratulatory purpose without requiring a continued attention to Italy's depressing downward spiral.

Italian Decline

The Bravo, on the other hand, paints a considerably grimmer picture of the decline of Italy. In practical terms, *The Water-Witch* focuses on and is set in the United

States, the nation on the rise, and thus its tone stays predominantly optimistic, whereas *The Bravo* focuses on the nation in decline and takes its tone from that more disquieting national moment. The latter novel dwells obsessively on the decline and implied death of the Venetian republic and does not shrink from representing the end of the historical cycle. Its examination of Venice's self-destruction, although undertaken nominally to illustrate how the U.S. republic differs from the Venetian one, actually raises the specter of aristocratic tendencies within U.S. society similar to the ones that ensured Venice's downfall. *The Bravo* wrestles with the logical extension of Cooper's statement in *The Water-Witch* that nature has "set limits to *all* moral and political ascendency"—not just to Italy's ascendency, but theoretically to the ascendency of the United States as well.

Cooper's darker meditations on cyclical history's ravages can be usefully glossed through his comments on the painting series *The Course of Empire* by Hudson River School artist Thomas Cole.[17] *The Course of Empire* (1836), itself a visual narrative of imperial eclipse, depicts the rise and fall of an empire over the course of five canvases. The empire's conquest from without is preceded by corruption within. Scholars have interpreted the middle canvas, showing the empire at the height of its power, as alluding to contemporary critiques of "King" Andrew Jackson through the image of the emperor surrounded by his adoring mobs; Alan Wallach, among others, argues that the cautionary tale inherent in the progression through the paintings would have been well understood as directed backhandedly at the United States.[18] International history thus takes on intranational significance in *The Course of Empire*, as it does also in *The Bravo* and other imperial eclipse narratives that I discuss in this book.

Cooper thought extremely highly of Cole and his *Course of Empire*, calling the series "the work of the highest genius this country has ever produced" and "one of the noblest works of art that has ever been wrought." He agreed with Cole's vision of humanity and history. Cooper writes, "In the lifetime of a nation,—for nations like individuals have a life-time, bounded by birth and death—there is a summit-level, up to which, it may be said, it carries itself, and down from which it is carried. Moving forward by the force of native energies and passions, there arrives a time when energies are exhausted, and passions vitiated." From that point on, "it is caught in the arms of avenging, irresistible destiny, and hurried down to extinction."[19] In *The Bravo*, he chooses to chronicle a moment in Venice's headlong rush to dissolution, to watch its "avenging, irresistible destiny" at work. In the process, he suggests the possible direction of U.S. destiny as well.

When Cooper says that "nations like individuals have a life-time," instead of saying that *most* nations, like individuals, have a lifetime, he dooms the United States to the same birth and death that Cole delineates in *The Course of Empire*.

The constraints of a universalist historical logic challenge U.S. exceptionalism, and as seductively coherent as the cyclical theory of history made the material of the human past, U.S. Americans struggled between the intellectual magnetism of the cyclical hypothesis and their addiction to national exceptionalism. Some produced elaborate justifications for why the exception proved the rule—why the United States was exempt from a pattern that had governed the course of all previous empires.

Many espoused the idea of religious millennialism, a historical logic that potentially offered competition to cyclical history. In one version of the millennial framework, the United States, the divinely blessed nation, would act as a spur to the establishment of God's kingdom on earth, facilitating a movement of humanity out of history and away from the laws that had controlled its processes before.[20] No longer would time move in an eternal circle; it would now progress to a higher plane, all because of the United States' extraordinary character and destiny as a nation. The seemingly inescapable pattern of imperial rise and fall would itself become obsolete, as God's empire supplanted humanity's empires.

A distinct (though sometimes overlapping) form of exceptionalist thought, one that predominates in *The Bravo*, grounded itself on the United States' unique political constitution as a democratic republic. Republicanism, with its emphasis on popularly elected representatives dedicated to the common good of society, seemed to many a particularly estimable and beneficial mode of government, worthy of an exemption from the cyclical pattern. Unfortunately, republicanism's track record—in Athens, Sparta, and Rome, as well as more recent early modern examples—did little to alleviate concerns about inevitable societal degeneration and decline. However, the conditions of the United States varied enough from these previous failed examples to provide hope for a different outcome.

Whereas previous republics in the Old World had been required to construct tortured and ultimately unsuccessful methods for producing the social equality necessary for a scheme of popular representation, U.S. society had not been founded on feudal or aristocratic systems that would have undermined its republicanism. As Gordon Wood writes, "[T]he New World seemed uniquely free of the constraining distinctions of social rank—a naturally egalitarian society, young, rustic, energetic, . . . without the stifling and corrupting refinement of the Old World." Furthermore, although classic republican theory regarded the extent of U.S. territory as an obstacle to the creation of a functioning republic, Federalists famously argued that a larger territorial scope would actually inhibit the formation of destructive factions (a theory that Cooper advocates in the preface to *The Bravo*). The availability of land would also guarantee more universal access to yeomanly virtue, so essential in a system in which power rested in the people. The scope of an empire could thus be effectively combined with the righteousness of a republic. Given the United States' geographic and social advantages and its originally conceived, cleverly designed Constitution, Wood writes, "The decay and the eventual death of the republican body politic now seemed less inevitable. . . . For the Americans at least, and for others if they followed, the endless cycles of history could finally be broken."[21] Republicanism could facilitate an escape from the rise and fall of empires pattern.

Cooper argued for this kind of exceptionalism in relationship to U.S. republicanism, a system so just that it might be able to tip the United States out of cyclical time and into progressive time, and which certainly precluded forecasts of U.S. decline based on Old World versions of republicanism. Cooper made *The Bravo* into an extensive exercise in distinction between the U.S. and Venetian "republics." Venice, too, for much of its history, had claimed the title of a republic, but by the nineteenth century it had categorically succumbed to the forces of cyclical history. Cooper therefore had to make the case that the so-called Venetian republic actually had no right to the name, and that its failure should not be used to predict the future of the United States. Cooper explicitly worked to "demonstrate the fallacy of a reasoning which is so fond of predicting the downfall of our own liberal system, supported by examples drawn from trans-atlantic states of the middle ages" (130).

These examples from the modern era seemed more damning than classical Athens, Sparta, and Rome because they also operated (after 1492) in a "trans-atlantic" world, with its reconfigured global commercial system and new rules. Cooper thus devotes special attention to undermining their claim to the mantle of a "republic," which implied popular sovereignty: "At the period of which we write, Italy had several of these self-styled commonwealths, in not one of which, however, was there ever a fair and just confiding of power to the body of the people, though perhaps there is not one that has not been cited sooner or later in proof of the inability of man to govern himself!" Venice, which Cooper judges the "most important" of Italy's pseudo-republics, had accrued a myth of exemplary stability and duration (130).[22] But Cooper endeavors to show that although "[m]uch was said of the venerable character of her polity," in fact "[t]here was a never-ceasing and a natural tendency to dissolution in her factitious system, which was only resisted by the alertness of her aristocracy" (254). Thus it did not necessarily follow from Venice's downfall at the end of the eighteenth century that even a long-lasting modern "republic" would ultimately and inevitably fail (a "reasoning" that would have had grim implications for the United States).

In his preface to *The Bravo*, Cooper bemoans the fact that "the world does not discriminate more justly in its use of political terms," complaining that the term *republic* had been applied inappropriately to both democracies and aristocracies (3). He distinguishes Venice, which he considers an aristocracy and therefore not properly a republic, from a true democratic republic by continually referring to it throughout the novel as a "self-styled," "titular," or "pretending" republic (76, 114, 130, 131, 254, 318). He aims in *The Bravo* to clear up the "utter confusion" that surrounds this issue by giving "his countrymen, in this book, a picture of the social system of one of the *soi-disant* republics of the other hemisphere" (3). Although, as we shall see, Cooper's critics would disparage his suspect Europhilic penchant for unnecessary Gallicisms—"soi-disant," instead of simply "so-called"—Cooper clearly writes for a U.S. audience of "his countrymen" and argues for a U.S. political exceptionalism. "Freedom" in European systems, if such there actually be, "depends on a principle entirely different from our own," and "so long as this vital difference exists between ourselves and other nations, it will be vain to think of finding analogies in their institutions" (3, 4). The quest to establish "this vital difference," the thing that set the United States apart from the early modern Italian city-states and the cyclical pattern in which they seemed to be embedded, occupies the whole of the novel.

The Bravo presents a running contrast between Venice and the United States. Cooper repeatedly explains Venetian society and politics with reference to the United States (24, 210, 254, 275, 318). For example, he describes Venice's "peculiar machinery of the state," its system of councils—the Council of Three Hundred (representatives from the established noble families), Council of Ten (a more powerful group chosen at random from among the three hundred), and Council of Three (the highest power in Venice, a secret body also chosen by lots with complete authority to act in any manner deemed necessary on behalf of the state, and with no oversight by the other councils or the public).[23] The reader, he assumes, will need this explanation, "for the name of a republic, a word which, if it mean anything, strictly implies the representation and supremacy of the general interests, . . . may have induced him to believe that there was, at least, a resemblance between the outlines of that government, and the more just, because more popular, institutions of his own country" (128). Instead, in the case of Venice, although monarchy had been avoided by limiting the power of the doge, the aristocracy ruled the state, a situation entirely different from the popular system of representation in the United States.

Cooper writes that "Venice, though ambitious and tenacious of the name of a republic, was, in truth, a narrow, a vulgar, and an exceedingly heartless oligarchy"—that is, a government controlled by the few (129). In contrast to the (theoretically) egalitarian society of the United States, "[d]istinctions of rank, as separated entirely from the will of the nation, formed the basis of Venetian polity" (130). Venetian government arose out of an aristocratic society and helped to solidify the privileges of the nobility at the expense of the people. Cooper embodies the aristocratic temperament most flagrantly in the character of Alessandro Gradenigo, a Venetian senator and member of the despotic Council of Three, whom Cooper sums up as a thoroughgoing aristocrat and "powerful advocate for vested rights" (76). Gradenigo reprimands a boyhood friend, a poor fisherman who protests the impressment of his young grandson and asserts that "God has given all feelings and nature alike"; Gradenigo tells him, to the contrary, that he should "remember thy condition, and the difference that God hath made between our children" (175, 62). The divine right of kings has been replaced by the divine right of the aristocracy.

Furthermore, although Cooper depicts Gradenigo's aristocratic philosophy as particularly callous and self-serving, the entirety of Italian society is built on unequal and unjust distinctions of birth. Cooper describes Don Camillo Monforte, one of the more admirable characters whose eventual escape from Venice represents one of the story's few victories, as a "feudal lord" who refers to people born within his ducal domains as his "vassals" (299, 21, 187, 203). When one of his servants hesitates to fulfill an order, Monforte reminds him of his status as "a being of my fiefs." Perhaps even more problematically, his servant, and most of the other common people in the novel, respond with "habitual deference" to the nobles, cowed by displays of aristocratic grandeur (21). A short-lived burst of mob resistance later in the story withers in the absence of a natural rights philosophy. Clearly, Italy is a feudal society, and true republican equality cannot be built on such a corrupt social foundation. Real republicanism, republicanism that could last the test of time, required a post-feudal society like the United States.

Venetian senators such as Gradenigo, instead of acting as representatives of the people's will, conspire to maintain their own power and keep the people in subjection. The novel's plot consists entirely of characters being trapped by and trying—generally unsuccessfully—to free themselves from the machinations of the state. Venice as a setting symbolizes the state's claustrophobic totalitarianism and illustrates how easily conspiratorial factions can put a stranglehold on popular liberty within the small space of a city-state, as opposed to the vast territory that the U.S. republic was fortunate enough to occupy. Cooper's Venice induces a kind of breathless absorption through the unalleviated evil of its atmosphere and the almost completely seamless embrace of its web.[24] Venice engrosses, whether in the literal or metaphoric imprisonment of characters within its confines or in the magnetism exerted by its unique culture. Cooper presents in vivid detail such distinctively Venetian customs as the routine wearing of masks, which both promotes carnivalesque play and symbolizes the stifling ethos of deception fostered by the state.[25] Masks confer a level of libertine freedom on their wearers but only as a brief reprieve from state surveillance. Cooper paints a compelling picture of an environment full of swift-moving gondolas, noiseless streets, and exotic architecture where state agents practice unremitting intrigues from which no one can be safe.

Nonetheless, however engrossing Venice may seem, to its inhabitants or to Cooper's readers, the larger historical narrative against which the novel's story plays itself out actually involves Venice's eclipse as a global power. The state's cruelty grows in inverse proportion to its waning power, as its leadership combats the restiveness of an increasingly abused and economically depressed populace. Venice employs ever more punishing measures to suppress the rebellion that continually threatens. But as a senator observes of the state's harsh laws, "[T]here is something unsuited to a falling fortune in . . . our laws. When a state is eminently flourishing, its subjects overlook general defects, in private prosperity, but there is no more fastidious commentator than your merchant of a failing trade" (260). Totalitarian control simply increases the pressures that threaten to tear Venice apart and renders it more susceptible to outside conquest.

Although the novel ends with an invocation of evil Venice, holding "its vicious sway, corrupting alike the ruler and the ruled," it begins with the city-state's dwindling influence and power, which forms the wider framework in which its utter malignancy must be interpreted (362). Early on in the first chapter of the novel—approximately where Cooper placed his articulation of cyclical history philosophy in *The Water-Witch*—he calls our attention to the "fallen fortunes" of Venice in the present day; however, "at the period of our tale, the city of the isles, though no longer the mistress of the Mediterranean, nor even of the Adriatic, was still rich and powerful. . . . Men lived among her islands in that state of incipient lethargy which marks the progress of a downward course" (6). Though not yet in dire straits, Venice is "marked" as declining. Even commoners can see that "the republic is a little aged . . . the leap of the winged lion is not as far as it was" (14). When one of them attempts to champion "the great deeds of the Queen of the Adriatic" by beginning, "Thou forgettest that Venezia has been—" his companion interjects, "Zitto, zitto! that *has* been, caro mio, is a great word with all Italy. . . . It is better, Gino Monaldi, to be one of a people which is great and victorious just now" (15). Throughout the novel, Cooper repeatedly makes this kind of allusion to Venice's decline (31, 52, 70, 147–48, 150, 169–70, 254, 259).

Venice's rulers work to keep this knowledge from the populace by manipulatively stoking their patriotism: in the Piazza San Marco, "the improvisatore, secretly employed by a politic and mysterious government, recounted, . . . in a language suited to the popular ear, . . . the ancient triumphs of the republic"; the cheers of the crowd "were the reward of the agents of the police, whenever they most administered to the self-delusion and vanity of their audience" (89).[26] But the aristocracy themselves also seem prone to this blindness.[27] On hearing the sounds of an angry mob in the streets, "some listened in admiration . . . and they believed that St. Mark had gained a victory, in that decline, which was never exactly intelligible to their apathetic capacities" (255). Similarly, the state kept up the ritual of the "marriage of the Adriatic," the renewing of the commitment vows between Venice and the sea, long after it became farcical to suggest that Venice dominated the waves:

> [S]everal of the ministers of the northern and more maritime states, who were witnesses on the occasion, had scarcely concealed, as they cast glances of intelligence and pride among themselves, their smiles. . . . neither the increasing feebleness of the Republic, nor the known superiority of other powers on the very element which this pageant was intended to represent as the peculiar property of St. Mark, could yet cover the lofty pretension with the ridicule it merited. Time has since taught the world that Venice continued this idle deception for ages after both reason and modesty should have dictated its discontinuance; but, at the period of which we write, that ambitious, crapulous, and factitious state was rather beginning to feel the symptomatic evidence of its fading circumstances, than to be fully conscious of the swift progress of a downward course. In this manner do communities, like individuals, draw near their dissolution, inattentive to the symptoms of decay, until they are overtaken with that fate which finally overwhelms empires and their power in the common lot of man. (92–93)

In just over a century, Venice will be an Austrian colony with no autonomous government. Already, Venice has been eclipsed by "other powers," personified by the smirking ambassadors. Cyclical history has Venice in its grip, and the (perhaps willful) blindness of Venetians to their empire's decline masks awareness of the uselessness of state machinations.

And, the novel suggests, this might be the blindness of the United States as well. Despite their inevitable implication "in the common lot of man," U.S. Americans remained dangerously inattentive to potential symptoms of imperial "dissolution." Flattered by their nation's status as a republic, they paid too little heed to the pretensions of an aspiring U.S. aristocracy, which would mire the country in corruption and despotism if it gained control of the government. Cooper, in *A Letter to His Countrymen* and other writings, expressed concern about the sly power of the Whig-dominated Congress, especially in the controversy over the Second

National Bank, a power struggle between the executive and legislative branches of government. Democratic president Andrew Jackson alleged that the bank functioned to monopolize wealth in the hands of the country's Whig elite, allowing them to pervert and corrupt the political process. In Cooper's pro-Jacksonian view of the bank controversy, U.S. congressmen often acted suspiciously like Venetian senators, dressing up oligarchy in the trappings of republican democracy.[28]

Robert Levine details Cooper's increasing fears, registered in *The Bravo*, of forces in society and government whose conspiratorial activities were weakening the United States' commitment to freedom. In Cooper's portrayal of the insidiously oligarchical Venetian senators, Levine identifies contemporary fears about secret coalitions of groups like the wealthy Freemasons, who were believed to be undermining the fabric of the republic and perverting the legal system in order to cover up their evil deeds and secure ever-greater political and economic power for themselves.[29] Marius Bewley has noted that Cooper "had his eye steadily on the American scene" in *The Bravo*: the novel "was written as a warning of the kind of oligarchy that might, under the cover of nominally republican institutions, get control of the government of the United States."[30] Although the United States had no system of nobility akin to the feudal lords of Venice, Cooper believed that the Whig Party desired to institutionalize its power as an aristocratic governing class.[31]

In *A Letter to His Countrymen*, Cooper wrote, "I knew there existed at home a large party of *doctrinaires* [the French aristocratic party, used here to describe the Francophilic Whigs], composed of men of very fair intentions, but of very limited means of observation, who fancied excellencies under other [political] systems" (15). The admiration of these aristocratic Whigs for foreign constitutions threatened to undermine U.S. political exceptionalism, which rested precisely on the fundamental difference between U.S. republicanism and other schemes of government. If the United States could not claim to be exceptional, then it could not avert, or even long delay, the dissolutive energies of cyclical history. Whigs gravitated toward what Cooper saw as the same oligarchic system that had corrupted and doomed previous republics. So, "with the painful conviction that many of my own countrymen were influenced by the fallacy that nations could be governed by an irresponsible minority, without involving a train of nearly intolerable abuses, I determined to attempt a series of tales, in which American opinion should be brought to bear on European facts. With this design the Bravo was written" (12).

Given the "painful" concerns about his countrymen with which he began the novel, Cooper's project of national distinction falters. He shows successfully that Venice did not deserve the title of "republic," but in the process he creates doubt about the term's aptness to describe the United States. Perhaps neither "self-styled republic" deserved an exemption from cyclical history. He writes in the preface to *The Bravo* that "so long as this vital difference [of popular sovereignty] exists between ourselves and other nations, it will be vain to think of finding analogies in their institutions," but the Whigs conspired to circumvent popular sovereignty and thereby exposed the United States to the force of Old World analogies. The oligarchic aspirations of the Whigs created a spatiotemporal contact zone that brought together times and places that Cooper strove to hold distinct. For Cooper, then, the international history of Venice served to diagnose and warn against intranational political tendencies that imprisoned the United States within the logic of cyclical history.

U.S. Oligarch

Despite Cooper's patriotic motives for writing *The Bravo*, the novel met with a hostile reaction from many critics. The Whig press leveled especially harsh criticism, no doubt partly motivated by partisan resentment toward Cooper and his resolutely Democratic political viewpoint.[32] In an autobiographical fragment written in 1844, by which time Cooper had become thoroughly disenchanted with the U.S. cultural scene, he describes his sense of the reason for the critical backlash: "As this was the first of my books in which the scene was laid abroad, since Precaution [an 1821 novel of manners set in England], I was abused as a deserter from my country, and all sorts of silly twaddle was uttered, for laying the scene of this book in Venice."[33] His abandonment of "American materials" in favor of Venetian ones constituted literary treason.

Cooper expresses "contempt" for this "silly twaddle," defiantly stating, "I will lay the scenes of my books wherever I please." He refuses the conflation of foreign settings with desertion of his country because, for him, national principles don't have to be wedded to national things. Foreign settings can in fact be the best opportunities to engage with national principles. This theory enables him to claim, "*Au reste*, The Bravo is perhaps, *in spirit, the most American* book I ever wrote" (4:461).[34] He makes a similar claim in his earlier *A Letter to His Countrymen*, where he insists that *The Bravo* "was thoroughly American in all that belonged to it" (15). The Venetian setting occasioned Cooper's deepest engagement with American principles.

Cooper judges the public incapable of understanding this logic, because "thousands in this country, who clamor about such things, do not know American principles when they meet them, unless it may happen to be in a Fourth of July oration" (4:461–62).[35] They can recognize an American principle only when it comes yoked in a straightforward and unchallenging way to an American thing, such as a Fourth of July oration. They do not have the capacity to appreciate the exploration of American principles when decoupled from American things. And just like the oblivious Venetians who cheer at the recounting of the "ancient triumphs of the republic" as their empire declines, those who engage with American principles only in self-congratulatory Fourth of July orations (vehicles for recounting the ancient triumphs of the U.S. republic) risk a perilous cultural blindness about the present state of the United States.

Forces conspire against more challenging and urgent explorations of American principles. In *A Letter to His Countrymen*, Cooper argues that a U.S. writer will encounter obstacles if he decides "to take part frankly with the institutions and character of his country; the feelings of those who control public sentiment on subjects of this nature, are opposed to his success" (47). Disillusioned by attacks on what he regarded as highly patriotic literary projects, Cooper had come to the conclusion that the "American who wishes to illustrate and enforce the peculiar principles of his own country, by the agency of polite literature, will, for a long time to come, I fear, find that *his* constituency, as to all purposes of distinctive thought, is still too much under the influence of foreign theories, to receive him with favor" (98). "American literature" (in Cooper's sense, literature that is imbued with and devoted to American principles, whether or not it concerns itself with American things—an interesting way to reimagine the category) had no supportive U.S. audience.

Cooper particularly decries the practice of reprinting foreign literary reviews in U.S. journals, as had happened with some of his own reviews, because "[t]he habit of fostering this deference to foreign opinion is dangerous to the very institutions under which we live" (59). In his assessment, the culture of European aristocracy was antithetical to U.S. republicanism and therefore highly critical of writing that championed it; letting foreign reviewers dictate U.S. literary taste thus disempowered authors who sought to advocate and explore republican ideologies uniquely endemic to the United States. Cooper had written in an earlier piece on the controversy that "all the familiar thoughts and illustrations of English literature are in direct and dangerous opposition to our own system, and yet we are unwilling to support a writer in the promulgation of those that are in harmony with our profession," despite "the frank attitude of republicanism we profess" (110, Note A). He felt that a true republican author—as Cooper believed himself to be—had to fight against the slavish adherence to foreign principles of politics and taste exhibited by the press (particularly Whig newspapers) and the public at large. The people did not seem to appreciate his efforts to defend their natural rights.

However, Cooper's critics questioned his populist credentials. He seemed to fight for the people by belittling them. As we have seen especially in his more cynical 1844 account of *The Bravo*'s reception, Cooper expresses "contempt" for his fellow citizens who utter "silly twaddle" and simplemindedly consume the patriotic pabulum offered in Fourth of July orations. In their support of literary talent, their actions and attitudes don't match their professed republican principles. Although Cooper saw his philosophy as entirely ideologically consistent, his depiction of the U.S. public as undiscerning to the point of denseness about what actually constitute American principles, and himself as the unfairly maligned, staunchly loyal defender of those principles, does not seem in line with his abstract championing of the people. The contrast is certainly striking between his protestations for "popular rights" in *The Bravo* and his increasing disdain for the idiotic, mobbish masses as the years go by.[36]

Cooper understood the statement that "*Au reste,* The Bravo is perhaps, *in spirit, the most American* book I ever wrote" as indicating an enlightened and amplified kind of patriotism, so committed to national principles that it could see beyond mere superficialities. His critics, on the other hand, pointed to the linguistic pretension of Gallic gestures like the phrase "au reste" as ridiculous and inconsistent with his Democratic stance as a man of and for the people. "Au reste" and "soi-disant" suggested a desertion of the United States by Cooper more far-reaching than the simple adoption of foreign settings for his novels. Critics saw in Cooper a noxious investment in a Europhilic style of gentlemanliness, culture, and breeding, a class consciousness that tended toward anti-populist elitism. His denunciations of Whig aristocratic infringement on the rights of the people struck them as hypocritical given his inclinations toward a cultural, if not political, American oligarchy.

Predictably, then, Cooper's attempt in *A Letter to His Countrymen* to explain himself and the motives behind *The Bravo* did not appease his critics. It merely provided them with more fodder for their attacks. Edward Sherman Gould, who wrote under the pseudonym "Cassio" and who had penned a scathing review of *The Bravo* that Cooper censured in *A Letter,* published a parody in July 1834 called "The Man in the Claret-Coloured Coat to His Countrymen." It ridicules Cooper's bloated prose and pompous self-presentation and homes in on a personal condescension that colors the original document. The title evokes not only an emphasis on elegant clothing, consistent with Cooper's investment in being a gentleman with taste, but it also hints at an underlying betrayal of national principles: Cooper has turned "redcoat."

In the parody, Gould takes aim at Cooper's habit of interjecting French phrases into his writing: the man in the claret-colored coat confuses the word *despot* with *depot* but insists on rendering "*despot*" as "*dépôt.*"[37] Gould has the claret-coated man come out of his "classic and dignified retirement" to complain about his treatment at the hands of the "vulgar" press. He mocks this statement of Cooper's in the original *Letter*: "As to [a critic's] assertion that I took pride in being called 'The American Walter Scott,' it will be seen as quite gratuitous, and, if permitted to speak for myself on this point, I shall merely say that it gave me just as much gratification as any nick-name can give a gentleman" (55). Gould reserves his jab at this statement for the penultimate paragraph, writing, "It has become a common thing in France, England, Turkey, China, Russia, Egypt, and the city of Washington, to style me the *American Walter Scott*." The claret-coated man makes sure to point out the cosmopolitan, global reach of his conspicuously nonnational popularity ("the city of Washington" is the only U.S. place mentioned), although the randomness of the list of places where he is styled the American Walter Scott suggests not universal acclaim but perhaps instead a pathetic concern with his somewhat overinflated sense of importance.

But even as he makes gratuitous mention of how far his literary fame has traveled, the claret-coated man disdains the public's flattery in calling him the American Scott: "[T]he people seem to think that I ought to be flattered! by the degrading appellation! But I take this occasion to inform them that the title *'gives me just as much gratification as any* NICKNAME *can give a gentleman,'! ! !* . . . This is what I call republican independence." He considers the title of American Scott "degrading" either because nicknames aren't gentlemanly or because it turns the claret-coated man into a derivative of Scott. The man must "inform" the people of their mistake in presenting this title to him as a compliment. Gould adds capital letters and three exclamation marks to highlight his intense reaction to the striking haughtiness of Cooper's original statement.

Dorothy Waples rehabilitates Cooper's dislike of the "American Scott" moniker by pointing to his belief that Scott's romances often glorified the feudalist institutions of their medieval settings.[38] Cooper had devoted significant time and energy to endorsing deeply republican institutions in his writing as, for example, when he subtly critiqued Don Camillo Monforte in *The Bravo* for his assumption of superiority over his "vassals." Cooper therefore felt frustrated by the widespread tendency to emphasize the superficial resemblance between his romances and Scott's. Waples furthermore ascribes the vehemence of the attacks against Cooper to partisan spirit; his most merciless critics were all Whigs, who had a factional investment in eviscerating a declared spokesman for their political adversary, the Democratic Party.

But his critics do legitimately diagnose in Cooper an aristocratic arrogance at odds with his avowed Democratic populism. Cooper saw himself as a righteous defender of the principles of liberty integral to the American spirit and argued vociferously for that interpretation of his work. The fact that Gould's claret-coated man interprets his own spurning of a public compliment as an act of "republican independence" indicates the problem with that approach, though. His personal crusade to safeguard U.S. republicanism from foreign threat and domestic misunderstandings seemed to his critics like petulant and conceited self-absorption. They pointed to apparent inconsistencies in Cooper's philosophy: his time spent hobnobbing with the aristocracy in Europe (the claret-coated man remarks pompously that "while visiting nations I received special attention from all the nobility without exception"); his vitriolic defense of the landlords in the anti-rent controversy of the 1840s; and his elitist and anti-populist sentiments in, for example, the Effingham novels, which valorize the spiritual and social superiority of gentlemanly landowners over the coarseness of demagogues and their rabble. For many, Cooper's personal condescension and investment in being one of the landed New York gentry undercut his diatribes about democratic liberty and the sanctity of the rights of the people.

The aristocratic superciliousness already in evidence in the 1834 *Letter to His Countrymen* becomes more prominent over the course of the 1830s and '40s. In a revised preface to *The Water-Witch* published in 1851, Cooper abandons his earlier paean to national progress, in which he had claimed, "America has preceded, rather than followed Europe, in that march of improvement which is rendering the present era so remarkable." He instead predicts a dark future for U.S. society. He mentions patroons, wealthy Dutch landowners who formed an important part of the colonial New York society that he depicts in *The Water-Witch*:

> the genus seems about to expire among us. Not only are we to have no more patroons, but the decree has gone forth from the virtuous and infallible voters that there are to be no more estates.
>
> "All the realm shall be in common, and in Cheapside shall my palfrey go to grass."
>
> The collected wisdom of the State has decided that it is true policy to prevent the affluent from investing their money in land! The curse of mediocrity weighs upon us, and its blunders can be repaired only through the hard lessons of experience. (8)

The same person who had lauded "the more just, because more popular, institutions" of the United States in *The Bravo* now speaks with biting sarcasm of the "virtuous and infallible voters." The quotation in the middle of the passage comes from Shakespeare's *Henry VI, Part 2*, in which Jack Cade and the Peasants' Revolution are disparaged as the workings of an inane mob.[39] The enfranchisement of the peasants would mean chaos and a leveling of hierarchies and standards that

Cooper characterizes as "the curse of mediocrity." Although he believed that great injury would be done to the interests of the people if an oligarchical class burrowed into the institutions of government, he also believed that the interests of the people would be served by encouraging a moral aristocracy, ennobled by investment in the land, which could exert a benevolent effect on the institutions of culture.[40] According to Cooper, the anti-rent agitation and subsequent legal revisions broke up large estates and in the process broke up the moral fabric of society.

In the end, it seems that Cooper developed some of the blindness that he thought characteristic of his Venetian senators. He did not recognize the inevitable waning of the patroon way of life and the inexorable weakening of the power of the landed gentry. He fought so hard against the feudal ideology in romance that he did not recognize it in the reality of his landowning neighbors. His dislocation of American principles from American things allowed him to defend liberty abroad—and in the abstract—while neglecting its domestic exigencies.

As he sensed his way of life disappearing, he was "rather beginning to feel the symptomatic evidence of its fading circumstances, than to be fully conscious of the swift progress of a downward course. In this manner do communities, like individuals, draw near their dissolution, inattentive to the symptoms of decay, until they are overtaken with that fate which finally overwhelms empires and their power in the common lot of man."

Caught in the grip of what might therefore be considered a personal, socioeconomic eclipse, Cooper also produced in his representations of Italy a narrative of collective, imperial eclipse. The United States, a rising power, had surpassed the great Italian city-states of the early modern period. But it seemed to be reenacting some of the same self-destructive sociopolitical mistakes that Venice had made. Cooper's efforts to educate his U.S. readers about the dangers facing their nation resulted mostly in scorn rather than gratitude, and so he contemplated his country's future with ever-increasing gloom.

2
Calculating the Consequences
Property Fears in Prescott's *Conquest of Peru*

Cooper described nineteenth-century Venice in *The Bravo* as "the ruins of what, during the Middle Ages, was the mart of the Mediterranean" (24). Venice's medieval heyday came to an end when new geographies reconfigured the patterns of global commerce in the early modern period. The Americas as a source of European wealth after 1492 diminished Venice's centrality to a now-transatlantic world of trade and initiated the city-state's lingering decline. However, modernity had only begun to pile up its casualties. In the rapid-fire succession of eclipsed empires during this period, indigenous American empires that had enjoyed their own "medieval" (that is, pre-Columbian) prosperity also suffered eclipse in the form of conquest by the Spanish.

William Hickling Prescott, a Boston historian, wrote two influential accounts of Spanish conquest in the Americas: *History of the Conquest of Mexico* (1843) and *History of the Conquest of Peru* (1847). Although most critics now focus on *The Conquest of Mexico,* I will be focusing primarily on *The Conquest of Peru*, analyzing it as a narrative of imperial eclipse in which international Peruvian history sparks intranational anxiety in Prescott. Conquest represents a more sudden and violent kind of imperial eclipse than the gradual decline that Cooper depicts as overtaking Venice, but conquest similarly signifies that a once flourishing and powerful empire has fallen victim to the cyclical history pattern. Resemblances between that fallen empire and the nineteenth-century United States would therefore be cause for concern.

In his introduction to *The Conquest of Peru*, which describes life under Incan rule, Prescott defensively emphasizes the contrast between the essentially proto-communist economic system that operated in Incan Peru and the more beneficial capitalist one that was operating in the United States in the nineteenth century—just as Cooper had attempted to distinguish Venice's pseudo-republicanism from true U.S. republicanism. Despite what Prescott depicted as the Incas' totalitarian disregard for individual freedom, though, preconquest Peru's social and economic system was actually more successful in guaranteeing a minimum quality of life to all its participants than U.S. laissez-faire capitalism. Heavily invested (financially and psychologically) in laissez-faire capitalism, Prescott therefore actively championed the wisdom of the U.S. system. The ideological disquiet revealed in Prescott's strenuous arguments about the glories of capitalism arose not only from the seeming success of Incan proto-communism but also from what that success might forecast, given the increasing popularity of communist and socialist movements in the United States in the 1840s. Prescott diagnosed elements of Peruvian thinking at work in these alternative economic logics emerging in his own society.

Prescott's principal objection to communism concerned its interference with personal property. Prescott regarded the right to acquire and retain property as fundamental to individual liberty, a core belief and political priority that he shared with other wealthy and influential Whigs. He also regarded property as fundamental to overall economic health, because the possibility of acquiring personal wealth provides the incentive to participate energetically in competitive commerce.[1] Therefore, in detailing Prescott's account of the deadening economic effects of communism, I will also be discussing other indicators of economic weakness related in Prescott's mind to the lack of personal property guarantees.

Because of his underlying commitment to property rights, Prescott's critique of communism actually proceeded from a much broader worry about contemporary social reform movements that threatened the sanctity of personal property. Postconquest Peruvian history continued to inspire Prescott to address this broader worry. In *The Conquest of Peru*, after the Spanish overthrow the Incas, a second-order narrative of eclipse occurs in which the tumultuous reign of the Spanish conquistadors yields to the authority of the Spanish crown. Resemblances between radically unstable conquistadorial Peru and nineteenth-century U.S. culture therefore spelled trouble for the United States, just as resemblances to Incan Peru did. So, while Incan Peru's proto-communism inspired Prescott to write back against communistic property schemes in his own society, efforts in conquistadorial Peru to end native slavery inspired Prescott to write back against U.S. abolitionism, which sought to strip slaveholders of what the law generally regarded as their property. Prescott foresaw that abolition would lead to massive social upheaval in the United States, akin to the civil wars that had convulsed conquistadorial Peru.

Communism and abolitionism thus became the unexpected bedfellows in Prescott's general anxiety about the state of U.S. property rights in the 1840s. Although these movements sought to redress social injustices that limited the freedom of the poor and the enslaved, Prescott could not countenance their challenges to a freedom that he saw as more urgent to maintaining individual liberty and societal well-being: the freedom of personal property from infringement. In this social calculation, Prescott exemplified the attitude of conservative northeastern Whigs.[2] But like Cooper's commitment to the idea of a landholding moral aristocracy, Prescott's pro-property ideology put him on the wrong side of history. He espoused a middle-ground position—antislavery but antiabolition—that was rapidly being abandoned in the late 1840s. As the Civil War approached and the ideological middle disappeared, Prescott suffered his own personal form of eclipse. The experience of increasing social and political marginalization may have led Prescott and Cooper to identify more closely with the eclipsed empires of the early modern period than with its ascending powers. They seem to have gravitated toward the fallen empires even as they sought to distinguish their country from them.

This line of argument, however, contradicts the thrust of much scholarship on Prescott, which reads his conquest histories primarily as a commentary on the conquerors, not on the conquered. Identification with the conquerors makes more sense as a framework for understanding Prescott's earlier history, *The Conquest of Mexico*, on which most critics focus. Immensely popular when first published in 1843, *The Conquest of Mexico* acquired new meaning when the U.S. war with Mexico—the so-called second conquest of Mexico—happened a few years later.[3] Taking their cue from this historical context, and from the United States' obvious imperial ambitions in that conflict, most critics examine *The Conquest of Mexico* to gauge the extent of Prescott's investment in a conquistadorial mentality: the primacy of Euro-American civilization over indigenous American barbarism and therefore the legitimacy of the Spanish subjugation of the Aztecs (and, by implication, the U.S. subjugation of nineteenth-century Mexico).[4] In other words, they tend to examine the extent of Prescott's identification with the Spanish conquerors, not with the indigenous conquered.

In *The Conquest of Peru*, however, I see a different emphasis as dominant, one that follows from the varying positions that Peru and Mexico held in the U.S. imagination. Despite the parallels that encouraged Spanish conquistadors—and modern critics of Prescott's histories—to treat Peru as a replay of Mexico, nineteenth-century hemispheric politics argue for making some distinctions between the two.[5] The United States in the nineteenth century did not have a consequential territorial interest in Peru, as it did in Mexico.[6] Although the Monroe Doctrine technically encompassed the whole southern continent with its rapacious hemispheric vision, it remained without teeth for several decades, and when enforced, was invoked only for situations in closer geographic proximity to the United States. Thus, as Katherine Manthorne argues, U.S. representations of South America "must be read as something more than the direct . . . corollaries to U.S. policies of expansion and penetration into the territories of the south."[7] This suggests that the customary focus within Americas studies on nineteenth-century U.S. connections to northern territories such as Mexico and the Caribbean might be usefully augmented by more attention to the distinct cultural logics that concretized around more southerly locations.[8] The idea of the contact zone—so central to how I understand the connections forged in imperial eclipse narratives between the United States and fallen empires—clearly manifests somewhat differently in contiguous and noncontiguous territories.

Given its place in nineteenth-century hemispheric politics, Peru wouldn't have triggered thoughts of U.S. territorial expansion and incorporation as automatically as Mexico did. Prescott therefore has greater room in *The Conquest of Peru* to engage in other forms of imperial self-reflection. He identifies the United States as much with the conquered Incas as he does with the Spanish conquerors, even if his identification comes in the form of a defensive rejection of Incan economics prompted by his recognition of modern U.S. counterparts to Incan economic philosophy. Furthermore, the subjugation of the conquistadors by the Spanish crown, a second layer to *The Conquest of Peru*'s narrative of imperial eclipse, changes the signification of Prescott's discovery of resemblances between the United States and the Spanish. These resemblances, too, function to correlate the United States with an eclipsed empire. Both stages of Peru's conquest—the Incas succumbing to the conquistadors and the conquistadors succumbing to the crown—inspire Prescott to fear for U.S. property rights, facing the dual threat of a communist redistribution of wealth and a destabilizing abolition of slaveholders' "property."

Peruvian Communists

Prescott's survey of Incan civilization in the introduction to *The Conquest of Peru* presents preconquest Peru as, in effect, a massive proto-communist state. The Inca ruled absolutely, surrounded by a privileged class of nobility, while the vast majority of the populace existed without personal property, the fruits of their labor swelling the coffers of the government. In return, though, the state took entire responsibility for their social welfare.[9]

What Prescott apparently found especially noxious about this system was that the Peruvians "had no money, little trade, and hardly any thing that could be called fixed property" (754), had "little property of any kind" (762), and "had nothing that deserved to be called property" (817). He believed that the "fiscal regulations of the Incas, and the [restrictive] laws respecting property, [we]re the most remarkable features of the Peruvian polity" and also deeply "repugnant to the essential principles of our nature" (755, 752). The ability to acquire property allows for the possibility of social advancement, so "[t]he great hardship of the Peruvian was, that he could not better his condition. . . . The great and universal motive to honest industry, that of bettering one's lot, was lost upon him. The great law of human progress was not for him. As he was born, so he was to die" (762). In the stifling immutability of this social arrangement, "the power of free agency—the inestimable and inborn right of every human being—was annihilated in Peru" (817).

This despotic Incan suppression of human liberties, according to Prescott, both fostered and was facilitated by the submissiveness of the people. He proclaimed the Peruvian tendency toward accepting authority "unprecedented in the history of man" (817). Their passivity and lack of economic incentive meant that "[t]he Peruvians, though lining a long extent of sea-coast, had no foreign commerce" (805). Prescott notes that "they were not a commercial people, and had no knowledge of money" (811). Although Peru therefore seems in some ways idyllic, an economically innocent Eden, Prescott clearly believed this state of affairs to be unnatural and unjust, artificially created through the inhibition of free action and the prohibition against property—in other words, the denial of basic human rights. Economically paralyzed, Peruvians were less commercially proactive than they otherwise would have been.

But Prescott also reluctantly admits that Incan rule had some benefits and virtues. The fact that this repressive system "should have so successfully gone into operation, and so long endured, in opposition to the taste, the prejudices, and the very principles of our nature, is a strong proof of a generally wise and temperate administration of the government" (817). The effectiveness of the Incan government manifested itself most clearly in its dependable social guarantee of a minimum standard of living to each Peruvian: "[I]f no man could become rich in Peru, no man could become poor" (762). The heights of economic achievement were sacrificed to banish the lows of economic privation. Prescott writes that the Incas' "manifold provisions against poverty . . . were so perfect, that, in their wide extent of territory,—much of it smitten with the curse of barrenness,—no man, however humble, suffered from the want of food and clothing." Through big government ("manifold provisions"), the Incas achieved "perfect[ion]" in ensuring the welfare of the people throughout the large state of Peru, a fact that even causes Prescott to invert the savage/civilized dichotomy of Europe and native America, albeit briefly: "Famine," Prescott writes, "so common at that period in every country of civilized Europe, was an evil unknown in the dominion of the Incas" (818).

Prescott not only saw virtue in the effectiveness of the Peruvian social welfare system, he also recognized the value of social aid coming from the state, not from more local or individual sources. He writes, "When a man was reduced by poverty or misfortune, the arm of the law was stretched out to minister relief; not the stinted relief of private charity, nor that which is doled out, drop by drop, as it were, from the frozen reservoirs of 'the parish,' but in generous measure, bringing no humiliation to the object of it, and placing him on a level with the rest of his countrymen" (762). Here the long arm of the law, though still despotic in nature, brings equality back to the social sphere and serves the humanitarian purpose of providing the poor with material aid while preserving their dignity.[10]

In the end, though, because Prescott believed that "[t]he best aid . . . is that which enables the handicapped to help themselves," he "rejected the ancient Peruvian economy because, in eliminating poverty, it made the individual a creature of the state."[11] He ultimately cannot countenance this social system, regardless of its merits, because the radical limitations placed on the Peruvian people's "free agency" stunted their capacity for self-reliance and personal enterprise.[12] Richard Kagan has characterized Prescott as "firm in the belief that progress required liberty in the guise of democratic institutions, freedom of worship and of expression, and laissez-faire economics." William Charvat concurs, noting that "like most of his generation"—though not all of his generation, a fact of which Prescott was aware—he "assumed that the beneficence of laissez faire was unarguable, and that a competitive economy was best for both individual and society."[13] It certainly benefited Prescott as an individual. Unsurprisingly given his personal wealth (he both inherited and married into mercantile fortunes), the Peruvian rejection of personal property, a situation in which "no man could be rich," did not sit well with the Brahmin historian (762).[14]

Therefore, as Cooper had explicitly championed U.S. republicanism in *The Bravo*, Prescott explicitly argues for the superiority of U.S. laissez-faire capitalism and its corresponding social structure to the stifling control and protection of preconquest Peru. And just as Cooper's project in *The Bravo* to demonstrate the superiority of U.S. republicanism had ultimately backfired, *The Conquest of Peru* would ultimately raise doubts about the validity of Prescott's attempt to distinguish U.S. property arrangements from Peruvian ones on the basis of their greater liberatory effect. Nonetheless, Prescott at least initially argues that the U.S. system was designed to promote the freedom of each individual, so radically constrained in Peru. Prescott extols "our own free republic, where every man, however humble his condition, may aspire to the highest honors of state,—may select his own career, and carve out his fortune in his own way . . . where the collision of man with man wakens a generous emulation that calls out latent talent and tasks the energies to the utmost; . . . where, in short, the government is made for man,—not as in Peru, where man seemed to be made only for the government" (819). In contrast to Peru, then, social advancement is possible for all (or, at least, everyone "may aspire" to the highest honors in the land, whether or not those honors are actually attainable). In the U.S. system, competition calls out only what is best in human nature. The potentially violent and unsettling "collision of man with man" results only in "generous" emulation, in which achievement inspires other achievement. In this gentlemanly atmosphere, no governmental intervention is necessary to restrict economic activity, and innate human ambition operates without constraint.

The glowing language of Prescott's description of free-market capitalism in this passage presents capitalism as a clear moral imperative. As David Levin remarks of Prescott and his generation of historians, they "saw something of that connection between Protestantism and capitalism which Weber and Tawney have more recently established; but in the romantic histories the connection often serves to elevate the economic motive rather than to lower the religious one." According to Levin, Prescott believed that "when one acts for the spirit of commerce, one adheres to a progressive principle."[15] Because the Peruvians, "though lining a long extent of sea-coast, had no foreign commerce," they were therefore impeding progress. In contrast, the "hardy temper" of "the members of the great Anglo-Saxon family . . . has driven them to seek their fortunes on the stormy ocean, and to open a commerce with the most distant regions of the globe" (805). The Anglo-Saxon race, with greater genetic mercantile propensities, therefore embodies progress—as does the United States, which in Prescott's view was the most highly evolved Anglo-Saxon civilization in the history of the world.

But he still cannot dismiss the virtues of Incan Peru so easily. At its core, the contest between the U.S. and Incan systems centers on each society's treatment of its most lowly and disadvantaged members. In the United States, "every man, however humble his condition, may aspire to the highest honors of state,—may select his own career, and carve out his fortune in his own way." In preconquest Peru, "no man, however humble, suffered from the want of food and clothing" (818).[16] In the United States, the poorest of the poor have the freedom to try to improve their situation. In Peru, the poorest of the poor are safeguarded from extreme physical suffering. Prescott's language offsets the appeal of the U.S. liberty to pursue advancement with its potential tenuousness: every man *may* carve out his own fortune, which implies both the permission to do so and the conditional nature of the result—he may or may not actually end up carving out his own fortune. In contrast to the potentially subjunctive mood of the U.S. promise, the Incan social services are described in the indicative mood: no Peruvian in fact did suffer from the want of food and clothing. The U.S. system as Prescott depicts it sets up conditions of wild possibility, whereas the Peruvian system administered substantial actualities. Obviously the former system would work better for the few who managed to actualize the possibility (as Prescott and his family did).[17] The latter system would work better for the vast majority who couldn't ever actualize that possibility, and who in the United States would therefore be subjected to the dark side of the "collision of man with man" that Prescott describes so admiringly.

The subjunctive mood of Prescott's description of the United States also stems from it being a present-day civilization whose story is still being written and therefore is uncertain in its outcome. "[T]he empire of the Incas has passed away" and can therefore be fully assessed in the indicative mood (819). On the other hand, "the other great experiment [in the New World] is still going on,—the experiment which is to solve the problem, so long contested in the Old World, of the capacity of man for self-government. Alas for humanity, if it should fail!" (819–20).

Here, at the height of Prescott's rhetorical juxtaposition of the United States and Incan Peru, his confidence falters. The choice to label the U.S. principle of self-government an "experiment" belies the seeming certainty of the prediction that it "is to solve the problem" of man's capacity for self-government. The phrase "is to" could be read as expressing the sense of "will," as in that the United States will solve the problem, a brash claim that the United States will in fact prove man's capacity for self-government and thereby ensure the possibility of political freedom for the whole human race. On the other hand, "is to" could also be read as expressing merely the purpose behind the experiment, namely, that it is intended to solve the problem. Prescott clearly cannot safely assert that this experiment will meet with success, given his somewhat histrionic conclusion, "Alas for humanity, if it should fail!" Although committed to the propriety and efficacy of the U.S. model, Prescott himself raises the specter of its failure.

This moment of doubt seems prompted in part by the idea that the "great experiment" of the "empire of the Incas has passed away," eclipsed by the Spanish empire (which itself, in turn, would later be eclipsed). In thinking about how great civilizations end, Prescott naturally starts wondering if, when, and how his own civilization might fail. As he writes to a correspondent, "History . . . is the voice of the past,—the infinite past, addressed to the present. . . . And when [the citizen of a republic] sees how fragile a thing liberty has been, how it has passed away like a dream from the fairest spots & finest races of the world, he will comprehend the perils which beset it in his own land, and will learn how to avoid them."[18] In fact, the greatest threat that Prescott saw to the United States in the 1840s lay in moral admiration for anticapitalist social structures like preconquest Peru's. Just as Cooper had descried Venetian senators in U.S. Whigs, Prescott found the problems of his fallen empire cropping up in the United States.

In a May 30, 1848, letter to Pascual de Gayangos, his Spanish correspondent and indefatigable research agent,[19] Prescott wrote that he believed that "we here [in the United States] are safe" from the kind of revolutions that convulsed Europe in 1848, "[u]nless, indeed, the communist philosophers should get up a division of property for the benefit of the millions. But I think there is too much principle, as well as property in this community, to endorse such speculations."[20] The U.S.

system of personal property seemed to Prescott both the most likely target of destabilizing revolutionary energies and the most effective damper on such energies (having so much property would keep people from agreeing to any redistributive meddling with property rights). He saw property as the operative factor in national politics; to one correspondent, he characterized the fundamental conflict of the 1844 presidential election as "property versus no property," and wrote to another, "If suffrage could be limited to those who have property at stake . . . this would be a perfect government."[21] Suffrage limited in this way (as it had been up to a few decades earlier) should in theory sufficiently safeguard the interests of property, but Prescott's "*I think* there is too much principle, as well as property in this community" still suggests concern with the possible endorsement of "communist" "speculations" by members of his own class.[22]

Although communism as such had not made significant inroads into U.S. social activism in the 1840s, an increasing number of people during this period, even people of property in Prescott's own community, were turning to philosophies that critiqued capitalism's competitive individualism and increasingly concentrated ownership of the means of production in the hands of the few. The National Reform Association, which began in the United States in 1844 and which Marx recommends in *The Communist Manifesto*, popularized an "Agrarian" agenda of "radical and democratic land redistribution"; "most radically and essentially, [the Agrarians] wanted to limit the amount of land any individual could own" so that government land in the West, the primary target of their efforts, would be dispersed evenly, thus alleviating some of the social inequities arising from industrialization in the East by providing a refuge for the impoverished working classes.[23] Given that "in the young republic, land and property were almost synonymous terms," Prescott likely had in mind groups like the National Reform Association when he wrote about his fears of a communistic division of property.[24]

This conclusion is supported by his bewildered and resistant description of Incan land policies in *The Conquest of Peru*. He writes of the Incan division of land "*per capita*, in equal shares among the people," in strict accordance with the size of families and reapportioned each year to maintain parity and keep pace with births and deaths: "a more thorough and effectual agrarian law than this cannot be imagined" (756).[25] The label "agrarian" does not simply indicate legislation concerned with land and land use in general but more specifically implies a law based on "the principle of a *uniform* division of lands" (*OED*, "Agrarianism"; emphasis added). The term often had deeply pejorative connotations in Prescott's day; as one of his contemporaries remarked in an attempt to debunk popular misconceptions about the movement, "Even the charge of irreligion has not been found more effective against the advocates of improvement or change than that of Agrarianism,—by which is meant hostility to existing property-institutions, and a determination, if possible, to subvert them."[26]

The Incas' skill at subverting existing property institutions seems to befuddle Prescott. When the Incas assimilated newly conquered territories into the empire of Peru, a "division of the territory was then made . . . [in which] the share of each individual was uniformly the same. It may seem strange, that any people should patiently have acquiesced in an arrangement which involved such a total surrender of property" (770). Prescott provides various explanations for this strange acquiescence. He suggests that garrisons of armed soldiers inhibited resistance to the new system and that perhaps the Incas endeavored to meddle as little as possible with existing proprietorships or that the conquered tribes weren't civilized enough to mind infringement of their property. He even casts doubt on the credibility of the sources that describe this acquiescence to agrarianism: "According to Velasco, even the powerful state of Quito, sufficiently advanced in civilization to have the law of property well recognized by its people, admitted the institutions of the Incas, 'not only without repugnance, but with joy.' . . . But Velasco . . . believed easily,—or reckoned on his readers' doing so" (771n). Prescott cannot believe that a radical communistic reform would be welcomed. He clearly considers this mainly from the perspective of property owners whose holdings would be reduced, rather than from that of the poor for whom this might constitute a significant enfranchisement. Given his assertion in the letter to Gayangos that "there is too much principle, as well as property in this community, to endorse" a communist division of property in the United States, he must explain away the seeming success of the Incas in convincing even property owners to consent to agrarianism.

In common usage, "the word Agrarians comprehend[ed]" "Socialists, Communists, Fourierites, and so forth," and thus agrarianism constituted a fairly formidable social force.[27] The National Reform Association, which remained largely a working-class movement, collaborated with movements that had wider social support, including so-called utopian socialist groups.[28] The theories of utopian socialists like Robert Owen, Henri de Saint-Simon, and especially Charles Fourier gained a dramatic following in the United States in the late 1830s and '40s, leading F. O. Matthiessen to dub this period in American letters "The Age of Fourier."[29] Just outside Boston, the Brook Farm commune—begun in 1841 and converted into an official Fourierist phalanx in 1844 as Prescott worked on the introduction to *The Conquest of Peru*—attracted Nathaniel Hawthorne as a resident and many other leading figures in the New England literary scene as visitors or contributors to its magazine the *Harbinger*.[30]

At places like Brook Farm, utopian socialists conducted experiments in communal living and cooperative labor arrangements. According to Carl Guarneri, utopian socialists argued that their more equitable social structure would provide the antidote to "the uncertainty and inequality of competitive individualism." Utopian socialism arose in response to the societal problems associated with industrial capitalism, and the suffering caused by these problems in turn made utopian socialism's alternative economic vision dangerously attractive in the eyes of capitalist apologists like Prescott. "[T]he urgency of the utopian socialists' rhetoric, [and] the importance of their short-lived achievements" became exaggerated because capitalism was especially vulnerable to critique during this period.[31] Confidence did not then run high in the inevitable dominance of capitalism as a system: "[I]n the 1830s and 1840s it was far from evident that the new economy could or would overcome its difficulties," according to Eric Hobsbawm.[32]

Capitalism's difficulties included a seemingly inherent, societally devastating tendency toward instability. The Panic of 1837 and subsequent severe depression, which lasted until 1843, played a particularly important role in helping to launch the popularity of utopian socialism and other communistic movements in the United States. When "many Americans [sought] a theory to explain their plight, . . . Fourierism put the panic and the depression in a larger and novel structural perspective: [it] indicted the competitive economic system for bringing hard times."[33]

Although largely insulated by his wealth from the worst effects of the economic crisis, Prescott had to make alternate arrangements for his first book, *History of the Reign of Ferdinand and Isabella, the Catholic* (1837), when his initial publishers went bankrupt in the wake of the Panic of 1837.[34] Prescott's letters from 1837 to 1843 refer often to the crisis and reveal his anxiety about the economy, both in his dire rhetoric describing the situation and in his precipitate declarations of a return to financial health.[35] In these letters, he partakes to some extent in the anxiety and conservative agenda that fueled what recent critics have called "Panic fiction": literature written in the late 1830s and early 1840s that directly discussed the economy, attempted to pinpoint rational causes for extreme market downturns, and tried to shore up the stability of middle-class identity even as members of the middle class were suddenly going bankrupt. This stabilizing often involved positing a new relationship to, rather than a rejection of, the market, and therefore in the end functioned to entrench further the cultural logic of capitalism and existing class relations.[36]

In a related effort at ideological damage control through redefinition, Prescott belittled the ideas of communist "philosophers" (a label that itself often connoted impracticality for him) as "speculations," or unsound conjectures that risk much in the expectation of an advancement that may prove illusory.[37] "Speculations" in the 1840s in fact more commonly referred to the catastrophic financial practices that helped to create the Panic, for example, the purchase of western land on the assumption that its value would rise and that it could be resold for a profit.[38] In his letter to Gayangos, then, Prescott evades criticisms of free-market capitalist "speculation" by redefining the term as its economic opposite: the risk philosophy of communism rather than the risk philosophy of capitalism.

Whigs also produced narratives of U.S. economic health and opportunity that contradicted reformers' pessimistic assessments. These "rosy," "indelibly conservative" interpretations "coupl[ed] paeans to national economic growth with persistent references to extraordinary social fluidity and unrivaled popular access to the burgeoning economic opportunities."[39] As Marvin Meyers puts it, "The Whigs distinctively affirmed the material promise of American life as it was going."[40] The ringing optimism of Prescott's depiction in *The Conquest of Peru*'s introduction of the possibility for unfettered social mobility in the United States clearly partakes of this habitual Whig capitalist apologia.

Guarneri points out that "poverty and unemployment [resulting from the depression] belied the Whigs' utopian confidence," but even social facts like poverty could be contested.[41] In an 1848 letter to Henry Hallam, in which Prescott contrasts European and U.S. social conditions in terms of their relative tendency to incite popular unrest, he asserts that "poverty is unknown" in the United States, because "[i]f a man is at all straightened, he has only to open the western gate that leads to the boundless & bottomless prairies, where bread will come to him for the asking."[42] Prescott here participates in a discourse that "self-consciously vaunted [the United States] as the very solution to such old world problems as hunger and want, and even to social stratification itself."[43]

To whatever extent Prescott papered over his anxieties about the health of U.S. society by making assertions like these, the West's role in the process that he describes as "equalizing conditions" seemed to him essential in keeping U.S. democracy functional: "But no such physical—& therefore unforced means of equalization exist in the old countries of Europe."[44] Laissez-faire, according to Prescott's argument, was a viable strategy in the United States because migration and the size of U.S. territory naturally prevented severe class stratification. So no "forced" program of "equalization," like "the communist philosophers [getting] up a division of property for the benefit of the millions," was necessary.[45] But Agrarianists, who also recognized the West's central role in providing an outlet for the eastern poor, argued that the "millions" couldn't go West because capitalistic land speculation had driven prices so high—hence the Agrarianist emphasis on land ownership reform, including the kind of property-limiting proposals most worrisome to Prescott.[46] Thus even the "boundless & bottomless prairies" of the West, seemingly the perfect way to avoid the social and economic evils that had inspired the

1848 European revolutions, actually dragged Prescott more deeply into contemporary debates over the status of property in U.S. society.

The economic context to which Prescott was responding has generally been overlooked, but his writings do register the dramatic ups and downs of the U.S. economy in the late 1830s and '40s and convey concern over the social reforms that some of his contemporaries advocated to deal with the fallout from economic unpredictability and increasing industrialization. I would argue that Prescott's writing from 1843 to 1848 reflects a "post-Panic" mentality.[47] During this period, the economic depression had largely ended and Prescott could therefore paint free-market capitalism in glowing, idealized terms in his introduction to *The Conquest of Peru*. But his text still subtly reveals residual economic fears in his otherwise unnecessary defense of the U.S. economic system and his otherwise disproportionately vehement condemnation of Incan restrictions on property and competitive commerce. The spectacle of preconquest Peruvian society had touched on a spot that remained sore.

Unlike most writers of the day who commented on economic matters, Prescott did not set out to address the state of the U.S. economy; instead he came to it, unintentionally, through the back door of Incan Peru. He initially regarded the introductions to his conquest histories merely in their functional relationship to the remainder of the story: "My design is not to go minutely into the previous civilization of the Mexicans and Peruvians, only just so far as to interest the reader in the destinies of the conquered races."[48] But in each case, he got drawn in to these civilizations; the introductions took on lives of their own and greatly exceeded the time that he had allotted to write them. At the beginning of his labor on *The Conquest of Peru* introduction, Prescott commented in his working notebook that he had not gotten "sufficient knowledge of the ground, & its capabilities, yet, to feel a lively interest in it." Once he had engaged in some research and study, however, he decided that in the introduction, "I shall be able to exhibit the structure of a social polity, altogether remarkable, & quite interesting."[49]

The depth of his research and his immersion into the minute details of Incan Peru gave him the opportunity to recognize parallels between Incan policies and radical reforms being proposed in his own day to deal with increasing social inequality.[50] Becoming engrossed in the particularities of Incan Peru led Prescott to seemingly unplanned meditations on the precariousness of property rights in his own culture, a historical resemblance that he might not have noticed had his study of Incan Peru been briefer and more perfunctory. His rigorous historiographical method thus facilitated the creation of a spatiotemporal contact zone between the Incan empire and the nineteenth-century United States. International history, in the form of Incan agrarianism, led him to reflect on an intranational problem—

threats to property—and inspired him to write an encomium to the system of laissez-faire capitalism.

Spanish Capitalists

Yet Prescott manages to undermine this championing later in *The Conquest of Peru*. He himself raises an ominous historical precedent for the solution that he suggests will solve the problems of U.S. capitalism, that is, economically disadvantaged classes moving to the West in search of opportunity unavailable to them in the East. The Spanish conquistadors embodied this entrepreneurial spirit and socially beneficial capitalist redistribution but represented a distinctly dystopian version of it. The rapacity of the vulgar Spanish capitalists, as Prescott portrays them, manages to cast Incan communism in a more flattering light, one to which even Prescott is susceptible, despite his anxiety about communistic leanings.

As we have seen, Prescott lauds the U.S. system in which "every man, however humble his condition, may aspire to the highest honors of state,—may select his own career, and carve out his fortune in his own way." No one in his history better exemplifies this exploitation of potential social mobility than Francisco Pizarro, the conqueror of Peru. Born the illegitimate child of a woman of "humble condition" (834), he was "early cast upon the world to seek his fortunes as he might" (1097). Through his efforts in Peru, he became a knight of the royal order of St. Jago, the governor and captain general of Peru (the highest offices then available in the land), and a marquis; "thus was the fortunate adventurer placed in the ranks of the proud aristocracy of Castile, few of whose members could boast . . . their elevation from so humble an origin" (1017). Prescott marvels in his history at the rags-to-riches story of Pizarro, "a man who, born in an obscure station in life, without family, interest or friends to back him, has carved out his own fortunes in the world, and, by his own resources, triumphed over all the obstacles which nature and accident had thrown in his way" (888).

The newly discovered lands of the Americas opened up the social possibilities of medieval Spain, allowing men of low birth with skill in exploration and soldiering to gain wealth and enhance their position. The New World therefore created an economic and social environment for Spaniards analogous to Prescott's representation of opportunity in the U.S. republic. Although for the most part poorly educated and born without privilege, the conquistadors (including Gonzalo Pizarro, Francisco's brother, and Diego de Almagro, his partner, both also illegitimate and both eventually in contention for control of Peru) became men of property and consequence in the New World.

These men prioritized the commerce that the Peruvians had neglected. The sea-coast that provided such a ready occasion for trade with other countries and that had gone undeveloped under the rule of the Incas, was soon dotted with bustling Spanish settlements, "destined to become hereafter the flourishing marts of commerce" (1013). Pizarro anticipated the growth of traffic with a visionary clarity: he founded Lima by a harbor that promised "a commodious haven for the commerce that the prophetic eye of the founder saw would one day—and no very distant one—float on its waters" (1006).

The conquistadors seem invigorated by a capitalist spirit that should shine in comparison with Peruvian economic stagnation, according to the contrast that Prescott sets up in his introduction, but he in fact recoils from the conquerors' money-making spirit, their "ferocious cupidity." He labels them "the scum of [Spain's] chivalry," "irresponsible individuals, soldiers of fortune, desperate adventurers" (1232, 1120). He frequently characterizes them as rapacious and greedy, and states over and over again their core motivation: "the love of gold" (947), "the lust of gold" (1096), "the love of lucre" (1216). With visions of El Dorado spurring them on, "gold and the Cross were the watchwords of the Spaniard. The spirit of chivalry had waned somewhat before the spirit of trade" (988).

In their self-interested pursuit of gain, the conquistadors certainly manifest "the collision of man with man" that Prescott mentions in his description of U.S. society, but at no time do they evidence the "generous emulation" that in Prescott's scheme supposedly results from such collisions. In fact, the word *collision* never intimates anything positive when Prescott uses it in the rest of his history. It always refers to a violent engagement between warring factions jostling against each other for advantage, generally with destructive results.[51] In the majority of cases, "collision" refers to dissensions among the Spaniards, who waged endless civil wars with each other to determine who could claim ultimate power in Peru. Pizarro, whose selfish machinations enraged his enemies and alienated his allies, fought off multiple challenges before being assassinated. His brother Gonzalo, similarly, led a revolt against representatives of the Spanish crown that ultimately resulted in his execution as a traitor. Book 4 of the history is entirely given over to the "Civil Wars of the Conquerors," as the conquistadors destroy each other and Peru in their quest for wealth and power.

Prescott calls attention to the contrast between the Spaniards' dissolute prodigality with Peru's resources and the Incas' traditionally careful stewardship of them. Meditation on Spanish excesses prompts a shift in his moral assessment of Peru before the conquest. Abandoning his execrations on Incan despotism from the introduction, Prescott eulogizes a veritable utopia under the Incas: "a country well advanced in the arts of civilization; institutions under which the people lived in tranquility and personal safety; the mountains . . . whitened with flocks; the valleys teeming with the fruits of a scientific husbandry; the granaries and warehouses filled to overflowing; the whole land rejoicing in its abundance." This land of plenty, this earthly paradise, morphs into the dystopic prospect of Peru postconquest, after "the flocks were scattered, and wantonly destroyed; the granaries were dissipated; the beautiful contrivances for the more perfect culture of the soil were suffered to fall into decay; the paradise was converted into a desert" (1095). The Spanish commitment to commercial development steadily stripped Peru of its resources and "wantonly destroyed" the sophisticated agricultural system so crucial to the Peruvians' sustenance, because their goal was profit, not good governance.

Spanish avarice thus tampered with the Peruvian way of life and took unconscionable advantage of the native population, because "while they taxed the strength of the native to the utmost [in their system of forced labor], [they] deprived him of the means of repairing it, when exhausted." In contrast, the Incas seem like model leaders: "[U]nder his Incas, the Peruvian was never suffered to be idle; but the task imposed on him was always proportioned to his strength. He had his seasons of rest and refreshment, and was well protected against the inclemency of the weather. Every care was shown for his personal safety" (1121). Prescott had argued in the introduction that although the Incas faithfully safeguarded the welfare of their subjects, the lack of individual freedom in preconquest Peruvian society nonetheless violated inherent human rights and outweighed the benefits of the arrangement. After the spectacle of Spanish exploitation, however, Prescott reverses his earlier emphasis. He highlights the "care" taken with the Peruvian's safety more than the obligation under which he labors. Furthermore, the phrase "his Incas" conveys a sense of affection and affiliation between the Peruvian and his leaders and even grammatically makes the Incas a kind of emotional and civic possession of their people, whereas in the introduction Prescott had asserted that "man seemed to be made only for the government" in Peru, instead of "the government [being] made for man" (819).

Postconquest, the defects of the Incan system pale in comparison with the cruelties of the Spanish one, and the Incas seem positively beatific next to Pizarro and his army. One reviewer of *The Conquest of Peru* goes so far as to say that "in all the arts of government . . . the Incas were immeasurably superior to the Spaniards. . . . In every light in which we can view the subject, we must be compelled to award the Incas wisdom and beneficence superior to the Spaniards, and to acknowledge they approached nearer to the idea of a Christian civilization," specifically with regard to their provision for the general welfare of their people compared to the utter disregard of the Spanish for the same.[52]

Prescott believed that "commerce was [both] the mother, [and] the child of freedom." In general, "The Whigs thought of economic progress as providing the basis for all other kinds of progress."[53] The conquistadors represent a major stumbling block to this philosophy. Their promotion of commerce did not translate into increasing liberalism, social advancement, or broad-based opportunity in Peru: "[I]t was little to [the Peruvian] that the shores of the Pacific were studded with rising communities and cities, the marts of a flourishing commerce. He had no share in the goodly heritage. He was an alien in the land of his fathers" (1095). Participation in commerce also didn't ennoble the Spaniards, given their relentless infighting, depredation of Peru's natural resources, and abuse of the indigenous population. To Prescott, the conquistadors, with their Christianity and better technology, symbolized "progress," but they brought brutality rather than betterment to Peru.

They were also unforgivably vulgar. Prescott champions social mobility in the abstract while he scorns the concrete embodiments of social mobility. He scoffs privately at Pizarro, a "hero that could not even write his own signature!" and even worse, a "hero that can't read!"[54] Like many social elites who favored national economic development, Prescott resented the resulting erosion of traditional patterns of social hierarchy and deference. Gregory Alexander writes, "Dialectically situated with the optimism over the Market Revolution was deep ambivalence about the new and quite evident society developing in many parts of the country and nostalgia for . . . a premodern culture" characterized by "social hierarchy and privilege, . . . order, security and regularity."[55] Prescott was a progressive in his economic philosophy but a reactionary in his social attitudes.

In *The Conquest of Peru*, this results in a conflicted underlying argument. Although in the introduction Prescott explicitly asserts the superiority of free-market capitalism over state-mandated communism, the emotional thrust of the text as a whole actually endorses Incan institutions with respect to the tenor of social relations that they encouraged. In comparison with the anarchy and devastation unleashed on Peru by the capitalist conquistadors, the order and stable hierarchies of proto-communist Incan Peru become increasingly attractive—a "paradise," in fact (1095).[56] Yes, the Incas achieved this social stability through limitations on personal freedom, but Prescott emphasizes this fact less and less as he gravitates psychologically toward the societal result, at least in contrast to the coarseness of the Spanish nouveau riche: "[W]hen we contrast the ferocious cupidity of the conquerors with the mild and inoffensive manners of the conquered, our sympathies . . . are necessarily thrown into the scale of the Indian" (1096).

The history of Peru assails Prescott's capitalist, pro-property ideology from two different directions: by furnishing the spectacle both of a well-run, stable, humane communist state and of a truly loathsome group of property-hungry capitalists. I do not mean to suggest that Peru shakes Prescott's commitment to capitalism and property—his commitment remains firm—but that when he is forced to specify and defend his economic ideology, some of the ambivalence, logical contradictions, and moral compromises of his position become clear. He favors economic development but cringes at the manners of the masses who might take advantage of that development; he favors a free capitalist system but actually enjoys the social orderliness of a benevolent despotism.

This ambivalence necessarily retroactively tarnishes his glorification of the United States and its economic system. Prescott, as we have seen, sets up a contrast between preconquest Peruvian institutions and nineteenth-century U.S. institutions in his introduction. He then associates the field of economic opportunity in which the conquistadors displayed their bold commercial character with that of the United States and its citizens by employing the same language to describe both. He furthermore represents the Spanish policy in Peru as acquisitive and morally problematic to such a degree that the despotic Incan proto-communist state emerges as the more admirable social structure. By analogy, then, the U.S. model also suffers in comparison with the Incan polity. Even as Prescott attempts to promote the glories of laissez-faire capitalism, his text paradoxically presents a historical exhibition of some of its worst features, undermining the economic moral high ground he claims in the introduction and legitimating the very critiques of capitalism that he was trying to refute, critiques that were fueling communistic movements in the United States.

By casting free enterprise in such a negative light that even Prescott himself starts to admire the Incan system, the conquistadors hinder Prescott's case for the superiority of U.S. capitalism over Incan communistic property arrangements (and, by implication, over nineteenth-century U.S. schemes for a communistic redistribution of property). However, the conquistadors present an additional problem for Prescott. They enjoyed their conquest of the Incas for a brief time but then suffered their own eclipse. As Prescott writes in the preface to *The Conquest of Peru*, outlining the key features of the history that he will relate: "The conquest of the natives is but the first step, to be followed by the conquest of the Spaniards,—the rebel Spaniards, themselves,—till the supremacy of the Crown is permanently established over the country" (727). The forces of the Spanish monarchy had to subdue the rogue conquistadors who defied the authority of the crown and sought to control Peru themselves. In effect, Prescott's history contains a second narrative of eclipse, in which, after the Incas yielded to the conquistadors, the days of the conquistadors gave way to the days of centralized Spanish imperial power.

Just like resemblances between Incan agrarianism and U.S. proto-communism, therefore, similarities between nineteenth-century U.S. culture and the conquistadorial period in Peru boded ill for the United States. The ungentlemanly conquistadors' rise to power signaled an overturning of traditional social hierarchies akin to the changing demographics of power in the United States in the 1840s, which tended to sideline Whig elites such as Prescott in favor of less pedigreed figures.[57] The radical instability of Peru under the conquistadors' leadership suggested the danger of such nonelites gaining power.

The conquistadors' passion for gold may also have reminded Prescott of contemporary debates over specie: in his 1836 Specie Circular, Andrew Jackson had responded to rampant land speculation by mandating that only hard currency could be used to buy government lands in the West. According to many Whigs, this bullionist policy undercut the value of paper currency, caused massive inflation, and precipitated the Panic of 1837.[58] Political cartoons of the time depict Jackson and likeminded Democrats in crazed pursuit of "the gold humbug."[59] Gold functioned very differently in colonial Peru than it did in the United States during the Panic period: whereas U.S. banks tried to avoid runs by suspending specie payments and issuing paper currency instead, thus making gold scarce, the conquistadors faced a superabundance of gold with the sudden availability of Incan spoils. Prescott writes about the massive inflation that resulted in Peru: "The effect of such a surfeit of the precious materials was instantly felt on prices. The most ordinary articles... rose in value, as gold and silver, the representatives of all, declined" (996). So although gold was more available in Peru than in the United States, the underlying issue remained the same: the destabilization of currency's symbology—its ability to stand as a reliable "representative" of value. The conquistadors' greed for gold had undermined Peru's economic system in ways familiar to Prescott, writing in the wake of the Panic of 1837.

Gold had been abundant in Peru before the advent of the Spanish, but the Incas had checked its destabilizing potential: "[N]one of the ore . . . was converted into coin, . . . the whole of it passed into the hands of the sovereign for his own exclusive benefit" (747). This despotism had restrained economic progress and individual liberty, but clearly the conquistadors' introduction of a system of currency and private property did not automatically usher an economic utopia into being in Peru. In fact, property continued to be a vexed subject in the conquistadorial period, in ways that yet again reminded Prescott of conflicts over property rights in his own society.

Prescott argues that the lack of personal property rights under Incan rule meant that "[t]he power of free agency—the inestimable and inborn right of every human being—was annihilated in Peru," and therefore, the Spanish introduction of a system of personal property should have increased individual liberty (817). However, a key form of personal property on which Spanish conquistadors insisted—slaves—complicated the equation of property rights with individual liberty. Slaves, regarded as property but also theoretically possessing "the inestimable and inborn right of every human being" to free agency, undermined Prescott's attempt to characterize the United States as more free than Incan society because of its system of personal property.

But although the institution of slavery delegitimized Prescott's claims in the introduction to *The Conquest of Peru*, he defends property rights even when they undermine particular individuals' liberty. In the deeply unstable early days of the colonial period, Peru was convulsed by the conflict over slavery. Slaveholding conquistadors violently resisted well-meaning but dangerously abrupt attempts to abolish slavery. This history fueled Prescott's fears about the likely consequences of a push for immediate abolition in the United States. Whatever evils slavery may have entailed, Prescott saw more social devastation resulting from the schemes of abolitionists—whether in conquistadorial Peru or the nineteenth-century United States.

Spanish Abolitionists

The "natural liberty of the subject" that Prescott discusses so confidently and uncomplicatedly in his analysis of Incan Peru fractures into competing prerogatives in colonial Peru: the native peoples' right to self-ownership versus the conquistadors' property rights (819). The conquerors-turned-colonists staunchly maintained their own personal freedom as subjects of the Spanish empire and protested interference from the Spanish crown with their slave labor, ceded to them legally by the *encomienda* system, in which indigenous peoples were allotted to colonists for their use in mining and agriculture.[60] For Prescott, contemplating a Peru shaped by this system, the native right to liberty came into irreconcilable conflict with the colonists' right to hold property, and Prescott upholds the primacy of property. He resolutely refuses to discuss slavery as an issue of race or the disenfranchisement of the enslaved, instead electing to consider it from an economic perspective, as a question of the property rights of the slaveholder.

Predictably, the encomienda system encouraged widespread abuse in Peru and across the Spanish Americas. Indigenous peoples were subject to unrelenting brutality, without redress. The protests of critics like Bartholomé de las Casas, who railed against the outrages being visited upon the native population, provoked the Spanish government in 1542 to institute a sudden change in policy. A new code of laws, known as the New Laws, forbade the enslavement of the natives, outlawed new encomienda allotments, including those acquired by way of inheritance (meaning that the whole system would pass away in less than a generation), and stripped Spaniards of existing allotments of slave labor in the case of brutal treatment.[61] These laws threatened to beggar many of the colonists. During a period of already great unrest in the early days of colonial Peru, these laws, in Prescott's words, "broke up the very foundations of property, and, by a stroke of the pen, as it were, converted a nation of slaves into freemen" (1125)—just as the Emancipation Proclamation would do in the United States in 1863.

Prescott's commitment to individual liberty should cause him to applaud these measures, and indeed he does characterize them as "salutary in essential points." But he expresses deep reservations about their practicality, saying that "in the remote regions of America, and especially in Peru, where the colonists had been hitherto accustomed to unbounded license, [this] reform . . . could be enforced thus summarily only at the price of a revolution" (1125). The colonists, who "trembled for their property" (1134), adamantly and belligerently argued that "any laws which prejudiced property and rights within a kingdom required the ratification and consent of the leading citizens of that country."[62] The newly appointed viceroy of Peru, Blasco Núñez Vela, who had committed himself to a strict enforcement of the New Laws, met with widespread hostility: "[I]n one place where he took up his quarters, he found an ominous inscription over the door:—'He that takes my property must expect to pay for it with his life'" (1131). He nonetheless persisted, with what Prescott paints as unappealing and impolitic inflexibility, in implementing reforms intended to secure the right of natives to their own labor. He died in a resulting conflict with the colonists.

Núñez Vela's rigidity, though in the service of a virtuous principle, did more harm than good. Prescott critiqued Bartholomé de las Casas on similar grounds. In his estimation, "just and benevolent people" who "felt deep sympathy for the wrongs of the natives," could be pardoned for doubting "whether [Las Casas's] scheme of reform was not fraught with greater evils than those it was intended to correct" (1123–24). Prescott therefore condemns the approach of the Dominican priest: "Las Casas was the uncompromising friend of freedom. He intrenched himself strongly on the ground of natural right; and, like some of the reformers of our own day, disdained to calculate the consequences of carrying out the principle to its full and unqualified extent" (1124). Prescott finds himself espousing the practical limits of freedom, the prudence of placing constraints on the natural rights of human beings. He thereby compromises on the philosophy that he used in his introduction to distinguish so clearly between the virtue of the U.S. republic and the calculating despotism of the Incan state.

This compromised attitude toward liberty prompts him to "calculate the consequences" of principle pursued without caution, whether in the case of Las Casas or the "scheme[s] of reform" proposed by "the reformers of our own day." With this, he may be referring to the general tendency of philanthropists to sacrifice realism for idealism and efficacy for vain imaginings. But given the fact that Prescott labels "Las Casas and the Dominicans [as] the abolitionists of their day" in *The Conquest of Mexico* (678), and given the heavy parallels between the encomienda debate and the argument over abolition in the United States in the decades before the Civil War, Prescott likely has in mind outspoken abolitionists like John Quincy Adams, who campaigned feistily against slavery in his years as a congressman in the 1830s and '40s.

Prescott wrote of Adams, "He is a most remarkable man certainly, planting himself on the right ground, and half making it wrong by the manner he defends it. He is a very qualified blessing . . . who can refuse his sympathy to him in the contest with the arrogant South? But it is a pity to bring the great local divisions of the land into conflict more than is necessary."[63] Prescott clearly believed that the brash and ungentlemanly manner of Adams's defense of the abolitionist cause exacerbated sectional tensions "more than [was] necessary." The importance of putting an end to slavery's evils did not justify disregarding all other priorities like diplomacy and maintaining the Union, and these other priorities limited what could be claimed as "necessary" in the fight against slavery.

Prescott therefore judged radical abolitionists' advocacy of "immediatism"—the immediate emancipation of all slaves without provisions for compensating slaveholders—unnecessary and foolhardy. Such a sudden and radical step would wreak havoc on the economy of the South and infringe catastrophically on the property rights of southern slaveholders: the major justification cited by southern states for secession and the grounds of a charge of despotic northern encroachment on their rights to life, liberty, and property. James Huston notes that "proslavery advocates called abolitionists . . . socialists" because they believed that abolitionists did not respect the idea of property.[64] And indeed they did not, in the conventional manner of economic conservatives like Prescott.

Prescott, an antislavery Whig, did see and condemn the wrongs done to slaves, but he also believed firmly in the principle of property. He therefore eschewed the more extreme abolitionist (as opposed to simply antislavery) camp. As William Charvat writes, Prescott "disapproved of the institution, but refused to subscribe to the abolitionist attitude that the freedom of the Negroes was more important than the preservation of the Union and the constitutional rights of the slaveholders," including their right to property as guaranteed by the Fifth Amendment to the Constitution.[65] He feared the consequences of emancipation, and certainly did not want such a sweeping transformation to take effect immediately. Given that in his analysis, "the efforts of our out & out abolitionists have retarded the cause of emancipation of the negroes," he believed that the gradualist or incrementalist model of social change would be more effective in securing the desired ends, and more palatable than sudden revolution with its attendant uncertainties and dangers.[66]

Prescott's abhorrence for sudden revolutions arose in part from the natural conservatism of wealth, which condemned any tumult likely to endanger property. As Charvat and Michael Kraus observe, "Security for wealth was definitely a fundamental consideration with Prescott."[67] But Prescott's concern also no doubt proceeded from the lessons of history, which taught that revolutionary changes in social or economic policy often spark counterrevolutions, as they did among the Spanish conquistadors in colonial Peru (and as they would in the era of the U.S. Civil War).

The Spanish government ultimately decided that enforcing the radical change involved in the New Laws "would be for the interests neither of the country nor of the Crown" (1132). "On mature consideration," Prescott writes, "this was judged impracticable in the present state of the country, since the colonists, more especially in the tropical regions, looked to the natives for performance of labor, and the latter, it was found from experience, would not work at all, unless compelled to do so" (1225). The exigency of the colonists' need for workers rendered "impracticable" the complete emancipation of the native from the compulsion to work on another's behalf. The polity of Peru therefore continued to extort native labor as a kind of personal tax, even as it terminated the "most odious" manifestation of slavery, meaning that "every Indian vassal might aspire to the rank of a freeman" (1125, 1226). This wording stands in stark contrast to Prescott's self-congratulatory characterization of the U.S. republic as a place where "every man, however humble his condition, may aspire to the highest honor of the state." In the context of the slavery issue, though, that uncircumscribed sphere of personal aspiration could not realistically be extended to all people in the United States any more than it could be to the indigenous peoples of Peru, Prescott believed.

The historian thus concurred with the insights formed by consulting "mature consideration" in the handling of fraught social circumstances like native servitude. In this, he sides with Pedro de la Gasca, the first reasonably successful viceroy of Peru, whose "common sense" Prescott particularly admires, because "while his sympathy with mankind taught him the nature of their wants, his reason suggested to what extent these were capable of relief. . . . He did not waste his strength on illusory schemes of benevolence, like Las Casas, on the one hand; nor did he countenance the selfish policy of the colonists, on the other. He aimed at the practicable,—the greatest good practicable" (1231). La Gasca's utilitarian policy, in which common sense curbed sympathy and government representatives pursued only that which could feasibly be accomplished, causes Prescott to describe him to Pascual de Gayangos as "that great and good man" whose "administration is a bright spot, almost the only one, in the Conquest of Peru."[68]

La Gasca's policies accorded with Prescott's espousal of a gradualist model of social change. According to Prescott, La Gasca accomplished "more potent, and happily more permanent" successes than the convulsions precipitated by the conqueror's martial glories; "as he thus calmly, and imperceptibly, as it were, comes to his great results, he may remind us of the slow, insensible manner in which Nature works out her great changes in the material world, that are to endure when the ravages of the hurricane are passed away and forgotten" (1232). Prescott prefers an "insensible" movement toward the future, an unnoticeable easing along the path, jarring no one and nothing in the process. To those who would characterize such an "insensible" movement as unable adequately to perceive or to react to the current distresses of the oppressed—insensible *to*, rather than insensible *by*—he would respond that gradualism may be more slow, but it is also more sure of achieving the desired result.

Prescott advocates this position in *The Conquest of Mexico*, where he discusses "the great question of slavery" in its sixteenth- and nineteenth-century manifestations:

> [Slavery] in the sixteenth century, at the commencement of the system, bears some resemblance to that which exists in our time, when we may hope it is approaching its conclusion. Las Casas and the Dominicans of the former age, the abolitionists of their day, thundered out their uncompromising invectives against the system, on the broad ground of natural equity and the rights of man. . . . In one important respect, the condition of slavery, in the sixteenth century, differed materially from its condition in the nineteenth. In the former, the seeds of evil, but lately sown, might have been, with comparatively little difficulty, eradicated. But in our time, they have struck their roots into the social system, and cannot be rudely handled without shaking the very foundations of the political fabric. It is easy to conceive, that a man, who admits all the wretchedness of the institution and its wrong to humanity, may nevertheless hesitate to adopt a remedy, until he is satisfied that the remedy itself is not worse than the disease. That such a remedy will come with time, who can doubt, that has confidence in the ultimate prevalence of the right, and the progressive civilization of his species? (678)

Prescott advocates waiting for a remedy for slavery that will bring real health back to the national body, instead of eradicating the disease at the expense of its well-being. He professes confidence that "such a remedy will come with time" and will be worth the wait, although that confidence is undermined by his framing of that assertion in the form of a question—"who can doubt?"—which problematizes the inevitability of progress toward a less evil society. The impotence of this gradualist posture is implied in his statement that "we may hope [slavery] is approaching its conclusion" in the nineteenth century; hope must be put in the conditional sense when he cannot condone radical solutions like the abolitionist disregard for constitutional proprieties.

He does describe slavery in terms of "evil," "wretchedness" and "wrong." His strategy of deferral perpetuates his contact and complicity with such an institution, and as he observes in a discussion on Mexican indigenous labor laws, their provisions for care and religious instruction of the natives do not mitigate their immorality: "[W]hat avail good laws, which, in their very nature, imply the toleration of a great abuse?" (636). Nonetheless, he seems generally willing to accept the consequences of his accommodationist stance in order to preserve the political, legal, and fiscal status quo and avoid "shaking the very foundations of the political fabric." The position on slavery that he articulates in *The Conquest of Mexico* is borne out by his disapproving representation in *The Conquest of Peru* of the way that Las Casas and Núñez Vela's impractical schemes court a violent response from the slaveholding conquistadors. La Gasca's practical, gradualist approach to mediating between the two camps embodies for Prescott the only sane way for U.S. politicians to proceed as they work to repair a society similarly divided over the slavery issue.

To find evidence of anxiety over slavery in *The Conquest of Peru*—a text written during the U.S. war with Mexico by an author responsible for one of the most widely read and imaginatively influential books of that conflict—is unsurprising. Slavery was deeply entangled in the stakes of the war. Acquisition of Mexican land by the United States meant a potential increase of slaveholding territory that worried the antislavery community and led to widespread opposition to the war in the North.[69] So one might expect to find the specter of slavery looming over Prescott's Peru. But accessing this issue through the vehicle of the war and its emphasis on U.S. identification with the perspective of the conqueror (including the fraught processes of expansion and incorporation) overdetermines the fears that one finds in *The Conquest of Peru*. As a Whig writing in a time of imperial growth, Prescott should be concerned about the extension of the institution of slavery. Instead, he seems most disquieted about contemporary efforts to end the institution, a fear arising out of his study of the conquered of Peru.

In a representation of conquest written in an era when the United States was beginning to thresh out its own identity as an increasingly powerful empire in relationship to places like Mexico, one would expect Prescott to be contemplating

U.S. similarities to the rising imperial power of Spain. This does happen to some extent, but he also contemplates U.S. similarities to what he sees as the economically moribund culture of Incan Peru and the destabilizing factions of conquistadorial Peru, both ultimately eclipsed by a centralized Spanish empire. In *The Conquest of Peru*, despite the triumphalist potential of the early modern episode that Prescott relates, he worries over what makes empires fail every bit as much as he analyzes what allows them to flourish.

The Disappearance of the Middle Ground

Prescott's defense of property rights leads him into difficult argumentative and moral territory. He maintains that U.S. capitalism constitutes a more moral because more free economic system than Incan proto-communism does, while in the same text he represents the very free but totally immoral capitalistic conquistadors as a plague worse than the Incas. He also maintains that the Incas' restriction of individual freedom in denying Peruvians the right of personal property constituted inexcusable tyranny, while slaveholders' restriction of individual freedom in denying their slave "property" emancipation could be excused in the service of societal harmony. Freedom, which early in his history he strenuously extols as an individual right and the mark of an enlightened civilization, therefore neither guarantees a moral society nor trumps property interests when they conflict. The history of challenges to property in early modern Peru forces Prescott into defenses of the U.S. property system that reveal the moral compromises he makes in stressing the preservation of social stability and security for wealth, his de facto top priorities.

Any moral discomfort that Prescott might have experienced due to his logically contorted ideology would have added to the distress caused by eroding support for his position. The antislavery but also antiabolitionist philosophy became increasingly embattled in the 1840s and increasingly difficult for Prescott to maintain. According to William Scott, writing about social attitudes toward property in the nineteenth-century United States, a large antislavery faction at the 1820 Missouri Compromise debates believed that "[s]lavery was immoral, but men must regulate their lives according to practical necessity, not abstract theory. Therefore southern property in slaves had to be honored."[70] Although this camp was large in 1820, more staunchly abolitionist attitudes gained ground in the decades that followed, so when Prescott expresses this viewpoint in the late 1840s, he is defending a position being abandoned even by members of his own political party.

Around the time that Prescott was writing *The Conquest of Peru*, the Whigs began to splinter into antislavery "Conscience" and proslavery "Cotton" factions (one scholar labeled 1844–48 the "period of political disintegration" in Massachusetts politics).[71] The Free Soil Party, active from 1848 to 1852 in campaigning for slavery-free western territories, picked up members among antislavery Whigs. These developments made middle-ground positions like Prescott's difficult. Just as La Gasca attempted to mediate between the demands of the abolitionist Las Casas on the one hand and the property-preserving colonists on the other, Prescott attempts to stake out a position from which he can both condemn the institution of slavery as the Conscience Whigs were doing and defend southern property rights as the Cotton Whigs were doing.

In this attempt, he follows the political logic of Daniel Webster, the antislavery, pro-Union Whig politician best known for his assistance in brokering the Compromise of 1850, which Prescott publicly supported, and which prohibited slavery in some western territories at the expense of concessions to southern interests such as a revitalized fugitive slave law.[72] Webster's work with the compromise resulted in his abrupt fall from favor in the North and the end of his senatorial career. Daniel Walker Howe notes that "the protection of property" as a value motivated Webster to support the compromise; he furthermore notes that "Webster's fundamental dedication to the defense of property" underlay all of his stances on a wide range of social and political issues.[73] I argue that the prerogative of property likewise dominated many of Prescott's attitudes, and likewise consigned him to a middle-ground position rapidly being eliminated in U.S. society in the 1840s.

Webster, a constitutional lawyer as well as a politician, acted as counsel in a number of key Supreme Court cases impacting the system of private property in the United States, including *West River Bridge Company v. Dix* (1848), in which he unsuccessfully argued against Vermont's power of eminent domain as justification for an 1843 decision to seize a privately owned bridge. Webster cautioned the Court that a judgment against the West River Bridge Company would send the United States down a slippery slope, because if "the legislature, or their agents, are to be the sole judges of what is to be taken, and to what public use it is to be appropriated, the most levelling ultraisms of Anti-rentism or Agrarianism or Abolitionism may be successfully advanced."[74] Webster here lumps together seemingly very different social reform movements under the single conceptual umbrella of threats to property: anti-rentism (the tenants' rights philosophy that emerged in the New York anti-rent war in response to large estate owners' near-feudal control over their tenants; it asserted a tenant's right to purchase the rented land eventually), agrarianism, and abolitionism.[75] For Webster, these radical "ultraisms" all aim at social "levelling," pulling property owners down to the level of the masses: forced equalization, in Prescott's terms. Webster claims that broad interpretations of the Fifth Amendment's provision for government seizure of private property for the purposes of "public use" would allow agrarianist-minded legislatures to redistribute land to broaden public stakeholding in the republic and allow abolitionist-minded legislatures to emancipate slaves in the interest of the public good.[76] He articulates a sense of U.S. property rights as the potentially vulnerable target of multiple radical reform efforts, but importantly, he fails to persuade the Court to adopt his logic.

Prescott clearly shared the apprehension that Webster expresses in the *West River Bridge* case because he takes the time to mount counterarguments of his own against these property challenges. William Scott has argued that antebellum debates over the concept of property focused on potential legislation to ensure democratized land ownership, in part as a way to address the growth of a propertyless class of wage laborers, and also focused on whether slaves could justifiably be considered property and how that would affect emancipation and slaveholder compensation.[77] Prescott's *Conquest of Peru* therefore takes up, even if only obliquely, two of the major strands in property theory in the decades before the Civil War. As we have seen, Prescott argues, first, for the importance of personal property even given the social evils that can flow from capitalistic individualism and a free market; and second, for slaves to be considered as property, if not in theory, then at least in practice, and the consequent impracticability of immediate abolition without compensation. To Prescott, both communism and abolitionism were misguided social reform schemes, ostensibly directed at creating a better society by redressing the injustices of a capitalist system of property, but actually dangerously radical in the revolutionary havoc that they would wreak on U.S. society.

Prescott's stance on property, equality, and social change exemplifies the philosophy of old-guard, wealth-conscious Whigs, a group caught in the middle during this era between two steadily coalescing, increasingly antagonistic sectional factions. By the 1850s, northerners would largely unify under the antislavery, proabolition banner.[78] But in the 1840s, not all northerners had acquiesced to this social agenda. People like Prescott rightly foresaw the violence and social havoc that would result from the North pursuing an abolitionist course. In addition, the moral urgency of emancipation had not yet taken universal precedence over every other social concern; antislavery Whigs like Prescott could still envision the concept of abolition as merely one subcategory subsumed under the larger issue of property rights, and could therefore argue for the greater exigency of defending personal property against agrarian and abolitionist challenges.

However, as evidenced by the way that the Compromise of 1850 actually produced a more polarized society, middle-ground positions like Prescott's were rapidly disappearing. *The Conquest of Peru* speaks to a moment just before the strict bifurcation of U.S. society into sectional camps, allegiance to which superseded all other agendas. To Prescott's eyes, the international history of early modern Peru raised the specter of some intranational problems confronting the United States: Incan Peru's lack of personal property mirrored contemporary communist objectives, and conquistadorial Peru offered a precedent for efforts to abolish property in slaves. Peruvian history thus evidently inspired Prescott to articulate a defensively all-encompassing pro-property ideology, a viewpoint that in the context of the late 1840s identified him with a social position on the verge of being eclipsed.

3 Inquisition

Religious Tolerance and Motley's *Rise of the Dutch Republic*

Spain's American conquests in the early sixteenth century catapulted it into a stratospheric rise, transforming it into the most powerful and extensive empire in the world. However, it did not long retain this unqualified position of global eminence. Domestic economic troubles and European wars in the late sixteenth century undermined Spain and precipitated the beginning of its decline. Prescott argued for this interpretation in his unfinished late-career *History of the Reign of Philip the Second, King of Spain* (1855–58). In the opening remarks of this work, Prescott briefly sketched what he saw as the main contours of the narrative that he had created about Spain over the course of his histories of Ferdinand and Isabella's reign, the American conquests, and this final history of Philip II: Spain, "consolidated into one empire" under Ferdinand and Isabella, with "territory extended by a brilliant career of discovery and conquest" during the reign of Charles V, "had risen to the zenith of its power" under his son, Philip II. However, at this point, it had "already disclosed those germs of domestic corruption which gradually led to its dismemberment and decay."[1] In Prescott's depiction, Spain had succumbed to the rise and fall of empires pattern, which caught the empires of the early modern period up into a seemingly inescapable domino effect.

John Lothrop Motley, another Boston historian, also argued in his 1856 *Rise of the Dutch Republic* that Philip had already begun to lose his grip on Spain's dominance. Motley writes that the "Indian revenue, so called, was nearly spent," and that Philip, the "possessor of all Peru and Mexico[,] could reckon on 'nothing worth mentioning' from his mines."[2] In Motley's interpretation, desperate greed therefore combined with religious bigotry to motivate the persecution of the people of the Netherlands, another key holding of the Spanish empire. The property confiscated from victims of the Inquisition would produce "a torrent of wealth, richer than ever flowed from Mexican and Peruvian mines," to alleviate Spain's financial woes (2:103). This policy of persecution inspired the conflict that became Motley's great subject: the Dutch revolt from Spain.

Starting in the late sixteenth century, the Netherlands began to wrest its independence from the Spanish empire. The surprising success of the Dutch revolt against mighty Spain revealed Spanish weaknesses even at the height of its power, and the loss of the Netherlands further weakened the Spanish empire. Although Motley does not dwell on this era as the beginning of the end for Spain (he devotes too much energy to depicting Spanish infamy to undermine it constantly with reminders of Spain's growing weakness), he does make clear that the larger context for understanding this moment in history involves the eclipse of Spain by the rising power of the Netherlands.

He writes that in the course of its struggle with "the most potent empire upon earth," the Dutch Republic "becom[es] itself a mighty state, and binding about its own slender form a zone of the richest possessions of earth, from pole to tropic, finally dictates its decrees to the empire of Charles" (1:iv). Philip II and William the Silent—the Prince of Orange who masterminded the first phase of the Dutch independence movement—symbolized their respective countries and embodied the shift in power, despite William's assassination well before the Dutch Republic got fully free of Spain.[3] Philip in his campaign against the Dutch "was by the same process to undermine his own power forever," and, had he been able to see the future, he "might have beheld his victim [William], not crowned himself, but pointing to a line of kings . . . and smiling on them for his" (2:87, 2:88). Given that William's great-grandson would, through his alliance with the Stuarts, assume the throne of England in the Glorious Revolution, William's line was thus associated not only with the great state of the Netherlands but also with the English empire, the successor to global dominance upon Spain's decline. The Dutch revolt, according to Motley, constituted the turning point in the fortunes of Spain, although Philip—like Cooper's oblivious Venetian senators—could not see it.

However, Motley's history presents a variation on the imperial eclipse theme. Unlike the other authors of imperial eclipse narratives (with the possible exception of Cooper in his approach with *The Water-Witch*), Motley devotes his energies primarily to exploring the rising rather than the falling power. He called his history *The* ***Rise*** *of the Dutch Republic*, and he wrote that "our subject, which is the rise of the Netherland commonwealth," precludes significant attention to "the decline of the Spanish monarchy" (2:225).[4] This variation in focus changes the tone of the history from generally elegiac to triumphal, as we root for the Dutch underdogs to overthrow their Spanish oppressors.

The spatiotemporal contact zone that Motley works to construct links the United States not with declining and tyrannical Spain but with the up-and-coming Dutch. His text tends toward national self-congratulation instead of national anxiety, and therefore usefully shows the other main tendency in nineteenth-century U.S. nationalist discourse (even though some of his reviewers' more pessimistic associations with this same episode in early modern history once again indicate the availability of the more anxiety-producing type of contact zone). The Dutch rise, a noble and inspiring story, involved an audacious revolution, fought against incredible odds by men of great valor committed to principles of civil and religious freedom. The Dutch revolt reminded Motley of a revolution much closer to home: the U.S. Revolutionary War had also pitted an untried colonial force against the greatest power in the world at the time, in a contest over the rights of the people to refuse oppression and demand personal liberty. Reading about the Dutch revolt and feeling awe at Dutch victories therefore squared with and actually helped to reinforce nationalist pride in the U.S. Revolution and in its great hero Washington, whom Motley explicitly likens to the champion of the Netherlands, William the Silent.

William, a powerful advocate for religious tolerance, had utterly rejected the worldview of the Spanish Inquisition and had instituted a forward-thinking culture of free worship in the Netherlands, an achievement that Motley particularly admired. He associated it with the fact that two centuries later, the U.S. republic would also embrace religious tolerance as a core value and provide exceptional guarantees of free worship to its citizens—after a brief hiccup with the persecution-prone New England Puritans, at least. But some of Motley's reviewers believed that religious tolerance of the type that William had so beautifully embodied was not only scarce among the Puritans but was also becoming endangered in the United States in the 1850s. Anti-Catholic groups, vehement in their antipathy toward the Romish religion, were working to suppress the spread of Catholic influence in the country, just as Philip and the Inquisition had worked to suppress Dutch Protestantism two centuries earlier. In the connections that these particular reviewers drew between international history and intranational problems, the story of the Dutch revolt from Spain did not necessarily predict good things ahead for the U.S. republic, which on the issue of religious tolerance sometimes resembled Spain more closely than it did the rising star of the Netherlands. These reviews thus draw out and articulate the more typical form of the imperial eclipse narrative that remains latent in Motley's determinedly triumphalist account of the Dutch revolt.

The Dutch Washington

Although the relevance of early modern Dutch history to the United States may now seem obscure, it constituted a "usable past" for Motley, in Van Wyck Brooks's famous phrase (which Brooks explained using the example of Motley's treatment of the Dutch).[5] Motley's framework for understanding history involved recurring motifs and echoes, such that the Dutch revolt from Spain could foreshadow the U.S. revolt from England, William the Silent could foreshadow George Washington, and William's emphasis on religious toleration could foreshadow the First Amendment to the U.S. Constitution. Motley sought to use Dutch history to strengthen U.S. commitment to the civil and religious liberties for which William and the Dutch had also fought.

Motley's historiography is no longer frequently read or discussed by critics, but in his own day, he garnered a significant audience for his work. The story of the Dutch revolt seemed to connect with the reading public: in the first year after its publication, *The Rise of the Dutch Republic* sold about fifteen thousand copies in the United States and another fifteen thousand in England.[6] The history proved so popular that in February 1857, a U.S. reviewer wrote, "So rapid, general, and brilliant has been its success, that we feel ourselves already entitled to presume in the progress of our remarks, that our readers have familiarized themselves with its contents."[7]

Motley's efforts to demonstrate the contemporary relevance of his subject no doubt helped it to connect with readers. Although many of the parallels that he identified between the sixteenth-century Netherlands and the nineteenth century involved nationalist associations between the Dutch revolt and the U.S. Revolutionary War, he also wrote with international audiences in mind (as Prescott did as well: intensively researched historiography from this period drew on and addressed itself to an international network of historians and archivists and lent an internationalist focus to the scope of historians' intended audiences). Instead of following the logic of his Revolutionary War comparison and associating Philip II's Spain with George III's England, Motley courts an English readership by associating both the United States and England with the rising power of the Netherlands. For example, in his preface, he gives an explanation of his work's interest for English audiences: the Dutch Republic's global commercial empire "must always be looked upon with interest by Englishmen, as in a great measure the precursor in their own scheme of empire" (1:v). The mercantilist and maritime emphasis of the Dutch empire made it a useful prototype of the English empire. Early modern history could serve as imperial self-reflection not only for the United States but also for England, and Motley's optimistic concentration on the Dutch rise avoided uncomfortable reflections about whether the rapid Dutch decline might also presage the downfall of English and U.S. global power.

Motley addressed English audiences not only because his worldview as a working historian was necessarily internationalist but also because he operated within an Anglo-Saxon racial framework that united the fortunes of the Netherlands, England, and the United States. According to Motley, the history of the Anglo-Saxon race wound through the histories of all these countries, consistently illustrating a genetic predisposition toward liberty.[8] In a lengthy "Historical Introduction" that precedes the history proper, Motley writes, "Love of freedom, readiness to strike and bleed at any moment in her cause, manly resistance to despotism, however overshadowing, were the leading characteristics of the race in all regions and periods, whether among Frisian swamps, Dutch dykes, the gentle hills and dales of England, or the pathless forests of America" (1:39). The Dutch revolt therefore had counterparts in both preceding and subsequent eras, in what Motley refers to as "the perpetual reproductions of history" (2:190). A contemporary Dutch historian, Guillaume Groen van Prinsterer, characterized Motley as writing in a mode of "perpetual anachronism."[9]

Motley reads the Batavian rebellion against Rome in 69–70 C.E. as a "remarkable foreshadowing of the future conflict with Spain" (1:17). "The power of Rome, overwhelming, although tottering to its fall," clearly parallels that of imperial Spain, a connection strengthened by references to Charles V as Caesar, Philip II as Tiberius, and the bloody-minded Duke of Alva—governor of the Netherlands from 1567 to 1573 and promoter of the Inquisition—as Nero (1:1, 1:99, 2:266, 2:211). The Batavi, a Germanic tribe in what became the Netherlands, revolted under the leadership of Claudius Civilis.[10] Civilis bears "more than a fanciful resemblance" to William the Silent, who would later wage another heroic struggle against a mighty tyrannical power on the same ground (1:17). At crucial moments both would be deserted by their Celtic allies (the Gauls in the case of Civilis and their descendents the Walloons in the case of William), but they would nonetheless exhibit Germanic vigor in the pursuit of freedom.

Just as the Batavian revolt prefigured the Dutch revolt, so the Dutch revolt prefigured other freedom fights and constituted, in one critic's words, Motley's "favorite preview of Lexington and Concord."[11] Motley writes that the "maintenance of the right by the little provinces of Holland and Zealand in the sixteenth, by Holland and England united in the seventeenth, and by the United States of America in the eighteenth centuries, forms but a single chapter in the great volume of human fate; for the so-called revolutions of Holland, England, and America, are all links of one chain" (1:iv). Although Motley intends his "chain" image to express a progressive interpretation of history, its antiexceptionalist logic chains the United States to early modern empires in a way that generally caused anxiety for imperial eclipse authors when it involved a cyclical temporality: grim international history reemerging as intranational troubles. However, Motley's more triumphalist account focuses on a source of national pride rather than on an intranational weakness: the Dutch revolt and the Glorious Revolution meant that the

U.S. Revolutionary War had an august lineage of Anglo-Saxon struggles devoted to the ideals of freedom and progress.[12]

Importantly, this lineage meant that none of these "so-called revolutions" were actually revolutionary. "Like the actors in our own great national drama," Motley writes, "these Netherland patriots were struggling to sustain, not to overthrow" (2:511). The Dutch wanted to "sustain" traditional civil rights, not create upheaval for its own sake—an attitude of conservative progress especially appealing to Whigs such as Motley (see also 1:vi, 1:428, 2:248, 2:368, 3:616).[13] As with Prescott's investment in a gradual abolition of slavery, Motley's vision of history shies away from rupture and instead embraces a gradual unfolding of democratic principles by Anglo-Saxon agents of human progress.

If these unrevolutionary revolutions blurred into each other for Motley, so did their leaders. The heroism of William the Silent, the Dutch prince who sacrificed comfort, fortune, and ultimately his life to secure freedom for the Netherlands, put him on par with the great George Washington. In his preface, Motley calls William "the Washington of the sixteenth century," and he writes in his concluding chapter that "no man—not even Washington—has ever been inspired by a purer patriotism" (1:vi, 3:625). Washington's already stratospheric reputation in the United States gained further luster from comparison to the revered founding father of the Dutch Republic—called, like Washington, the "Father of the country" (3:610). On the other hand, Motley clearly aimed to secure U.S. interest in the story of the Dutch revolt by making this analogy to a national idol.

In Motley's assessment, both William and Washington partook of a Protestant ethos. As he wrote to a correspondent, "I tell you without Luther, there would have been no William of Orange, no Washington."[14] Martin Luther and the Protestant Reformation had laid the foundation of freedom upon which these later heroes built. Motley and many others believed that the Protestant mentality encouraged the independence of spirit so necessary to the later struggles for political rights; in addition, religious liberty remained a key priority for the leaders of these later struggles. William "was the champion of the political rights of his country," Motley wrote, "but before all he was the defender of its religion. Liberty of conscience for his people was his first object. To establish Luther's axiom, that thoughts are toll-free, was his determination" (2:490).

To reinforce this impression, Motley repeatedly emphasizes that William took every opportunity to defend religious toleration. Before his conversion, when he still counted himself a Catholic, William nonetheless strenuously objected to the persecution of Dutch Protestants by the forces of the Inquisition, not only because of the brutality employed but also because people should be allowed to worship as they see fit (1:241–42, 1:275, 1:301, 1:341, 1:365, 1:373–74, 1:428, 1:456, 1:484–85, 1:507). After he converts to Lutheranism and then Calvinism, William objects as strenuously to violence done to Roman Catholics by overzealous Protestants and routinely institutes a policy of religious toleration in the territories under his sphere of influence (2:16–17, 2:66–72, 2:244–45, 2:368, 2:381, 2:385, 2:474–75, 2:482, 2:520, 3:20–21, 3:61–62, 3:83, 3:94, 3:617, among others).[15] Motley has a tendency, when listing a series of various policies instituted by William, to italicize the provisions for religious freedom, setting them apart and calling the reader's attention to them as especially important features of William's political philosophy.

Acting as a foil to all of this tolerance, Philip II, the Duke of Alva, and the other agents of the Inquisition pursue universal religious conformity with violent fanaticism; rooting out Reformist heresy and reestablishing the "ancient church" of Rome trumped all other concerns.[16] Although references to Inquisitorial violence occur throughout the history, Motley describes the practices of the Inquisition at length in part 2, chapter 3, a section central to my overall argument about Motley. He describes how victims of the Inquisition were identified by the insidious culture of surveillance established by the "holy office," whose "familiars" wormed their way into the private sanctums of homes, "diving into the secrets of every fireside," such that a prisoner's accuser "might be his son, father, or the wife of his bosom, for all were enjoined, under the death-penalty, to inform the inquisitors of every suspicious word which might fall from their nearest relatives" (1:323). Once arrested, supposed heretics were subjected to "all the forms of torture which the devilish ingenuity of the monks had invented," in suitably atmospheric surroundings, "at midnight, in a gloomy dungeon, dimly lighted by torches," where the "victim—whether man, matron, or tender virgin—was stripped naked," placed on the rack, and stretched to elicit confessions of heresy (1:324). They were convicted in religious trials that made a mockery of due process and then executed by the thousands.

Motley goes into particularly gory detail describing the atrocities of Peter Titelmann, an inquisitor in the Netherlands, who approached his work "with a jocularity which hardly seemed human" (1:331–32). He caused a man to be "hacked to death with seven blows of a rusty sword, in the presence of his wife, who was so horror-stricken that she died on the spot before her husband" (1:333). Titelmann inflicted a similarly sadistic punishment on another blasphemer: "[H]is right hand and foot were burned and twisted off between two red-hot irons. His tongue was then torn out by the roots.... With his arms and legs fastened together behind his back, he was then hooked by the middle of his body to an iron chain, and made to swing to and fro over a slow fire till he was entirely roasted" (1:335–36).

Motley seems to have worried that these almost pornographic descriptions of torture and killing might seem gratuitous, so rather than "let the reader deem that too much time is devoted to this painful subject," Motley answers the question: "Are these things related merely to excite superfluous horror?" (1:327, 1:337).[17] He argues that his lingering descriptions of ecclesiastical brutality form the only proper context in which to understand the subsequent Dutch revolt; the Netherlands could either rebel or be crushed body and soul by Spain and the Inquisition. The cruelty of people like Peter Titelmann "terrified many, but it inspired more with that noble resistance to oppression, particularly religious oppression, which is the sublimest instinct of human nature" (1:334). Motley's language here again calls up associations between the spirit of the Dutch revolt and the U.S. Revolutionary War, also an example of sublimely noble resistance to oppression in Motley's estimation.

The parallels between the two freedom fights meant that U.S. Americans "must look with affectionate interest upon the trials of the elder commonwealth"; echoing many other world history writers, Motley argues that the "lessons of history and the fate of free states can never be sufficiently pondered by those upon whom so large and heavy a responsibility for the maintenance of rational human freedom rests" (1:vi). In this same vein, he wrote to his father that he hoped "I may make some few people in the world wiser and better by my labour. This must be the case whenever a man honestly 'seeks the truths in ages past' to furnish light for the present and future track." Motley hoped that his story would strengthen his readers in their love of and commitment to freedom, the clear lesson of the Dutch revolt and the struggles of William the Silent. "If ten people in the world," he wrote, "hate despotism a little more and love civil and religious liberty a little better in consequence of what I have written, I shall be satisfied."[18] He worked to associate the Dutch revolt against Philip II and the Spanish Inquisition with Washington and the spirit of '76 via a tradition of Anglo-Saxon revolutions, and he used the sixteenth-century story of the rise of the Dutch Republic to reinforce his U.S. readers' devotion to the forms of civil and religious liberty that they enjoyed and for which William had also fought.

The American Inquisition

Although Motley primarily focuses on Washington and the Revolutionary War to demonstrate the relevance of the Dutch revolt to the United States, he does provide another American tie-in, this one with an actual material link to the history of the Netherlands. Motley writes in his preface that the doings of the Anglo-Saxon race are "essentially the same, whether in Friesland [an area in the Netherlands], England, or Massachusetts" (1:v). Many key events of the U.S. Revolutionary War—to which Motley is no doubt alluding—happened in Massachusetts, but Motley also certainly wants to suggest a connection between his tale and that of the Pilgrims.

This connection becomes more overt when Motley describes William's plan, conceived at a low point in Dutch revolutionary fortunes, to put all Netherlanders in boats and execute a mass national emigration (a rash plan, but one commensurate to Philip's order that everyone in the Netherlands, barring a few explicitly listed exceptions, be put to death): had the ships "taken the direction of the newly-discovered Western hemisphere," a "religious colony, planted by a commercial and liberty-loving race, in a virgin soil, . . . might have preceded, by half a century, the colony which a kindred race, impelled by similar motives, and under somewhat similar circumstances and conditions, was destined to plant upon the stern shores of New England" (3:49). Both groups had the Anglo-Saxon instinct for trade and freedom, and both contemplated a risky emigration to escape religious persecution. The Dutch in fact faced hardships even more severe than those experienced by the Pilgrims. Motley writes that upon reading the Edict of 1550 ordering the suppression of Protestantism in the Netherlands by violent means if necessary, an "American will judge whether the wrongs inflicted by Laud and Charles on his [the U.S. reader's] ancestors were the severest which a people has had to undergo, and whether the Dutch Republic does not track its source to the same, high, religious origin as that of our own commonwealth" (1:261).[19] Both the Dutch Republic and the United States originated as courageous bids for religious freedom in the face of spiritual tyranny.

But the Pilgrims didn't just resemble the Dutch spiritually; for a time they actually lived in the Netherlands. "The English Puritans," Motley reminds his readers, "fled for refuge to the Dutch Republic, and thence departed to establish the American Republic" (1:485). By virtue of their residence in the Netherlands from 1608 to 1620 and their subsequent departure for the New World, the Pilgrims thus literalized the emigration that William had only contemplated a generation earlier. While the Pilgrims actually had no interest in nation-building as such, Motley's conflation of their project with "establish[ing] the American Republic" exemplifies the teleological, proto-nationalist interpretation of their motivation then prevalent in New England. These founding fathers of the United States, as they were understood by Motley and his fellow New Englanders, had spent a formative period in the Netherlands, an experience shaped by the Dutch revolt that had raged in the decades prior to their arrival.

Fleeing from persecution by James I and Archbishop William Laud, the English Puritans who would ultimately establish the Plymouth Plantation went to the Low Countries, "where they heard was freedom of religion for all men," as William Bradford puts it in his chronicle of that community, *Of Plymouth Plan-*

tation.[20] (Bradford's manuscript had been lost for over a century but was rediscovered in the 1850s. Notice of its publication appeared in the July 1856 *North American Review*, in the same issue as a review of Motley's history.)[21] In 1608, when the Pilgrims left England, the Netherlands had an international reputation for religious liberty as a direct result of that region's experience of the Inquisition, its rebellion from Spain, and its subsequent institutionalization of freedom of worship.[22] After a brief stint in Amsterdam, the Pilgrims settled in Leyden, the town whose dramatic siege by the Spanish army in 1574 concludes volume 2 of *The Rise of the Dutch Republic* (2:557–82). The Pilgrims' reasons for leaving Leyden after their relatively happy twelve-year stay included, among other concerns financial and spiritual in nature,[23] the fact that a truce between the Netherlands and Spain was ending. This political shift jeopardized the Puritan community's ability to practice its brand of Protestantism in peace, and Bradford and his congregation felt that "the Spaniard might prove as cruel as the savages of America," so they resolved to go.[24] The Dutch revolt from Spain thus materially impacted the shape of the Pilgrim story.

Although Motley took advantage of the American tie-in that the Pilgrims provided to his history, and he appreciated the "high, religious origin" that they conferred on the United States by having risked so much to live in religious freedom, he saw flaws in the Puritan mentality. The New England Puritans did not extend to other religious groups the same freedoms that they themselves wished to enjoy. In *The Rise of the Dutch Republic*, Motley frequently mentions outbreaks of Protestant, especially Calvinist, violence toward Catholics, and he praises William for condemning this form of religious persecution as well as Spanish persecution of Protestants. William's belief that "[n]either monk nor minister should burn, drown, or hang his fellow-creatures" "was no small virtue, in that age. . . . We know what Calvinists, Zwinglians, Lutherans, have done in the Netherlands, in Germany, in Switzerland, and almost a century later in New England" (3:62). Motley here could be referring to the Quaker persecutions, the Salem witch trials, the treatment of Anne Hutchinson and Roger Williams, or any number of other Puritan inquisitions. He had also written disparagingly about the stern and unforgiving Puritans in his pre–*Dutch Republic* literary career. Motley's 1849 novel *Merry-Mount* (which describes the Puritan repression of the maypole revels at Thomas Morton's Merry-mount) "exposes the falsities of characterizing Puritans as ur-libertarians," according to John McWilliams.[25]

With Motley's claim that "[w]e know what Calvinists . . . have done . . . in New England," he suggests his position within the religious culture of his own day. Like many other prominent New England authors, including Prescott and Longfellow, Motley was a Unitarian. U.S. Unitarianism had emerged in the late eighteenth and early nineteenth century as the liberal opposition to orthodox Calvinists within the New England Congregationalist Church.[26] Unitarians rejected the concepts of the Trinity, predestination, and original sin; they espoused human reason as an important spiritual tool; and they shied away from doctrinal rigidity and thus professed a commitment to religious tolerance and freedom of conscience. Motley's insinuation regarding the persecutory potential of Calvinism, at which more orthodox Congregationalists might bristle, bespeaks a Unitarian mindset. Motley's representation of the Puritans corresponded to the attitude that nineteenth-century Unitarians typically held toward their seventeenth-century forebears.[27] To wit, although the Puritans deserved filiopietistic respect for their role in founding the United States, their rigid Calvinism and religious intolerance conflicted with a key value that Unitarians cherished and that Motley hoped to encourage with his account of the Dutch revolt: U.S. commitment to religious freedom. Puritan vices therefore had to be kept in mind along with their virtues.

Michael Davitt Bell has argued that nineteenth-century denunciations of Puritan severity and bigotry relied on "a myth of progress away from the errors of the fathers to the more enlightened views and practices of the nineteenth-century present."[28] But one of Motley's reviewers, a writer for the *Democratic Review*, questioned whether sufficient progress had in fact been made away from early modern forms of religious intolerance. Reviews of *The Rise of the Dutch Republic* are useful in drawing out the implications of Motley's history and will figure substantively in the remainder of my analysis; they illustrate that despite Motley's triumphalist intentions, a narrative of imperial eclipse nonetheless lurks in his text. The *Democratic Review* writer devoted his whole review (published in August 1856) to the issue of religious freedom: how it featured in Motley's history and the ways in which he saw it as endangered by recent developments in U.S. society. For him, the problem had not been laid to rest in the comfortably distant past.

He, too, stressed Puritan forms of persecution, pointing to their lack of respect for religious dissent within their own community: "The English refugees in America, none of them—save only Roger Williams, and the little band he collected around him, in Rhode Island—understood or practised [religious tolerance]. Fugitives for conscience sake, they persecuted in their turn. Their sole idea of religious liberty was liberty to think as they did."[29] He then uses Puritan religious despotism as a springboard to discuss modern incarnations of Philip II's spiritual bigotry. He lays the framework by praising the tolerant ideals that undergird the U.S. republic: he argues that the "great fundamental principle" so important to William of Orange—"free-conscience, and man's accountability only to God for his religious opinions"—has "now developed into such an immortal loveliness [in] the Democratic Republican Institutions of the United States of America." He characterizes the Dutch as "builders up of that system of free thought, and speech, and worship, wherein we now rejoice," and says that to William the Silent "we owe the true idea of religious liberty, the idea upon which this government has so firmly and happily rested for near a century."[30]

But excellence in U.S. institutions, systems, and foundational ideas doesn't necessarily mean that everyone in the country acts in accordance with those idealized abstractions. The reviewer identifies a troubling intranational phenomenon in conflict with the abstract U.S. commitment to religious freedom. After repeated expressions of admiration for William's tolerance, and just after his pronouncement on the narrowness of the Puritans' supposed "religious liberty," he explains, "We lay a particular stress upon this idea, because the old leaven of persecution is not even yet exhausted." He sees a very real, very present threat operating in the United States in 1856:

> The dominant idea of Know-Nothingism, and its proscription of men, in the nineteenth century, and on American soil, for worshipping God after a particular form, is nothing but the spirit of Philip II. of Spain, and his bloody servant Alva, in a new dress. Give it way. Allow it to gather force enough to work out its natural bent, and it would renew in New-York, Boston, Philadelphia, everywhere throughout the Union, the scenes of butchery which marked . . . the Netherlands of the sixteenth century. Strange that men should fail to see it. That they should fail to see that the spirit which originated and worked the Spanish Inquisition is the very spirit which to-day rears its unsightly head anew amongst us. It is true that the sixteenth century saw it crowned with more terrors than it has ever since displayed; but the serpents which coil about it are merely torpid, not dead, and ask only the grateful warmth of such a religious fanaticism as our political parsons seem bent on fomenting, to animate them to new life, to infuse a deadlier poison in their sting, and set an added horror on their crest.[31]

U.S. religious intolerance had created a spatiotemporal contact zone between the sixteenth-century Netherlands and "New-York, Boston, Philadelphia, everywhere throughout the Union." The spirit of Philip II and the Spanish Inquisition had cropped up again "in the nineteenth century, and on American soil," not among U.S. Catholics, as was frequently alleged in anti-Catholic propaganda, but among supposedly more liberty-loving Protestants.[32] The American Party, popularly called the Know-Nothings for their members' repeated insistence that they knew nothing of the group, gained force in the 1850s on a platform of extreme nativism (aimed specifically at Irish and German immigrants) and "No-Popery" (anti-Catholicism) that this reviewer sees as one step away from the brutalities of the Spanish Inquisition.

The Know-Nothings made startlingly great gains in state elections in 1854, having materialized as a political force overnight, capitalizing on widespread popular disgust with the existing parties, the potency of sectional issues like slavery and unionism, frustration with rising immigration, and a long-standing anti-Catholic trend in U.S. culture.[33] Anti-Catholic factions had unleashed relentless invective against Catholics and Catholicism for decades, denouncing the Roman Church as the Whore of Babylon, accusing the Pope and his devious Jesuits of plotting to overthrow the democratic United States, and depicting nunneries as dens of licentiousness where innocent girls were forced into sexual slavery to priests. Accusations of the latter kind had erupted into violence in 1834 when a mob burned an Ursuline convent in Charlestown, Massachusetts, an act that one observer felt might herald the onset of a "Protestant inquisition." This kind of violence continued, and in the mid-1850s, a number of Catholic churches were vandalized or destroyed, priests were attacked, and convents were violated.[34]

The Know-Nothings worked to capitalize on this kind of anti-Catholic climate and promised to rededicate government to the interests of "native" American Protestants. The organization required that its members be native-born Protestants sworn to resist "the insidious policy of the Church of Rome" and never vote for "foreigners and aliens, and Roman Catholics in particular."[35] In Massachusetts, where Know-Nothings had effectively complete control over the state government in 1855, they pursued what John R. Mulkern characterizes as "the legalization of state persecution of ethnic and religious minorities." For example, they passed legislation mandating that the Protestant King James Bible be read daily in public schools where Catholic schoolchildren would have to listen, a long-standing educational custom that U.S. Catholics resented and had strenuously resisted. Massachusetts Know-Nothings also proposed an amendment to the state constitution forbidding Catholics to hold public office.[36] Know-Nothings in Connecticut, Pennsylvania, Michigan, and most visibly in New York passed laws preventing Catholic bishops from owning real estate in their capacity as bishops, which aimed at reducing the wealth and political clout of the Catholic Church.[37]

By 1856, when it supported Millard Fillmore for president but achieved nowhere near its previous success, the American Party was dissolving, and its former members largely transferred their loyalties to the Republican Party, allowing the Republicans to become truly competitive with the Democratic Party. Although thus short-lived, the immense popularity of the Know-Nothings earns them a significant place in discussions of pre–Civil War politics. Staunch contemporary opponents condemned the group's bigotry as contrary to the tolerant spirit of the United States and potentially catastrophic to maintaining core U.S. values.

The *Democratic Review* author, writing for an ardently Democratic magazine, would obviously look with disfavor on the Democratic Party's main competition in 1856—the Know-Nothing American Party. And the Democratic Party's alliance with the New York Irish community, evident in institutions like Tammany Hall, would further predispose this author to condemn the American Party's nativist anti-Catholicism.[38] He uses Motley's history as a vehicle for expressing his concern about the Know-Nothings, drawing parallels between their proscriptive No-Popery stance and Philip II's brutal zealotry as different manifestations of the same inquisitorial spirit. Although he finds the connections that Motley seeks to draw between William's religious tolerance and U.S. freedom of worship compelling, he warns of an intolerant element of U.S. society that aligns more closely with the despotic and declining Spanish empire than with the rising power of the Netherlands.

Anti-Catholicism and Impartiality

The writer for the *Democratic Review* was not alone in making this more ominous connection between Motley's subject and U.S. society. Another reviewer, writing for the *Southern Quarterly Review* in February 1857, also found the Know-Nothings a pertinent modern context to demonstrate the contemporary relevance of Motley's history, but he goes a step further by implicating Motley himself in the problem of U.S. religious intolerance. He lauds William the Silent's religious liberality, which he finds "scarcely equalled in our times or country, after more than three quarters of a century of professedly universal and complete toleration. The recent politico-religious movement in the United States [that is, the Know-Nothing movement], was in direct contravention of the lessons taught by the precepts, the example, and the career of William of Orange." To this reviewer, the popularity of the American Party "shows how far the sentiment of a large part of the people of the United States of America still lags behind the toleration proposed by the illustrious founder of the United Provinces of the Dutch Republic."[39]

And according to the *Southern Quarterly Review* writer, Motley himself also lags behind William in his level of tolerance. The reviewer continues: "To these dispassionate views, Mr. Motley, though singularly fair and liberal in his appreciation of individuals, has scarcely raised himself." The reviewer admires Motley's abstract commitment to religious toleration, but he argues that Motley's writing does not consistently embody that tolerant mindset. His "history, while warmly and properly sympathizing with American sentiments, is at times Puritan in its tone, and more in unison with the feelings and practices of the sturdy companions of . . . John Winthrop, than with the more generous conceptions of the American constitution, and the tolerant spirit of legitimate American tendencies." Motley, who so deeply disapproves of Puritan intolerance, stands accused here of employing a puritanically intolerant tone in his writing. This constitutes "one of the chief blemishes of this truly splendid production. The ancient leaven of intolerance, so beguiling and so hard to be subdued, occasionally breaks out"—a harsh criticism in the generally gentlemanly rhetoric of nineteenth-century literary reviews.[40] In making this critique directly after his allusion to the Know-Nothings, the reviewer aligns Motley's ungenerous tone and Know-Nothing anti-Catholic intolerance as phenomena that undermine the "professedly universal and complete toleration" of the United States.

Motley certainly did not support the Know-Nothings. He once referred to their guiding spirit as "Jack Cadism" (mob rule, populism of the lowest common denominator, described through the same Shakespearean analogy that Cooper tended to use to describe the masses); Motley condemned the "abominations of the last legislature," when the American Party controlled Massachusetts government in 1855.[41] But both Motley and the Know-Nothings participated in the culture of anti-Catholic discourse prevalent in the mid-1850s. *The Rise of the Dutch Republic*, written in defense of religious toleration, is nonetheless a deeply anti-Catholic text.

Although clearly distinguishable from anti-Catholic propaganda literature by the depth of its historiographical apparatus and archival research, Motley's history does have thematic overlap with No-Popery screeds, which often lingered gloatingly over the horrors of the Inquisition as the best historical evidence of Roman Catholicism's evil inclinations. Ray Billington observes, "Nearly every book, pamphlet, or newspaper directed against Catholicism devoted some attention to the Inquisition" and "the tortures of the Inquisition were realistically depicted" as part of the sensationalized polemic forwarded by these works.[42] Motley himself alludes to the prevalence of these Inquisition exposés in his own discussion of the Inquisition: "Those who wish to indulge their curiosity concerning the details of the system, may easily satisfy themselves at the present day. The flood of light which has poured upon the subject more than justifies the horror and the rebellion of the Netherlanders" (1:324).

Motley suggests that his own discussion will not "indulge" the mere "curiosity" of his readers more than necessary to explain the causes of the Dutch revolt, thereby elevating his text above the lurid baseness of propagandistic Inquisition literature. However, he certainly engages to some extent in what Susan Griffin characterizes as "the vivid sadism of so much antebellum anti-Catholic fiction" in his descriptions of the tortures meted out by the inquisitors. His devilish monks committing dark deeds in gloomy dungeons furthermore draws on "that narrative treasure trove of anti-Catholic typology: the gothic." Thus, when Motley describes the Inquisition with such gruesome detail and conventionalized gothic tropes, he hits a thematic and stylistic note familiar from anti-Catholic writing of the period.[43] It may have been this blurring of his historiography with a lower-toned type of literature that urged Motley to justify the time that he devoted to the Inquisition as not "related merely to excite superfluous horror," but rather necessary to understand Dutch motivations.

As measured as some aspects of his research methodology seem, however, he engages in anti-Catholic rhetoric that approaches the vitriol of the propaganda literature when his tone is evaluated as a whole. The Catholicism of Motley's Philip II certainly qualified as fiendish. Philip was "most strict in religious observances" but "grossly licentious" (1:145), solicitous about the security of a saint's relics while the "devil's work" of a massacre was going on (1:188), and willing to renounce the religious persecution that he supposedly regarded as a sacred duty in order to secure the title of Holy Roman Emperor (2:479). Motley asserts that "no reasonable person could doubt that Christ, had he re-appeared in human form, would have been instantly crucified again, or burned alive in any place within the dominions of Charles or Philip" (1:330–31). But one could dismiss all of this as the perverted religiosity of the story's villain and do the same with the Catholicism of Philip's often demonic Spanish soldiers, who sacked Antwerp while carrying banners depicting Jesus and Mary: the "image of Him who said, 'Love your enemies,' and the gentle face of the Madonna, were to smile from heaven upon deeds which might cause a shudder in the depths of hell" (3:106).

However, Motley makes clear that the hypocrisy and abusiveness of Philip's Catholicism infect the Church of Rome as a whole. The church embodies "corruption" (1:70, 2:244), "power and depravity" (1:68), "absolutism and superstition" (1:257), a "foul disease" ready for Luther's harsh cure (1:76). Motley associates the church with imagery of morbidity, a common theme in anti-Catholic discourse: worship "irrevocably coffined with a buried language" (1:536–37) and the greed of "the ever-extended dead-hand of the Church" reaping financial gain from the sale of absolutions (1:29).[44] After the wholesale slaughter of Protestants in the Saint Bartholomew's Day massacre in France, the "Pope, accompanied by his cardinals, went solemnly to the church of Saint Mark to render thanks to God" and perform a Te Deum, a hymn of praise (2:389). Jesuits, predictably, don't come off well; "Jesuitism" and "Loyola" seem synonymous with deceptive sophistry (1:397, 1:419). As David Levin points out, the term *monk* always connotes nefariousness.[45]

Of course, the Protestant Reformation undoubtedly did have a legitimate case against the corruption of the church. And Motley mentions the existence of "[s]incere Catholics," "plain people, who loved the ancient Church" and deplored its current abuses (1:75, 1:72). But these people, like William, often end up converting to Protestantism. The *Southern Quarterly Review* writer says that in his condemnation of a Dutch nobleman for remaining Catholic, Motley judges "somewhat unjustly, for the historian of toleration."[46]

Motley presents the Catholics of the Low Countries as foiling the full realization of William's plan for his country when in 1579 the Catholic Walloon provinces reaffirmed their loyalty to Spain, at which the "friends of Romanism, the enemies of civil and religious liberty, exulted" (3:427). Motley suggests here that to be a friend to "Romanism" one must be an enemy of civil and religious liberty.[47] Accordingly, he attributes the Walloon defection in large part to "Catholic bigotry": "The Gallic element in their blood, and an intense attachment to the Romish ceremonial, which distinguished the Walloon population from their Batavian brethren, were used successfully by the wily Parma [Alexander Farnese, the Duke of Parma, the Spanish-appointed governor of the Netherlands] to destroy the unity of the revolted Netherlands" (3:416, 3:420–21). Race theory and religious prejudice combine in Motley's evocation of the predispositions inherent in the Walloons' "Gallic" blood; he had earlier described the Celtic Gauls, the "ancestors" of the Walloons, as "priest-ridden" and "superstitious," common terms in anti-Catholic rhetoric (1:4, 1:9). The Walloons, susceptible to manipulation by the Duke of Parma because of an irrationally strong attachment to a "ceremonial" (which connotes the trappings of religion rather than its essential principles), had thereby dealt a fatal blow to what the revolt might otherwise have been.

The forms of Catholic worship provoke Motley's disdain. He describes Catholic churches as filled with "gloom," "priests in effulgent robes chanting in unknown language," "the suffocating odors" of incense, "all combin[ing] to bewilder" the senses (1:555). A pageant to display an image of Mary is dismissed as "antiquated mummery" (1:557). Motley criticizes the great Gothic cathedrals as "opulent," as "gorgeous temples where paupers [were] to kneel" (1:555, 1:553). Motley may be channeling the attitudes of the Protestant Reformers with these comments, trying to convey their worldview, but he also clearly sympathizes with those attitudes. He does condemn the spate of image-breaking in 1566, during which Protestants sacked many of the Catholic churches in the Netherlands, but he minimizes the iconoclastic destruction and desecration as "only a tragedy of statues" (1:569).

Many of Motley's judgments about Catholic people and practices, when taken individually, may be reasonable, but collectively they amount to a relentless wave of anti-Catholic sentiment, one that did elicit contemporary notice. The writer for the *Southern Quarterly Review* was not the only critic to charge Motley with religious intolerance. As another reviewer remarked, "[T]he fault throughout Mr. Motley's book is the want, absolute and entire, of all sympathy with Catholicism, in its vigor as well as in its degeneracy. It is to him a thing of mere falsehood and sensuous superstition, and the secret of its higher influences is closed to him."[48] Modern critics have also observed that Motley's "histories were Protestant through and through," an example of the "hatred of Roman Catholicism" "running through the works of virtually all the great literary historians." But David Levin argues that the "distortions" in *The Rise of the Dutch Republic* "demonstrate that on the subject of Catholicism Motley was often the extreme rather than the representative" of the Romantic historians.[49]

Motley's tendency toward nativism no doubt had a symbiotic relationship with his anti-Catholicism. Motley did not appreciate the Irish influx of the late 1840s. He wrote to his father in 1852 that "Europe is decanting itself into America, a great deal more rapidly than is to be wished by us."[50] He expressed a similar sentiment to another correspondent, although couched in more colloquial language: "[W]hat possible use it can be to any body to come to this country, except to some Paddy who desires to become President of the United States, I cant imagine."[51] O. D. Edwards interprets Motley's "priest-ridden Gauls or Celts" as "no doubt Irish-Americans": *The Rise of the Dutch Republic* "was planned and its initial draft written in the Massachusetts of those years [the late 1840s, when immigration surged], years which yielded their fruit in the bitter nativist movement of the mid-1850s. Motley had some reason to fear the slavish hordes of Rome, as he doubtless saw them, and this, too, is an obvious point of origin for the burning anti-Catholicism of the book."[52]

Motley's manifest anti-Catholicism did not simply involve him in a moral contradiction—proclaiming the value of tolerance while consistently denigrating another religious tradition. It also undermined his bona fides as a rigorous and objective historian, as his reviews illustrate. The *Southern Quarterly Review* writer complains that in some of Motley's "censures" of his Catholic characters, "we miss that sturdy impartiality of judgment and large toleration, which William of Orange practiced, and which Mr. Motley presents to our admiration."[53] The word choice of "impartiality" in this assessment is especially significant, because it would have denoted not only religious broad-mindedness but also the mindset required to produce responsible historiography. As the discipline of history developed a more professionalized approach in the nineteenth century, historians were increasingly expected to handle historical subjects with impartiality in order to get at their truth, so Motley's clear anti-Catholic bias weakens his credibility as a historian.[54] A reviewer writing for the *Southern Literary Messenger* in 1858—

after protesting that Motley "sometimes forgets" "his duty to relate facts, without becoming an advocate or denouncer"—questions "whether the historian can become the apologist or advocate of men or systems, and still preserve his character of impartiality," implying that a historian's default mode would be a "character of impartiality" unless he throws it away with apology or advocacy.[55]

Motley had definite aspirations to being a modern type of historian. He studied at the University of Göttingen in Germany, a formative experience for many U.S. historians of this generation in exposing them to the historiographical methodologies of Leopold von Ranke and thereby committing them to high standards of documentary evidence.[56] In order to write the story of the Dutch revolt, Motley spent years immersed in manuscripts located in the archives of the Netherlands, Belgium, Germany, France, and England, a fact that he stresses in the preface, with two pages devoted to listing the various printed and manuscript sources that he consulted. Motley offers this narrative bibliography as proof that his history "is the result of conscientious research, and of an earnest desire to arrive at the truth" (1:vii). His expressions of gratitude to a number of foreign archivists and librarians who assisted him in his research further emphasize the rigor with which he pursued his primary sources (1:ix). Most of Motley's critics accordingly give him high marks for his original research and careful citation practices. Washington Irving mentions his "minute and unwearied research" admiringly, and Prescott commends his "scholar-like thoroughness of research" (no small compliment from a historian staunchly committed to archival rigor).[57]

But Motley doesn't embrace objectivity, the other key feature expected of modern historiographers.[58] He makes gestures toward impartiality, as when he says in the preface that accounts by "Catholic and Protestant, Monarchist and Republican, have been consulted with the same sincerity," an indication that he wishes to align himself with the empirical evenhandedness of Rankean historiography (1:vii). However, over the course of the history, he tends to characterize sources written by Catholics in ways that urge the reader to doubt their integrity.[59] For example, he prefaces quotations by attributing them to "a most bitter Catholic historian" or "a very bitter, but honest Catholic" or "a most bitter Catholic contemporary" (1:243, 1:571, 2:47; see also 1:254). The "bitter" label imputes to these writers a sour resentment that implies the need for a skeptical reading of the quotation in order to correct for a lack of objectivity in its tone. Furthermore, identifying a writer not by name but rather as a "bitter Catholic" inevitably associates the quality of bitterness with that writer's religious identity. Motley never uses the phrase "bitter Protestant" or anything similar to introduce a source.

He also associates Catholic historiography with "moralizing" rather than objective reporting, and with producing "panegryics" rather than balanced accounts (for example, 1:255, 2:232). Again, he never attaches these pejorative descriptors, which insinuate the subjectivity and partiality of Catholic writers, to Protestant sources. More revealingly still, Motley remarks in a letter to his wife that the writer of a particular history of England "is a Roman Catholic, but honest enough."[60] The prejudice implicit in his casual equation of Catholicism with an automatic assumption of dishonesty (a connection frequently made in nineteenth-century anti-Catholic discourse) belies the impartiality that he claims for himself in the preface and suggests that he is guilty of the same sectarian bias that he imputes to his Catholic sources.[61]

Motley's choice in his history to use disparaging language to introduce quotations from Catholic writers is consistent with his tendency toward overt moral commentary on his subjects. Although the liveliness of his narrative voice made his densely researched historiography readable and engaging for popular audiences, the didacticism of his style of writing conflicted with the impartial posture increasingly demanded of modern historians, leading a number of his reviewers to look askance at his vehemently opinionated rhetoric.[62] A reviewer for *Harper's New Monthly Magazine* wrote in April 1856 that Motley "betrays the influence of personal sympathy, and is more easily roused [than Prescott] to expressions of enthusiasm or of indignation. He describes, more as an actor in the scenes which pass under his review, and less as a cool and impartial spectator."[63] If Motley, with the insertion of his aggressively unignorable moral commentary, effectively writes himself into the scenes of the revolt, thereby metaphorically transporting himself to the Netherlands in the sixteenth century, he performs the reverse operation on his subjects. In violation of the historiographical tenet then in vogue that historical figures should be judged according to the standards of their own time, Philip "appears here [in *The Rise of the Dutch Republic*] not as he was in his own day, but as he would be if he were a New Yorker of the nineteenth century who could so act." This anachronistic depiction makes for "defective history."[64]

Motley esteems William of Orange's religious toleration so deeply and abhors Philip's religious bigotry so strongly that he trumpets his moral allegiance instead of stating the facts and letting the reader decide. His strident "moralizing" (precisely the quality that he attributes to his Catholic sources) involves him in self-contradiction, because it induces him to mirror the attitudes that he condemns. As one reviewer sums the paradox up, Motley is "tyrannical in judgment against tyranny, and having no tolerance at all for the intolerant."[65]

Motley faces the dilemma of a staunchly liberal Unitarian, namely, how to denounce religious zealotry without resorting to excessive condemnation of another person's conscience-driven religious beliefs. According to Daniel Walker Howe, "Unitarians claimed to be protecting religious toleration and freedom of conscience against repressive, cantankerous bigots," whether in the form of their Calvinist New England counterparts or, in Motley's case, Roman Catholics. Nonetheless, Unitarians "proved less tolerant than they imagined themselves to be."[66] Motley's intolerance of intolerance threatens to subvert his progressive agenda in applauding William's commitment to religious freedom.

The *Southern Quarterly Review* writer makes the extreme form of this critique, arguing that Motley's "Puritan" tone undermines his "American sentiments" of religious liberty and linking Motley to the Know-Nothings through their joint failure to embody the "large toleration, which William of Orange practiced, and which Mr. Motley presents to our admiration." Although Motley would certainly have disowned any association with the Know-Nothings, his representation of Catholicism in *The Rise of the Dutch Republic* participates in discourses commonly found in the anti-Catholic propaganda that helped to fuel the popularity of the American Party. These discourses included associations of Catholics and Catholicism with dishonesty, morbidity, and superstition as well as gory depictions of the Inquisition that showcased Catholic cruelty. That Motley was criticizing Catholics from a previous era doesn't serve to distinguish him clearly from denigrators of nineteenth-century U.S. Catholics, given "the logic [commonly employed in anti-Catholic literature] of describing the Catholic threat to nineteenth-century America by depicting sixteenth-century Italy or Spain."[67] The nativist No-Popery rhetoric of the Know-Nothings and Motley's consistently unfavorable representation of Catholicism thus arise from a shared discursive culture of anti-Catholicism in the 1850s.

Given the anti-Catholic aspects of his history's rhetorical genealogy, Motley arguably undermines his goal of furthering civil and religious liberty by his labors ("If ten people in the world hate despotism a little more and love civil and religious liberty a little better in consequence of what I have written, I shall be satisfied"). He puts himself rhetorically in league with the elements of U.S. society that the writer for the *Democratic Review* saw as the new face of the Inquisition, an American Inquisition, led by the Know-Nothings, or "Philip II. of Spain, and his bloody servant Alva, in a new dress." Unlike the accusations that foreign-born and foreign-sympathizing U.S. Catholics were plotting a new Inquisition on American soil, the *Democratic Review* writer locates the persecutory spirit of the Inquisition in proudly "native" American hearts.[68]

Motley attempts to argue that the meaning of the Dutch revolt for U.S. Americans is as a precursor to their own victorious struggle for independence, led by their beloved Washington, and their subsequent establishment of unparalleled levels of political and spiritual freedom for all citizens. In other words, Motley tries to suggest that studying the rise of the Dutch Republic was an opportunity to celebrate the rise of the U.S. republic. But the *Democratic Review* writer points to a darker interpretation, one only latent in Motley's history, in which the decline of Inquisitorial Spain might forebode the decline of the United States if it continues to embrace the kind of intolerant anti-Catholicism that the Know-Nothings propagated and in which even Motley's own rhetoric participated. In this interpretation, the United States once again—as in the other imperial eclipse narratives that I have discussed—appears uncomfortably similar to the empire being eclipsed.

4
The Vanishing Dutchman
Ethnicity in Irving's *A History of New York*

Given the fact that John Lothrop Motley required three large volumes to describe only the first thirty years of the Dutch Republic, one of his reviewers wondered "how many more will be required to recount the definite establishment of the Republic, its foreign and domestic wars, its internal discords, its revolutions, its conquests, its colonies, . . . its ascendancy, its wane, and its decay?"[1] Motley died before he could finish even the story of how the Dutch became fully independent, that is, "its ascendancy."[2] However, Washington Irving, from a very different perspective, covered some of the later material that Motley's Dutch histories left untouched. Irving published *A History of New York* in 1809, almost a half century before Motley's *Rise of the Dutch Republic*, but I have chosen to discuss him after Motley, because Irving treats a later period in the history of the Netherlands, one that centered around "its colonies," "its wane, and its decay." Considering Motley's and Irving's texts in this order reveals the cyclical pattern in which the Netherlands was caught up, along with every other important early modern empire, according to nineteenth-century historical philosophy: it rose to a position of great global power and then inevitably fell from that eminent position.

The Dutch "golden age," as seventeenth-century Dutch history is sometimes called, did not last long. The independence movement from Spain inaugurated a period of great prosperity and power in the Netherlands. It achieved significant global economic clout and initiated colonizing efforts throughout the world, including in the Americas, where it established the New Netherland colony in the early seventeenth century. It lost this territory to the British in the mid- to late seventeenth century. Irving's *History of New York* represents the 1664 British takeover of New Amsterdam, the capital of the New Netherland colony, as the eclipse of the Dutch by the English, another manifestation of the domino pattern that consistently structures nineteenth-century U.S. representations of early modern history.

A History of New York, from the Beginning of the World to the End of the Dutch Dynasty chronicles the fate of New Amsterdam from the beginning of the universe—

in typical Irving style—to its conquest by the British. Irving's text is sometimes called *Knickerbocker's History* in honor of its narrator, Diedrich Knickerbocker, a Dutch American historian interested in familiarizing the public with the glories of the Dutch colonial period in New York. (Irving reprises the Knickerbocker persona in, among other pieces, "Rip Van Winkle" and "The Legend of Sleepy Hollow," both included in the wildly popular 1819–20 *The Sketch Book*.)

Although New Netherland became the colony of New York after the British conquest, and later became the U.S. state of New York, *A History of New York* presents New Netherland not merely as one installment in the prehistory of the United States but rather as a kind of foreign land. The New Netherland period functions in the book mostly as international history, not proto-national history. Irving's text (like Henry Wadsworth Longfellow's *Song of Hiawatha*, which also challenges the assimilation of the history it tells directly into U.S. history as a proto-national period) can therefore productively be interpreted in light of the argument made by many modern scholars against superimposing the boundaries and frameworks that organize the United States anachronistically back onto a colonial period in which very different geographical and cultural logics structured North America. If we read New Netherland as simply early New York, then we can miss the ways in which *A History of New York* signals that the Dutch who controlled New Netherland were a people alien to Anglo-American culture. We can therefore also miss a central aspect of the critique that Irving levels at the nineteenth-century Dutch, stubbornly striving to maintain an ethnic identity distinct from, even alien to, the Anglo-American culture in which they were living.

In order to get at this dynamic, I will first examine the rhetoric used by Irving's narrator, Diedrich Knickerbocker, on its own terms; I will then discuss the politics of an Anglo-American author like Washington Irving putting such rhetoric into the mouth of a Dutch American speaker. Knickerbocker presents the history of New Netherland as the rise and fall of an empire, conforming to the standard cyclical pattern. He stresses the "extinction" of the Dutch era in 1664. He therefore depicts the condition of the ethnic Dutch in the early nineteenth century as one of cultural obsolescence, in which Dutch ways are being abandoned and people who identify with their Dutch heritage feel like foreigners in their own ancestral territory. Knickerbocker mourns the loss of the golden age of Dutch power in New Netherland because the end of New Netherland spelled the decline of his beloved Dutch culture. In response to the inexorable erosion of Dutchness, he advocates a religious adherence to traditional Dutch ways and applauds Dutch communities that cleave unto themselves to preserve a distinct Dutch cultural identity.

The picture of Dutch culture's fading fortunes that Irving has his narrator articulate does not reflect the reality of the Dutch situation in the early nineteenth century. Although the Dutch were under significant pressure from the forces of assimilation, *A History of New York*'s rhetoric of Dutch obsolescence and inevitable disappearance belies the actual size and strength of the ethnic Dutch community in New York and New Jersey at that time. The idea that the Dutch were vanishing had about as much legitimacy as the idea that Native Americans were vanishing—an apt parallel because Irving has his Dutch American narrator assent to his own cultural eclipse by presenting it as a foregone conclusion, as often happened in Anglo representations of dying Indians. Anglo rhetoric frequently sought to defuse the threat that supposedly alien racial or ethnic groups, such as the Dutch, posed to the (Anglo-)American melting pot; they did this by presenting them with only two options: assimilate or face extinction.

For the Dutch who would choose to resist assimilation, Irving's text works to make extinction the only alternative by exaggerating the Dutch desire for a distinct ethnic identity informed by communal tradition; Irving distorts this desire into Knickerbocker's ridiculously zealous clannishness and resistance to any innovations on a Dutch lifestyle imported straight from seventeenth-century New Netherland. As Irving parodies it through Knickerbocker, Dutch ethnicizing involved virtual secession from the United States and the embrace of an entirely anachronistic way of life, a doomed and self-destructive mindset. Irving's belittling depiction of Knickerbocker, and the Dutch more generally, as self-alienating and self-anachronizing actually performs the work of alienating and anachronizing them. For Irving, the backward, predominantly rural ethnic Dutch stand in the way of urban (Anglo-)American modernity, and *A History of New York* attempts to hasten them on their way to oblivion.

With this text, Irving conforms to many aspects of the typical imperial eclipse narrative pattern. He emphasizes the rise and fall of empires as the historical framework through which to view New Netherland, whose history he uses as a vehicle for critiquing intranational problems in the nineteenth-century United States. In the way that he satirizes Thomas Jefferson's policies through his portrayal of one of the Dutch governors, Irving produces a narrative of imperial eclipse very similar to the examples that we have seen thus far. However, in treating the intranational problem of ethnic Dutch resistance to assimilation, Irving complicates the typical pattern. The Dutch are both international and intranational subjects, a distinction further blurred because the ethnic Dutch (as he represents them) revere and seek to live as reincarnations of the New Netherland Dutch. Irving stigmatizes this excessive identification with the foreign past and does not try to induce reader identification with the early modern fallen empire, as other eclipse narrative writers do in order to alert their readers to the similarities between international and intranational problems. Irving creates distance between his readers and the New Netherland past through his satire of Dutch buffoonery, and so the facet of Irving's contemporary critique that focuses on Dutch ethnicization actually promotes less anxiety than usual, because the fallen empire's weaknesses reappear only among the equally buffoonish and doomed ethnic Dutch.

Certainly, Irving after a fashion "loved the Dutch even as he laughed at them."[3] Dutch material formed a significant and celebrated part of his oeuvre, and he would later effectively seek to inhabit the lost world of Dutch culture by moving to "Sleepy Hollow" (aka Tarrytown) and living in a kind of Disneyfied faux-Dutch house, Sunnyside.[4] But Irving traded in a nostalgic caricature of the people whose ability to live as a vital and vibrant nineteenth-century ethnic community he had worked to undermine in *A History of New York*.

Nonnational Netherland

Understanding New Netherland as a foreign land requires relinquishing a teleological interpretation of the colonial period as proto-national.[5] The North American colonies have often been construed—by nineteenth-century U.S. Americans and modern scholars—as the origin and infancy of nascent U.S. states. This logic presupposes that the United States was born not in 1776 or 1783 but in 1620, when the Pilgrims landed on Plymouth Rock, to take one possible starting point popular with New Englanders. At that moment, some would argue, the national spirit began to develop. Germ theories of the nation and its states disregard colonial borders, motivations for settlement, and political affiliations when they don't align with what became the various states of the United States. As Karen Ordahl Kupperman writes, "Historians, governed by their own partial assumptions, have conspired to reduce the international character of early modern North America to a simplified national model," but "it is anachronistic to allow later political distinctions to rule our view of the colonial period."[6]

The colonial period should therefore be recognized as "prenational"—in Wai Chee Dimock's terms, "a time when the nation-state was not yet on the planet."[7] Areas in what became the United States were not yet the United States, because the United States did not yet exist.[8] Reading the nation backward into prenational periods constitutes a suspect form of conceptual colonization, imposing the nineteenth- and twentieth-century spatial boundaries of the United States back onto sovereign territories and foreign times. Alta California in New Spain wasn't simply early California, Louisiana in New France wasn't simply the early U.S. Midwest, and the seventeenth-century New Netherland colony wasn't simply early New

York (not to mention the fact that Lenapehoking, the traditional homeland of the Lenape, also wasn't simply early New York).[9]

This historical reality matches the signals given by Diedrich Knickerbocker about the nature of his subject, which he generally describes as "city" or "province," not "state." As Jeffrey Insko has demonstrated, Irving's text can usefully be read in conjunction with the "state histories" of the early national era, including Jeremy Belknap's *History of New Hampshire* (1784–92) and Benjamin Trumbull's *Complete History of Connecticut* (1797).[10] Knickerbocker expresses a spirit of rivalry with New England historians such as Trumbull, whom he mentions specifically, and anticipates future competition from descendents of the settlers of New Sweden, "who may write a history of the state of Delaware" that contests his version of the interactions between the Dutch and the Swedes.[11] But these "state" histories devote the vast majority of their space to colonial history—in Knickerbocker's case, to "the province of Nieuw Nederlandts," made foreign by the odd orthography and by its status as a "province," a dependency of a distant empire, defined by its relationship to the Netherlands (425). I would argue, therefore, that Ed White more properly characterizes the genre when he labels Belknap and Trumbull's texts "provincial histories" and Irving's *History of New York* a "mock-provincial history."[12] As a province, New Netherland had a distinct political identity that cannot be absorbed into the province of New York—defined by its relationship to England—or the state of New York—defined by its membership in the U.S. nation.[13]

Knickerbocker also refuses the incorporation of New Netherland into a protonational narrative by emphasizing its temporal discontinuity with the history of British New York. When the British take over the city in book 7, chapter 9, Knickerbocker writes of "the final extinction of the Dutch Dynasty," referring to the three governors of the province during the Dutch period: Wouter Van Twiller, Wilhelmus Kieft, and Peter Stuyvesant. "Extinction" suggests a complete discontinuance of this era, as does the word "extinguished," also used to describe this moment of transition (718). In 1664, as Knickerbocker represents it, a historical rupture in the political identity of the city occurs: New Amsterdam ceases to be, and New York begins. This elides the period in 1673–74 when the Dutch regained control of the city, a reversion that would disrupt the clean historical break that is produced by Knickerbocker's rhetoric of extinction.

Knickerbocker's historical rupture disallows an evolutionary national narrative. Certainly, New York does inherit various customs and cultural forms from New Amsterdam. Knickerbocker writes in his preface of "one of the grand objects contemplated in my work, which was to trace the rise of sundry customs and institutions in this best of cities, and to compare them when in the germ of infancy, with what they are in the present old age of knowledge and improvement" (379). Representing the city with the familiar trope of an organic lifespan—"infancy" to "old age"—Knickerbocker indicates that continuities exist between the Dutch past and the New York present.[14] New York's Dutch inheritances allow this chauvinistic Dutch historian to argue for the preeminent relevance of his ancestors and his history to his New York readers—a constant and explicit goal throughout the *History*. However, although the city, its people, and its customs remain, New Netherland ends with the British takeover.

Knickerbocker solidifies this impression by describing the history of New Netherland as the rise and fall of an empire. He cites "*Gibbon's Rome*" as an aspirational model for his historiography, and he is accordingly drawn to depicting "the decline and fall of your renowned and mighty empires" (381, 718). His chapter on the British takeover is called "Containing reflections on the decline and fall of empires, with the final extinction of the Dutch Dynasty" (718). In it, he rehearses the cyclical historical logic that structured nineteenth-century history textbooks and informed the fears of imperial eclipse narratives. Knickerbocker traces the historical contours of the Assyrian empire, "extending its domains over the fairest portion of the globe" but "terminating ingloriously"; next, "its successor," the Median empire, "accumulating strength and glory over seven centuries" but "finally overthrown"; then the Grecian empire, the Roman empire, and the Saracenic empire all meet the same fate (719). Knickerbocker proceeds to place New Netherland into this pattern: "each had their rise, their progress, and their fall—each in turn has swayed a mighty scepter—each has returned to its primeval nothingness. And thus did it fare with the empire of their High Mightinesses, at the illustrious metropolis of the Manhattoes" (720). New Netherland fell victim to the same cyclical pattern that had toppled every other major world empire.

Casting New Netherland in the role of a fallen empire functions to insert a clear break between the Dutch and Anglo-American periods. Historically, empires didn't often evolve into nations; republican nations devolved into empires (a common fear in this era about where the United States was heading). These empires then eventually succumbed to "nothingness." So the word choice "empire" calls to mind a world historical pattern not conducive to a teleological narrative in which New York grew organically out of New Netherland. As with the language of "extinction" that Knickerbocker uses, the language of empire stresses the discontinuity between Dutch New Netherland and British New York.

Admittedly, characterizing a small colony as an "empire" reflects Knickerbocker's delusional Dutch partisanship, which seriously aggrandizes the greatness of New Netherland and consequently of his history. Irving also pokes fun at the histrionic rhetoric to which a rise and fall paradigm could give birth. This is especially clear when he has Knickerbocker articulate an exaggerated version of the pattern earlier in the book: "[E]mpires *of themselves*, are nothing without an historian . . . who cheerfully records their prosperity as they rise—who blazons forth the splendour of their noontime meridian—who props their feeble memorials as they totter to decay—who gathers together their scattered fragments as they rot—and who piously at length collects their ashes" (379–80). But even as Irving mocks the excesses of rise and fall rhetoric, this passage affirms that his text's representation of history is structured by and in dialogue with that historiographical convention. Tellingly, in an 1848 preface to a revised version of the *History*, Irving himself employs the same rhetoric, describing his decision to limit his subject "to the period of the Dutch domination, which, in its rise, progress and decline, presented that unity of subject required by classic rule."[15]

In *A History of New York*, the "fall" of New Netherland—its conquest by the British—is preceded by its "decline," which weakens it internally and sets it up for conquest. As Martin Roth writes, the "degeneration of the Dutch lubbers into disputatious democrats" and the subsequent "conquest of New Netherlands by the Yankees . . . represent the inner and outer (spiritual and historical) aspects of the same degenerative process."[16] The turning point for the Dutch comes in book 4 with the "reign" of Wilhelmus Kieft, the second of the three Dutch governors. Irving calls Kieft "William the Testy" (a spoof on appellations like William the Silent), because his improvidence and hasty hot temper cause him to make many political blunders and institute many counterproductive policies. Kieft encourages populist unrest that he then can't control; under his administration, demagogues agitate the townspeople at public meetings, and "the mob, since called the sovereign people"—a group that Irving elsewhere labels the "greasy multitude"—frustrates his attempts to govern (544, 551).

As with other narratives of imperial eclipse, this malfunction in the international past evokes a corresponding problem in the intranational present. The depiction of Kieft in *A History of New York* clearly satirizes Thomas Jefferson, a fact recognized by readers at the time and by critics since then.[17] Irving, a Federalist, did not appreciate Jefferson, his Democratic-Republican Party, or their vision for the nation's future. As we will see, Irving casts doubt in the *History* on the wisdom of Jefferson's ambition to make the United States into an agricultural society. Irving also repeatedly expresses antidemocratic sentiments, as when he compares the populist assemblies of New Amsterdam to "those sapient convocations called popular meetings, prevalent at our day," in which the inebriated "mobs of America" make political decisions influenced by party bosses whose machinations "entrap the suffrages of the greasy mob" and thereby subvert the liberty of the republic

(545, 546, 528).[18] These kinds of parallels bring the problems that vexed the New Netherland empire home to the United States in the nineteenth century.

Despite Irving's comic tone, then, *A History of New York* displays much the same kind of disquieting historical philosophy that other narratives of imperial eclipse do.[19] As Robert Ferguson writes: "Knickerbocker finds history to be cyclical rather than progressive. . . . His narrative of decline from the reign of Wouter Van Twiller to the end of New Amsterdam under Peter Stuyvesant is told in exactly those terms that every good whig lawyer from John Adams to Daniel Webster employed to express fear of republican collapse."[20] The historical logic governing the rhetoric of the text interprets history as a relentless succession of empires rising and falling. This pattern bodes ill for the United States, given that its claims to historical exceptionalism are undermined by the parallels between its political troubles and the causes of New Netherland's decline. Irving uses the history of New Netherland as an opportunity to present a critical message about Jefferson (and many other aspects of nineteenth-century U.S. society, including city politics, regional tensions between New York and New England, and even nationalist historians).[21] *A History of New York* thus conforms to the template of imperial eclipse narratives in which the international history of a falling empire becomes a vehicle for commentary on intranational problems.

But Irving's text does offer some variations on the typical narrative of imperial eclipse. In the context of the *History*, "the Dutch" are simultaneously both an international and an intranational group—both the settlers of New Netherland and their descendants living as an ethnic community in the nineteenth-century United States. One of the intranational problems that Irving's satire targets is in fact stubborn resistance to assimilation on the part of the ethnic Dutch, who (in Irving's depiction) identify so closely with the golden age of their ancestors' New Netherland "empire" that they effectively opt out of allegiance to the nineteenth-century United States and become spiritual citizens of a foreign land: New Netherland. The international and the intranational thus collapse into each other in a more complicated and complete way in *A History of New York* than they do in the typical spatiotemporal contact zone created by narratives of imperial eclipse.

Dutch Decline

One facet of the collapse of the intranational into the international in Irving's text is the way that the decline of New Netherland into "nothingness" seems to mirror the decline of Dutch ethnic culture. By the early nineteenth century, when Irving wrote *A History of New York*, the distinctive ethnic identity of the Dutch community of New York and New Jersey had been undermined by the forces of Anglicization that had been operating on the Dutch since the British conquest in 1664. Assimilative pressures threatened to erase the Dutch as Dutch. Diedrich Knickerbocker, with his obviously Dutch surname and his celebration of the era of Dutch power in the colonial period, presents Dutch culture as in decline in his own day, fading away and in need of the documentation that his history provides before it disappears forever.[22] His chronicle of past Dutch greatness has an elegiac tone, given that New Netherland gave way to the British and now Dutch culture itself was giving way before an alien Anglo-American culture.

When the British assumed control of New Netherland in 1664, tolerant policies and an English demographic minority allowed many elements of Dutch life in New York to continue unmolested, even as the colony's governing structures and legal systems became English. However, in the early eighteenth century, when political developments and shifting population numbers permitted, English authorities began aggressive efforts to Anglicize the Dutch. Viewing ethnic Dutch solidarity as an undermining force in the consolidation of English power in the colony, they threw up roadblocks to the formation of Dutch schools and thus weakened the generational transmission of the Dutch language taught therein. They also began to interfere with the autonomy of the Dutch Reformed Church, a cornerstone institution in the cultural life of the Dutch.[23] As these measures made themselves felt, and as English became the lingua franca of commerce, the Dutch community (especially the elite and the urban-dwelling Dutch) generally embraced bilingualism and then, over the course of the next few generations, increasingly turned entirely to English. Since, as Joyce Goodfriend argues, "the perpetuation of language is closely linked to the preservation of culture" and therefore "language behavior is a valuable index of ethnic consciousness," the decline of Dutch fluency in the eighteenth century suggests the erosion of a distinctly Dutch ethnic identity.[24]

This in turn put pressure on the Dutch Reformed Church, which experienced divisive disagreements in the eighteenth century over whether to allow preaching in English, and over the propriety of being governed by the Classis of Amsterdam in the Netherlands, a body that seemed increasingly foreign and removed from the concerns animating the American churches during this period. The Reformed Church suffered a chronic shortage of ministers, and church attendance declined. In the early nineteenth century, according to Firth Fabend, "the denomination was in danger of falling by the wayside."[25] Elton Bruins states that "Americanization took place in the American Dutch churches mainly as a survival measure; the American Dutch church adapted to some aspects of the American scene lest it simply go out of existence."[26] Identified heavily with the ethnic Dutch community, the church declined as Dutchness itself declined, especially after about 1750.

As a Dutchman, Diedrich Knickerbocker recognizes the fading fortunes of Dutch culture. In the context of ethnic declension in his own day, he expresses admiration for Peter Stuyvesant, the final provincial governor, who had steadfastly maintained his Dutchness even after the British takeover of New Netherland. According to Knickerbocker, Stuyvesant "railed continually at the degenerate innovations introduced by the conquerors" and demanded that nothing but the Dutch language be spoken in his house, where the "good old Dutch festivals . . . which are falling into sad disuse among my fellow citizens, were faithfully observed" (723, 724). In response to encroachment by British "innovations," Stuyvesant renewed his commitment to pure Dutch speech and customs, while in contrast Knickerbocker's "fellow citizens" have conformed to Anglo-American culture by allowing distinctively Dutch festivals to fall into "sad disuse." Knickerbocker specifically mentions New Year's, the feast of St. Nicholas (December 6), Paas (a two-day Easter celebration), and "Pinxster" (Pinkster, the Dutch name for Pentecost), all of which were particularly associated with Dutch festival culture in the colonial period. Although St. Nicholas would get a new lease on life in the nineteenth century due to his makeover as Santa Claus, the other Dutch festival traditions were disappearing at the turn of the nineteenth century.[27]

Knickerbocker singles out Dutch young people as especially careless concerning their ethnic heritage. Right at the beginning of *A History of New York*, in his prefatory note "To the Public," Knickerbocker expresses an anxiety about ethnic degeneracy. As the older generation of "venerable dutch burghers" prepares to be "gathered to their fathers," he fears that "their children engrossed by the empty pleasures and insignificant transactions of the present age, will neglect to treasure up the recollections of the past" (377). This kind of concern over the loss of history animated Anglo-American historians as the Revolutionary generation of '76 started to die off in the early nineteenth century; Knickerbocker's fear thus connects him to his historiographical brethren. Furthermore, though, in his case, it expresses a generational anxiety particularly acute for an ethnic community caught in the grip of assimilative forces.[28] The past that these Dutch children might neglect is the specifically Dutch past of the New Netherland period in colonial history.

Because of assimilation and the generational attenuation of ethnic pride, then, Dutch heritage and history were slipping away from public consciousness. An early nineteenth-century discussion about urban planning in New York City reflected this: a plan to name a series of streets after the great Dutch founders met resistance because city residents would be increasingly unfamiliar with those names in the years ahead. "Would they not," Elizabeth Bradley writes, "along with 'Coenties Slip' and 'Cortlandt Street,' just become the city's hieroglyphs, cryptic markers of a forgotten civilization?"[29] Although, as we shall see in the next section, it is significant that this assessment of Dutch obsolescence found expression in an urban context, it does speak to Knickerbocker's concern about the fading recollections of the Dutch colonial past.

Bradley describes Knickerbocker as a "self-appointed curator of the vanishing culture of Dutch New York."[30] He presents the history of New Netherland as threatened by "the widespread, insatiable maw of oblivion"; using that same language of "oblivion," which suggests that he views Dutch history as standing on the very brink of disappearance, he states that he aims to "withdraw the curtain of oblivion, which veils the modest merits of our venerable dutch ancestors" (381, 453). But because knowledge of Dutch history had become so rare, in order to construct his account he relies on "a host of well authenticated traditions from divers excellent old ladies of my acquaintance," as when he cites a story told to him by his grandmother, "a very wise old woman" (378, 456). Trusting to old wives' tales for learning about the colonial period certainly calls into question his credibility as a historian, but in addition to this joke at Knickerbocker's expense, it is important that these vessels of oral folk tradition are "old." Knickerbocker repeatedly describes the Dutch, in the seventeenth and nineteenth century, as "old" (477, 479, 492, 567, 591, 637, 673, 674, 697, 708, 721), "ancient" (726, 727), and even "antediluvian" (500). The only time that Knickerbocker ever associates the Dutch with youth is in his allusion to Anglicizing Dutch children, whose forgetfulness of their ethnic heritage calls into question how long they will be identifiable as Dutch. This aging community cannot keep its history going as its oral historians die off and its younger generations abandon their Dutch identity.

Knickerbocker seeks to rectify this situation with his work: "With great solicitude had I long beheld the early history of this venerable and ancient city, gradually slipping from our grasp, trembling on the lips of narrative old age, and day by day dropping piece meal into the tomb. In a little while, thought I, and those venerable dutch burghers, who serve as the tottering monuments of good old times, will be gathered to their fathers" (377). He offers his history as a substitute for these "tottering monuments," and just in time, because he describes himself as also old, in fact very near to death's door (453, 579, 582, 627). He concludes the history with the observation, "Already has withering age showered his sterile snows upon my brow; in a little while, and this genial warmth which still lingers around my heart . . . shall be chilled forever" (728). Knickerbocker partakes of the generalized decrepitude afflicting the Dutch community. But he does manage to finish the history before he gives up the ghost and thereby provides the Dutch colonial past with a chance at immortality, if not as a vital heritage celebrated by a thriving ethnic community, then at least as an important era in New York's history, irrecoverably lost in olden times but suitably memorialized by his historiographical "monument."

The epitaphic function of the history results in the distinctly elegiac tone of Knickerbocker's more meditative moments. He grieves for the period of Dutch supremacy, which he presents as a paradisiacal time. According to him, the "genial days of Wouter Van Twiller," the first governor, who reigned before William the Testy sent New Netherland into its decline, "may truly be termed the golden age of our city. There were neither public commotions, nor private quarrels; neither parties nor sects nor schisms; neither prosecutions, nor trials, nor punishments" (474). In summary, during this Edenic era, "every thing was better than it has ever been since, or ever will be again" (487).[31] He admits that he "cannot look back on the halcyon days of the city . . . without a deep dejection of the spirits"; a "sentimental historian" like Knickerbocker cannot "recal the most prosperous and blissful eras, without a melancholy sigh at the reflection, that they have passed away forever!" (453).[32]

He sees a stark contrast between the golden age of the seventeenth century and the current "degenerate age for which I am doomed to write" (483). He speaks gloomily of "the abominations she [the moon] every night witnesses in this degenerate city" in "these degenerate days," "at this degenerate day" (487, 492, 622). In typical Knickerbocker fashion, this forceful rhetoric of declension collides schizophrenically with his invocations of "this fair city," "the delectable city of New York," "my beloved island of Manna-hata!" (448, 445, 729). But even though he desires to tout the merits of New York City—and thereby argue for the importance of his history, which chronicles the city's origins—Knickerbocker feels deep ambivalence about the current state of the city, and his place as a Dutchman in it.

A kind of historiographical séance allows him to experience a consoling reconnection with the lost past of his ancestors. He nearly succeeds in revivifying the heroes of the New Netherland settlement: "I almost imagine myself surrounded by the shades of the departed, and holding sweet converse with the worthies of antiquity!" (454). But the fact that he can only "almost imagine" the resurrection of the past sends him into a pathos-ridden meditation on the implications of this irretrievable loss for his own sense of alienation in the present:

> Luckless Diedrich! born in a degenerate age—abandoned to the buffettings of fortune—a stranger and a weary pilgrim in thy native land; blest with no weeping wife, nor family of helpless children—but doomed to wander neglected through those crowded streets, and elbowed by foreign upstarts from

> those fair abodes, where once thine ancestors held sovereign empire. Alas! alas! is then the dutch spirit forever extinct? The days of the patriarchs, have they fled forever? Return—return sweet days of simplicity and ease—dawn once more on the lovely island of Manna hata!—Bear with me my worthy readers, bear with the weakness of my nature—or rather let us sit down together, indulge the full flow of filial piety, and weep over the memories of our great great grandfathers. (453–54)

Characterizing the present once again as "degenerate," Knickerbocker articulates more clearly what form that degeneration takes for him: the disappearance of a culture in which he had a place and the emergence of a culture to which he is an utter outsider. "The days of the patriarchs" seem to have "fled forever," and he desperately wishes them to "return" because he, who explicitly and proudly identifies himself as Dutch throughout the *History*, has been stranded in an age without a "dutch spirit." He is a vestige of an obsolete culture; he feels like the last of his race, the end of a line stretching back to his "great great grandfathers," but one that will die with him, given his lack of children. He has no sense of a possible future—other than perhaps through his history and the way it establishes a familial connection between him and his readers, who can weep with him over "our" ancestors (he frequently uses the first-person plural when talking about the seventeenth-century Dutch as "progenitors"; see, for example, 377). He never makes clear if he believes that his readers are actually Dutch or if he hopes that his history will somehow make them Dutch by convincing them of their Dutch heritage as New Yorkers. But even this fragile connection to futurity is framed as a mutual mourning for the dead. Adrift in the present, Knickerbocker yearns for the "sweet days of simplicity and ease" of the New Netherland past. As Martin Roth writes, Knickerbocker "desperately needs a spiritual ancestor in order to sustain his alienation in the present."[33]

The once "sovereign empire" of his people has been conquered and overrun. As a result, he has been alienated, "crowded" out by "foreign upstarts," new arrivals from what seems to him like another country (perhaps New England, the abode of a foreign race of Yankee Jonathans toward which the New York Dutchman feels endlessly hostile). He has become "a stranger and a weary pilgrim in thy native land" which, due to its domination by foreigners, he can no longer justifiably think of as his native land, in the sense of it being therefore his spiritual possession. Peter Antelyes points to Irving's repeated use of the "stranger" trope, often to describe his own alienation from the United States, as a consequence of his long sojourns in Europe.[34] In reapplying this trope to a Dutch American man's sense of cultural marginalization, Irving adds another layer to what Paul Giles calls "the emphasis on the philosophical implications of distance" in his work, so evident in the *The Sketch Book*'s meditations on the relationship between the United States and England.[35] The foreign land that Knickerbocker must negotiate is New York.

Dutch Persistence

Despite the ways in which Diedrich Knickerbocker's elegy for the lost Dutch past reflects a real cultural decline that the Dutch community had experienced over the course of the eighteenth century, Irving's narrator gives a skewed impression of the actual historical situation of the Dutch in the early nineteenth century. His rhetoric depicting the Dutch as an aged group on the brink of extinction, desperately in need of his memorialization lest their unique culture be lost forever, belies the fact that Dutchness was then alive and even thriving in some contexts. As when "last of the race" rhetoric dogged Native American communities—under stress but most assuredly still extant in the nineteenth century—and thereby facilitated removal policies by promoting a myth of inevitable native vanishing and supersession by Anglo-Americans, Irving creates an ideologically charged portrayal of the vanishing Dutchman.

Knickerbocker has in fact literally vanished, according to the frame narrative of *A History of New York*, leaving his writing behind as the only index of his former presence. The owner of the hotel at which he was staying reports that "he went out of a morning, with a bundle in his hand—and has never been heard of since" (375). Irving supported this fiction by publishing various notices to the same effect in New York City newspapers in the run-up to the book's publication. In one of them, a sketchy report indicates that "passengers on the Albany stage" saw a man matching Knickerbocker's description who "appeared to be traveling northward," which for a Dutchman would have been the equivalent of an Indian disappearing into the forests of the West, given that in the early nineteenth century the rural Hudson River Valley area remained a bastion for Dutchness.[36] Knickerbocker's disappearance echoes the vanishing of the Dutch as a whole: in a passage describing New England Yankee invasions into New York, he writes that "wherever these shrewd men of the east get a footing, the honest dutchmen do gradually disappear, retiring slowly like the Indians before the whites" (678).

This ethnic vanishing act helps to explain Knickerbocker's melodramatic leave-taking at the end of the book, which reads very much like the conventional farewell speech given by the stock character of the dying Indian. Knickerbocker takes "a sad farewell—which alas! must be forever" and consigns himself to the grave, hoping merely that his body can serve as "a humble sod of the valley, from whence shall spring many a sweet wild flower, to adorn my beloved Manna hatta"—a benedictional spirit eternally present in his ancestral lands, though now physically forever absent (728, 729). As David Murray observes of Indian farewell speeches, Knickerbocker's adieu serves as "an occasion for suitably comfortable melancholy reflections."[37]

In placing this kind of language into his Dutch narrator's mouth, and having him discuss the "extinction" of a vital Dutch culture at the fall of New Netherland, Irving treads the same problematic territory that Henry Wadsworth Longfellow would later cover in *The Song of Hiawatha*. Both Anglo-American authors write from the perspective of a racial or ethnic other and ventriloquize a resigned if mournful acceptance of their own cultural eclipse. Certainly, Irving approaches his subject with greater humor than Longfellow did, but as Robert Secor argues, "humor can be used aggressively" and "[t]here are few better indicators of the cultural anxieties and tensions behind ethnic attitudes than the jokes people tell."[38]

According to the figures of the 1790 census, the Dutch made up one-sixth of the population of New York and one-fifth of the population of New Jersey at that time. On the basis of this sizeable Dutch demographic, Marion Casey labels New York and New Jersey as the "most ethnic" states in the early republic (along with Pennsylvania and its substantial German population).[39] Although many members of this large Dutch community, especially in urban areas, spoke English by the turn of the century, Dutch language use continued throughout the nineteenth century and even into the twentieth. Many declarations of the language's impending demise came from Anglo commentators, whose bias against the Dutch makes their conclusions about linguistic extinction suspect.[40] The transition to English preaching in the Dutch Reformed Church in the late eighteenth century has often been read as an indication of the death of Dutch fluency, but many churches continued to offer Dutch preaching well into the nineteenth century. Furthermore, David Cohen points out that Dutch churches in many cases needed English preaching not because their congregants no longer spoke Dutch but rather because the Dutch still actively spoken in the United States had diverged sufficiently from the Dutch spoken by ministers trained in the Netherlands to impede clear communication.[41] Firth Fabend cites a story published in 1826 in the *Christian Intelligencer*, the Reformed Church's newspaper, featuring an older Dutch congregant slowly adjusting to the propriety of English preaching, indicating that even at that late date the Reformed Church still had to sell English to some of its adherents.[42]

As the existence of the long-running *Christian Intelligencer* suggests, the Reformed Church in the nineteenth century was a dynamic and vital cultural institution, still a cornerstone of Dutch ethnic life. It experienced a revival during the Second Great Awakening and helped to foster practices like "marrying Dutch," which assisted in preserving Dutch identity by promoting marriage within the ethnic community.[43] These kinds of practices reflect "Batavianization," a process named after the Batavi, the Germanic, proto-Netherlandic tribe whose revolt against the Romans also figures in Motley's *Rise of the Dutch Republic*. The opposite of Anglicization, Batavianization involved a self-conscious identification with all things Dutch.[44] Particularly in rural areas, the Dutch continued to embrace many distinctively Dutch practices and objects throughout the nineteenth century: building materials and architectural forms used in farmhouses, barns, and hay barracks; farming implements such as Dutch wagons, scythes, and plows and the accompanying farming practices; household items like the *kas* (a storage cupboard) and particular ways of structuring household space; and traditional foodways such as the preparation of *olekoeks* (Dutch doughnuts) and *sappaen*, a kind of porridge—both food items that Irving mentions (480, 630).[45] Dutch material culture, along with the Dutch language and Dutch forms of religious worship, had certainly not vanished in Irving's day.

Although—as Irving was fully aware—the Dutch were thus very much still extant as a distinct ethnic group when Irving had Diedrich Knickerbocker bemoan their impending demise, they were nonetheless negotiating a difficult cultural situation. Under pressure from the forces of assimilation, many Dutch people responded by clinging all the more tightly to their ethnic heritage.[46] This in turn gave their critics another weapon against them. Irving presents the Batavianizing impulse of the beleaguered Dutch community in marginalizing terms, stigmatizing it as clannishness, a common Anglo-American interpretation of Dutch ethnicizing.[47] Irving's othering rhetoric works in concert with assimilative messages to leave the Dutch with only two options: assimilate and entirely renounce the ethnic identity or be cast as *self*-marginalizers, insular and parochial in their stubborn adherence to Dutchness and therefore responsible for their own alienation from (Anglo-)American culture—a culture in reality quite hostile to them, as Irving's "jokes" at their expense attest.

Irving depicts Communipaw (now Jersey City, New Jersey) in terms that reveal both his awareness of the persistence of Dutch cultural life and his stigmatizing of Dutch clannishness. He describes Communipaw as "one of the numerous little villages . . . which are so many strong holds and fastnesses, whither the primitive manners of our dutch forefathers have retreated, and where they are cherished with devout and scrupulous strictness." In Communipaw, the "dress of the original settlers is handed down inviolate," including such old-fashioned and surely unflattering styles as "broad bottomed breeches." "The language likewise, continues unadulterated by barbarous innovations"; this linguistic purity does not elicit

Irving's admiration, given the fact that the abrasive Dutch language "has much the same effect on the nerves, as the filing of a hand saw" (438).[48] The village of Communipaw thus typifies the rural communities in which Dutch cultural forms and practices persisted into the nineteenth century, even as Irving mocks those cultural survivals and presents Dutch Communipaw as on the defensive: a haven into which Dutchness has "retreated."

Although Irving makes light of Communipaw's determined Batavianizing, other Anglo-Americans in this period represented ethnicizing as a real threat to the United States (and if Robert Secor's argument about the aggressive function of ethnic humor is accurate, Irving's mockery in fact indicates the seriousness of the problem rather than its insignificance). Cooper, another writer in what became known as the Knickerbocker group,[49] discusses the ethnic threat in the original 1830 preface to *The Water-Witch*, set in early eighteenth-century New York City, at which time even urban areas still had a significantly Dutch character. Cooper notes that New York used to be a United Provinces colony but that the British takeover "removed the danger": "Had the dominion of the Dutch continued a century longer, there would have existed in the very heart of the Union a people opposed to its establishment, by their language, origin and habits." Cooper maintains that despite the legacy of English, French, Swedish, Dutch, Danish, Spanish, and Norwegian colonization in what became the United States, "the people of the latter are more homogenous in character, language and opinions, than those of any other great nation."[50] Given that Batavianizing Dutch communities in the early nineteenth century were doing their best to maintain a distinct language, sense of origin, and set of cultural habits, they offered resistance to Cooper's idealized vision of the American melting pot and thus constituted a "danger" to the Union.

When Cooper groups the Dutch together with other U.S. ethnic groups supposedly absorbed into the homogenous American character, he indicates that the threat of Dutch ethnicizing comes in part from the way that it parallels the dynamic of assimilation and resistance in which other ethnic groups were also embroiled.[51] These groups taken together constituted a real challenge to the unity of the nation. Moreover, even though the relatively minimal U.S. Dutch ethnic presence today may make it difficult to reconstruct why the Dutch in and of themselves would present an intranational problem in the early nineteenth century, they represented a much larger and more salient proportion of the U.S. population in the early republic period, especially in New York and New Jersey, the main areas to which Irving imagined himself speaking in the initial 1809 edition of *A History of New York*, an early-career work addressed primarily to a regional audience.

After all, Irving mentions the existence of "numerous" communities like Communipaw, a sizeable group to be cleaving unto itself and refusing allegiance to the (Anglo-)American nation, as Irving portrays Dutch Batavianizing.

The clannishness of Irving's Communipaw Dutch makes them seem almost seditious. They affiliate themselves with a foreign past rather than the nation in which they actually live. On account of their self-imposed cultural isolation, the people of Communipaw "live in profound and enviable ignorance of all the troubles, anxieties and revolutions, of this distracted planet. I am even told that many of them do verily believe that Holland, of which they have heard so much from tradition, is situated somewhere on Long-Island . . . that the country is still under the dominion of their mighty highnesses, and that the city of New York still goes by the name of Nieuw Amsterdam. They meet every saturday afternoon, at the only tavern in the place, which bears as a sign, a square headed likeness of the prince of Orange" (438). Their willful blindness to "revolutions," and specifically the revolution that earned the United States its independence and deeply shaped its national identity, indicates an exasperating spiritual indifference to the nation to which they supposedly belong as citizens, but whose very existence they have contrived not to notice. In their shameful ignorance about their own country, the Communipaw Dutch metaphorically concede U.S. territory over to a foreign power by believing that Holland occupies Long Island. They still live in the world of the New Netherland province, near their sister city of "Nieuw Amsterdam" (note the linguistically alien "Nieuw"), and as provincials, they pledge allegiance to "their mighty highnesses," the governors who hold "dominion" over the province. The governors, although they act on behalf of the States-General of the Netherlands, at least live on American soil. But the loyalties of the Communipaw Dutch lie even farther afield than that. From "Rip Van Winkle," we know that the person whose image hangs in the village center, whether it be King George or George Washington, is understood by the townspeople as their spiritual and political leader. For the Communipaw Dutch, that leader is the Prince of Orange.

With this passage, Irving ratchets up the stakes of ethnic identification by associating it with disloyalty to the United States. Living in Dutch Communipaw according to Dutch cultural practices apparently entails foreign allegiances that effectively sever ties with the nation, and ethnicizing therefore becomes an act of secession. Irving has Knickerbocker characterize places like Communipaw as "our uncontaminated dutch villages" (481). In presenting the Dutch as desiring to hold themselves aloof from American "contamination" in sovereign patches of Dutch territory, Irving casts them as marginalizing themselves within U.S. society, even as his rhetoric actually clearly functions to marginalize them as clannish and unpatriotic. Despite the fact that many Dutch people actively supported the U.S. Revolution, Irving's portrayal works to foreclose the possibility of a Dutch American identity.[52]

Irving further stigmatizes Dutch ethnicizing by depicting it as a ludicrous anachronism.[53] He temporalizes ethnicity, painting U.S. Dutch Batavianization as backward and antimodern, an affiliation with a fallen empire of the past—New Netherland—rather than the cultivation of an ethnic identity in the present. Instead of simply celebrating their Dutch heritage, Irving's Dutch try to freeze themselves into carbon copies of their seventeenth-century forebears. They are wedded to what Werner Sollors calls "the static dream of ethnic cloning."[54] If being Dutch means being regressive, then by implication, assimilation and absorption into (Anglo-)American culture symbolize progress and modernity. Irving once again leaves the Dutch with two unpalatable choices through his anachronizing rhetoric: live like seventeenth-century Dutch dinosaurs or become nineteenth-century (Anglo-)Americans.

Irving has Knickerbocker espouse cultural backwardness, "lamenting the melancholy progress of improvement, and praising the zeal, with which our worthy burghers endeavor to preserve the wrecks of venerable customs, prejudices and errors, from the overwhelming tide of modern innovation" (489). Irving's Dutch avoid "improvement" and continue to embrace the old "prejudices and errors" simply on account of their status as community traditions. Knickerbocker applauds the "jealous reluctance that has ever distinguished our respectable dutch yeomanry; who adhere, with pious and praiseworthy obstinacy, to the customs, the fashions, the manufactures, and even the utensils, however inconvenient, of their revered forefathers" (458). Meticulous adherence to the old ways may be "pious" and "praiseworthy," but the Dutch mentality nonetheless embodies "jealous," "inconvenient" "obstinacy." Their deliberately anachronistic lifestyle makes them ridiculous—almost freakish—relics of a long-dead era.

This representation of "invariable Dutch custom" belies the actual adaptiveness of Dutch cultural forms as they interacted with an American context (429). Even though Irving describes the Dutch language spoken in Communipaw as "unadulterated by barbarous innovations," Dutch people in that area would actually probably have been speaking Jersey Dutch, a "creole dialect" distinguishable both from the Dutch spoken in the Netherlands and from Hudson-Mohawk Dutch, another dialect that had developed in the Mohawk Valley region by the time Irving wrote *A History of New York*.[55] More generally, Firth Fabend argues that the story of the U.S. Dutch in the nineteenth century "is one of cultural adaptation, as together, borrowing and modifying, giving and taking, resisting and relenting . . . they created a culture, a 'web of significance' that many interpreted as Dutch, but that was in truth a hybrid."[56] Dutchness changed and mutated even as it continued to be wielded as the unifying logic around which a self-consciously ethnic community cohered. In contrast, Irving's emphasis on Dutch resistance to innovation does not allow for any dynamism in Dutch cultural life.

Irving represents Dutchness in the nineteenth century as an anachronism inevitably doomed to extinction, like the New Netherland after which it religiously patterns itself. He associates Communipaw, a bastion of Dutch ethnic life, with the same fall of empires pattern to which New Netherland fell victim: in "some half a score of centuries yet to come . . . the great Communipaw, like Babylon, Carthage, Ninevah, and other great cities, might be perfectly extinct—sunk and forgotten" (437). The farcical element of this statement is not that Communipaw and the Dutchness it preserves will become extinct, but that Knickerbocker thinks the village so great that this extinction will take place a long time into the future, when in fact Dutchness already hovered on the brink of oblivion in Knickerbocker's own day.

Irving's particular ideological project leads to some alterations in the imperial eclipse narrative pattern as we have seen it operating thus far. Some blurring always occurs in these narratives between the international past and the intranational present, because authors recognize a discomfiting similarity between the two. But for Irving, that line is further blurred, not only because his intranational subjects—the ethnic Dutch—are descendants of his international ones—the New Netherlanders—but also because his intranational subjects intentionally emulate his international ones. The ethnic Dutch (as Irving represents them) actively seek to promote the collapse of the intranational present into the international past. However, because Irving's rhetoric marginalizes the ethnic Dutch into isolated bastions of a stubbornly anachronistic lifestyle, he actually contains the threat of the failed imperial past by quarantining its likeness among the ethnic Dutch, doomed to extinction as a discrete community anyway. The decline and fall of New Netherland forecasts only the decline and fall of the Dutch themselves. Once the Dutch have vanished, the (Anglo-)American nation as a whole can move forward into modernity unburdened by echoes of the early modern imperial past.

Unlike other writers of imperial eclipse narratives, then, Irving does not encourage his readers to be drawn into the lost world of the fallen empire, to experience it as anything absorbing or glorious (despite Knickerbocker's extravagant veneration of it as a golden age). Although Irving does do research into the history of New Netherland and offers a deeper look into that history than anyone had done to that point,[57] and so aligns with the archival emphasis of many of the imperial eclipse authors, he presents a caricature of New Netherland that invites the reader to laugh at it rather than be captivated by it. His comic mode works to disrupt reader identification with the fallen empire—the process by which readers of eclipse narratives are encouraged to become invested in and alarmed by the fate of a culture too similar to their own for comfort—because he is satirizing precisely the Dutch propensity for getting overly engrossed in the colonial past and trying to replicate it in the present.

Of course, Irving exaggerates this propensity so that he can stigmatize it through mockery, representing pride in an ethnic heritage as unpatriotic and the maintenance of a traditional ethnic identity as anachronistic.[58] Irving suggests that the Dutch disloyally cultivate the collapse of the intranational into the international, but that collapse is more properly understood as an effect of his own rhetoric about ethnic identity, which he presents as by its very nature prone to self-alienating and self-anachronizing behaviors. Unlike other imperial eclipse narratives that merely diagnose and critique an intranational problem, Irving's history actually seeks to neutralize the problem of ethnic particularity and refusal to assimilate by presenting the Dutch in dismissive terms, as irrelevant relics of the colonial Dutch period. He makes Dutch resistance to assimilation a laughing matter, which defuses the threat that they—and by association, other ethnic groups—pose to (Anglo-) American cultural homogeneity.

Irving's "jokes" about the Dutch had a serious marginalizing effect, as suggested by the frequency with which historians of Dutch American culture invoke Irving in order to debunk his characterization of the Dutch.[59] Another index of *A History of New York*'s serious cultural work can be found in the fervency of contemporary Dutch Americans' negative reaction to Irving's book. Many criticized its portrayal of their community and their ancestors.[60] The perception of some U.S. Dutch that the *History* was "nothing but a satire and a ridicule of the old Dutch people" lasted for decades.[61] In later versions of the *History*, Irving did try to tone down his mockery. He wrote in the preface to the 1848 edition that "at the first appearance of my work, its aim and drift were misapprehended by some of the descendants of the Dutch worthies. . . . I understand that now and then one may still be found to regard it with a captious eye." He claimed, however, that he had intended merely to draw attention to an aspect of the city's history with which most people were unfamiliar, at a time when "the peculiar and racy customs and usages derived from our Dutch progenitors were unnoticed, or regarded with indifference, or adverted to with a sneer."[62] But even in the phrasing of this defense, he signals Dutchness as other: "racy"—or characteristic of a distinct race of people, in the old meaning of the word—and "peculiar."

Irving directs his concession to the "descendants of the Dutch *worthies*," a term that suggests particularly the prominent and important people among the New Netherland settlers. Descendants of these notable citizens, generally among the upper strata of nineteenth-century U.S. society, had the social clout to make their displeasure known and induce Irving to make various revisions to the original edition to soften the satire on the Dutch.[63] However, poorer and less influential Dutch people would have had even greater cause for complaint than the elites. Whereas Irving sometimes speaks with a modicum of deference for "our respectable dutch citizens"—as for example when he attributes "uniform integrity" to the Stuyvesant descendants (377, 727)—he reserves unrelieved mockery for the laboring, rural Dutch, the "dutch yeomanry," who inevitably seem entirely buffoonish in their clannishness and backwardness (458, 713).

The concept of "yeomanry" had important political resonance in the early republic period because the major political parties disagreed over whether the United States should organize itself as a nation of freeholding "yeoman" farmers. Thomas Jefferson and his Democratic-Republicans advocated for this "agrarian ideal" and "celebrated agriculture as a livelihood, as well as a way of life."[64] Jefferson famously declared in *Notes on the State of Virginia*, "Those who labour in the earth are the chosen people of God, if ever he had a chosen people, whose breasts he has made his peculiar deposit for substantial and genuine virtue."[65] Although Jefferson's economic vision was not actually particularly nostalgic or anticommercial, Federalists painted its antiurban tendency as backward looking.[66] Irving, a city resident and a Federalist who opposed Jefferson's agrarian ideal, does not see much redeeming virtue in country folk, judging from his jokes about "yeoman" rubes.

Irving's Federalist sensibilities align with his assimilationist ideologies because the elite urban-dwelling Dutch tended to assimilate more readily than the rural Dutch did.[67] Irving does mention the Dutchmen "we may now and then see, stumping briskly about the streets of our city," but these figures' rarity and the peculiarity of their manners and dress, including a predilection for "old fashioned cocked hat[s]," marks these unassimilated Dutchmen as gauche outsiders, objects of the curious Anglo-American gaze (513). The urban environment had generally evolved beyond such backward displays of ethnic particularity.[68] The real significant remnants of Dutchness survived in the countryside, as when a farmer would keep accounts "by casting them up upon his fingers, and chalking them down upon the crown of his hat; as is still observed among the dutch yeomanry at the present day" (713; see also 543, 678). As the market revolution overtook Dutch farmers in the early nineteenth century, this kind of primitive accounting system suggested that they were out of step with what Federalists envisioned as the nation's commercial future.[69]

In Irving's *A History of New York*, the rural, regressive Dutch impede (Anglo-) American urbanity and mercantile modernity. Dutch villages and the backward culture that they sustain stand in the way of national progress. Similarly, Jedidiah

Morse wrote in his 1789 *American Geography* that Dutch farmers "seldom adopt any new improvements in husbandry, because, through habits and want of education to expand and liberalize their minds, they think their old modes of tilling the best"; they "generally follow the old track of their forefathers." Anglicization among the Dutch, such as Dutch children learning English in school, therefore signified "the buddings of improvement in the dawn of our empire," "dispelling the clouds of ignorance and national prejudice."[70] Like Morse and other Anglo-American commentators on the Dutch, Irving framed the disappearance of Dutchness as a victory for progress.[71]

The fact that the Dutch had not disappeared in the early nineteenth century, but rather were actively striving to maintain a distinct ethnic community, therefore posed a problem. Irving manages this problem rhetorically by presenting Dutch disappearance as inevitable and having his Dutch American narrator ratify Dutch extinction by mourning it as a foregone conclusion. Irving's Dutch voluntarily alienate and anachronize themselves, opting out of the national present, leaving the United States free to move into its future unburdened by ethnic dead weight—or discomfiting similarities to a fallen empire of the past. The Dutch in the New York and New Jersey area would indeed eventually largely assimilate, an outcome symbolized by the Anglicizing of Knickerbocker himself, whose name went on to grace a variety of non-Dutch products and endeavors, including an NBA basketball team.[72] But in the early nineteenth century, in the face of Dutch resistance to assimilation, Irving leverages the inescapability of the law of imperial rise and fall, which had brought down every great civilization in human history, to portray the Dutch—in both their international and intranational incarnations—as doomed to eclipse and, ultimately, to extinction.

5
Northmen and Native Americans
Longfellow's Resistance to Eclipse

The arrival of European colonizers supposedly put an end to the era of the Indian. U.S. Americans imagined that the eclipse of the North American Indian world by European and Euro-American empire had already been thoroughly accomplished by the nineteenth century. Although Native Americans—like the ethnic Dutch community—stubbornly persisted in existing, necessitating continuing removals and military conflict, the idea of the vanishing Indian backdated their defeat and cemented the decline of their civilization.

As Irving had done with his disappearing Dutchmen in *A History of New York*, Henry Wadsworth Longfellow drew from and perpetuated the cultural dominance of the vanishing trope in his long narrative poem, *The Song of Hiawatha* (1855). Hiawatha's disappearance into the lands of the West at the end of the poem has been central to critics' assessment of Longfellow's problematic racial politics. Daniel Aaron, on the first page of the introduction to the Everyman edition of the poem, writes that Longfellow "accepted the Red Man's inevitable extinction," and Lawrence Buell, in the introduction to the Penguin Classics Longfellow collection, sums up the poem as an embodiment of "the discourse of savagism: that is, nineteenth century liberal complacent-sympathetic construction of Indian culture as noble, exotic, and doomed."[1] *The Song of Hiawatha*'s nationalistic popular reception illustrates that the poem made available a fantasy of succession, of power passing from the vanished Indian to the Euro-American United States.[2]

However, I would argue that in addition to Longfellow's complicity with the racial politics of vanishing, a competing strand of *The Song of Hiawatha* actually resists the vanishing of the Indian in ways that belie the poem's nineteenth-century reception history, in which readers often gravitated toward the racist messages of the poem. To be sure, Longfellow's resistance to the vanishing Indian trope is impartial and imperfect, but the overall effect of the poem does not generate a resigned acceptance of Indian disappearance. Most narratives of imperial eclipse work to depict the culture of the eclipsed empire as vital and compelling, so that the dissolution of that culture can have maximum emotional impact and inspire anxiety over the resemblances discovered between U.S. society and the eclipsed culture. The vitality of the eclipsed culture holds meaning precisely in its relationship to the downfall that will ultimately overtake it. In contrast, *The Song of Hiawatha* not only works to depict the culture of the Ojibway (the people who now often call themselves Anishinaabe) as vital and compelling but also makes some attempts to forestall its dissolution by keeping Ojibway language and presence in the landscape alive.

Longfellow's resistance to native vanishing becomes most clear when viewed against the backdrop of certain elements of the poem's reception. Some early reviewers of his work obsessed over its Scandinavian sources. Longfellow, an accomplished linguist and dedicated student of world cultures, did indeed draw from Finnish, Swedish, Norwegian, and Icelandic influences. But the sheer eclecticism of Longfellow's many foreign and domestic influences makes his reviewers' concerted focus on the Scandinavian elements seem odd. This oddness can be explained by the fact that in the racial climate of this period, emphasizing Scandinavian influences often resulted in an equal and opposite de-emphasizing of Native American influences.

During this period, a theory that Vikings had discovered and settled in New England centuries before conveniently redrew the map of former Native American possessions in the area. This "Vinland" hypothesis possessed enormous cultural cachet in the period from the 1830s to the 1890s, due in part to the racial politics inherent in the idea of a pre-Columbian Viking foray into the Americas. The very concept of a European "discovery" of the New World, whether originally by Columbus or Leif Eriksson, sidestepped the question of prior inhabitants. Norsemen could therefore provide a convenient distraction from the troubling specter of Native American land claims. The prevailing tendency to connect or even confound Norsemen with Native Americans in descriptions of the New England landscape functioned to reinscribe the land's history as a Viking one rather than an Indian one; the former was altogether a far more comfortable prospect. The era of Viking empire had clearly ended and provided no hindrance to the rise of Euro-American empire. In fact, through their whiteness, Vikings actually helped to validate the racial ideology of Anglo-Saxonism that fueled U.S. manifest destiny.

Native Americans, on the other hand, interfered both symbolically and physically with Euro-American territorial entitlement. So the U.S. government removed them from the physical land while U.S. writers removed them symbolically from the history of the land, replacing them in some cases with Norsemen.[3] This politically convenient substitution also manifested itself in the plagiarism charges leveled at Henry Wadsworth Longfellow after the publication of *The Song of Hiawatha*. Critics accused Longfellow of imitating the Finnish epic *Kalevala*. In the process, they effectively nullified the poem's significant debt to indigenous imagination and cultural production.

Although Longfellow's poetry sometimes participated in and even helped to encourage this trend toward the privileging of Scandinavian over Native American history, he did try to resist the eclipse of the Ojibway in *The Song of Hiawatha* with his insistence on the Native American origin of his source materials and his determined inclusion of Ojibway language and place-names in the poem. By means of a markedly polyglot poetics, Longfellow represented the landscape as a tangled, dynamic anarchy that contradicted progressive narratives of the consolidation of European imperial control over the New World. To do this, he used some of the same techniques whereby Vinlanders made pseudo-Viking history seem vividly concrete for New Englanders who inhabited spaces where Vikings had once supposedly been: Vinlanders encouraged people to imagine the Vikings as tangible presences in the environment, in a process that I refer to as landscape architecture. In this vein, Longfellow encourages his readers to imagine Hiawatha and the Ojibway as continuing to be substantial occupants of the landscape. He thereby throws up at least a temporary roadblock to the progress of imperial eclipse.

In this chapter, then, I explore the perverse entanglement of Northmen and Native Americans in the story of *The Song of Hiawatha*. Taken together, the Vinland vogue and the *Kalevala* controversy paint a picture of a consistent redirection of public attention away from Native Americans—and, consequently, away from the crimes inflicted on Native Americans by Euro-Americans—and toward the Northmen. In his poetic method and his response to the *Kalevala* controversy, Longfellow resisted this Scandinavian diversion and the way it functioned to make Indians vanish.

Admittedly, I commit a cultural oversimplification in treating "the lands of the North" as a unified entity called Scandinavia. The area's history of internal colonization (Iceland has at various points in its history been controlled by Norway and Denmark, Finland by Sweden and Russia) troubles any sense of a singular, coherent tradition. For example, nineteenth-century Finnish nationalism, of which *Kalevala* was both an outgrowth and an inspiration, complicates the straightforward assumption of that country into a Scandinavian geocultural narrative. My rationale for adopting the rubric of Scandinavia despite its drawbacks is that the distinctions among Scandinavian countries were often not registered in the perception of the region held by those outside of it. In nineteenth-century U.S. parlance, the fuzzy concept of "Northmen" could and did encompass a variety of countries and a range of historical periods.[4] And sometimes that fuzzy concept acted to distract attention away from an equally fuzzy and romanticized—but in the United States, more politically problematic—concept: Indians.

This pattern of substitution indicates the reactionary power of a global imaginary when used as a tool for cultural misdirection. Wai Chee Dimock, in her theory of deep time, posits a "relativity of simultaneity . . . [where] two thousand years and two thousand miles can sometimes register as near simultaneity; . . . [time's] relational fabric is separately cut, stretching and bulging in odd places."[5] Although these temporal cuts transgress the constraining borders of the nation-state and therefore might seem to have utopian potential, the odd bulge that brings together nineteenth-century New Englanders and eleventh-century Viking navigators does not have that effect. With the Northmen discourse that this chapter examines, international history works to obfuscate intranational tensions instead of illuminating them, as narratives of imperial eclipse generally do. But whereas the idea of Scandinavia often seemed to efface vital forms of Native American presence, Longfellow's approach to language and landscape in *The Song of Hiawatha* strengthened the vividness of Ojibway cultural life and thus tried to stave off the cultural eclipse implied by the trope of the vanishing Indian.

Viking New England

Northmen had lived in New England—or so many in the nineteenth century thought. According to popular legend, Leif Eriksson and his crew of bold seamen had sailed up the Charles River around 1000 C.E. and established a settlement in what would become Cambridge, Massachusetts, and the surrounding towns. Although a Norse presence that far south is now generally discounted, the theory of Vinland—the name of the putative Viking settlement—gained widespread popularity in the nineteenth century, and the story of eleventh-century Vikings became imbedded in the New England landscape in both its literal and literary forms.[6]

Longfellow's poem "The Skeleton in Armor," first published in the *Knickerbocker Magazine* in 1841 and then reprinted in the collection *Ballads and Other Poems* in 1842, helped to promulgate this theory by strengthening the association between local landmarks and the Vinland story. The poem was inspired by the discovery of an actual skeleton clad in armor unearthed in Fall River, Massachusetts, in 1831. Many believed the remains were those of a Norse warrior buried during the days of the Vinland settlement. Longfellow's poem also features a stone tower that alludes to the tower at Newport, Rhode Island, commonly held at the time to be an ancient Viking church. In the poem, the tower is built by a Viking warrior for his stolen bride, who is buried beneath it after her death. Although Longfellow privately expressed some doubt about the Norse origin of the Newport Tower, he judged there to be sufficient public belief in that version of its construction to feature it in his ballad—and the result of the poem's success was to reinforce that belief.

The explosion of interest in a possible Viking settlement and the relics it might have left behind began in earnest in 1837, when Danish scholar Carl Rafn published *Antiquitates Americanae.*[7] He argued that ancient Icelandic sagas detailing the journeys of Leif Eriksson and subsequent adventurers supported a Viking discovery of the New World around the turn of the millennium. He published translations of those sagas and matched their geographic descriptions to elements of New England topography, and he claimed that the Newport Tower and the Fall River skeleton, among other local artifacts, dated to this era.

Many members of Rafn's New England audience latched on to his theory, agreeing that the sagas did seem to depict natural features of the New England area with perfect accuracy—unsurprising, given the regional prestige involved in locating the first European landfall and sustained settlement in the Americas on their very doorstep. New England's economic and cultural stature was diminishing during this period, and Vinland provided a compensatory source of regional status. Similar regionalist motivations, combined with ethnic pride, prompted the Scandinavian immigrant communities in the upper Midwest to rejoice over a rash of Viking finds that cropped up there in the later part of the nineteenth century. Domestic adherents to the Vinland theory found allies in native Scandinavians, such as the famed violinist Ole Bull, a Norwegian and a good friend of Longfellow's. Norwegians claimed Eriksson as a countryman (via Iceland) and thus had an investment in celebrating him as the true discoverer of the New World.[8] Bull encouraged the Vinland ferment, helping to raise support—including Longfellow's—for a statue of Leif Eriksson, which still stands on Commonwealth Avenue at Charlesgate, near Kenmore Square in Boston.

Rafn's *Antiquitates Americanae* touched off a spate of amateur archaeology as Vinlanders sought evidence to corroborate the textual hypothesis of a sustained Norse settlement. At the forefront of this effort was Eben Norton Horsford, the Harvard professor who invented baking powder and who also made a name for himself as a specialist in the Viking relics of New England.[9] Horsford and other devotees of the theory of New England's Norse origins redrew the mental map of the region, fleshing out what they thought had happened where and what remained in the landscape to prove it.[10]

Enthusiasts demonstrated how, from the center of Cambridge, where Longfellow lived, one could stroll to the site where Leif Eriksson's house had stood in 1000 C.E., or take a buggy ride to the heart of the Viking city of Norumbega, located in what had become Watertown, Massachusetts. One could visit Fall River to see the runic markings that Norsemen had inscribed on Dighton Rock and to view the site where the skeleton of the Viking warrior had been unearthed. One could travel a bit further still to Newport, Rhode Island, which boasted the famed tower featured in Longfellow's poem. One could also purchase a guidebook to point out other landmarks of the Vinland era.[11]

The power of the idea of New England's Norse past, sufficient to inspire a form of historical tourism, even for locals, proceeded from a consciousness of sharing space with History. The ability to locate traces of the Vikings in one's own backyard lent an especial thrill to life in the mundane present. The normal scenes of everyday living took place alongside the shades of great men long gone. Proponents of the Massachusetts landing theory made comments like this: Thorfinn Karlsefni, who followed Eriksson to Vinland, "planted the first colony in a.d. 1007, within a few rods of the present site of the Cambridge Hospital."[12] By using the Cambridge Hospital—now Mount Auburn Hospital—as a landmark to orient readers in a map of the Viking settlement that had flourished nearly a millennium before, this writer physically juxtaposes the present to the past, adding a frisson of delicious proximity to thoughts of Vinland. The emphasis on how close together the sites of the planting and the hospital are—"within a few rods," a rod being sixteen and a half feet, meaning that the epicenter of Vinland was maybe fifty feet from the hospital—betrays an excited wonder about such a historic, centuries-old enterprise having occupied the same ground regularly trod by nineteenth-century residents of Cambridge in their walks along the Charles River. Historical reconstructions like these encouraged New Englanders to picture that the Vikings had been, and their vestiges still were, *right here*, on the very spot where they now stood.

An experience of this kind of spatial immediacy facilitates a greater sense of temporal immediacy as well, by helping to overcome feelings of alienation from events that took place in a distant era. As one Vinlander wrote, "[T]hat Leif came up Symond's Hill seems to me as certain as a fact in the tenth century could be."[13] Clearly the topographical landmark to which he refers was not called "Symond's Hill" in the days of Leif Eriksson. But the writer chooses to call the hill by the name that he uses when *he* climbs it, and he expresses certainty about Leif's former presence on this hill, despite how fantastical the conjunction of his Symond's Hill and Eriksson's near-mythical progress into the New World seemed. The rhetorical impact of this sentence largely derives from making a claim about an era so far in the past that hypotheses about it always involve some level of conjecture, and rooting it in the incontestable solidity of a neighborhood landmark. The writer takes the groundless, abstract fact that Europeans once discovered the New World and, quite literally, grounds it, making ancient history seem tangible and immediate (to wit, the writer feels on intimate enough terms with Eriksson to refer to him by his first name).

Whether or not the writer of this comment consciously intended the effect that it creates, the conflation of hills past and present also functions to conflate the climbers. The writer, and anyone else who walks up Symond's Hill, becomes a new Leif Eriksson. By cresting the rise and recapitulating the steps of the discoverer into the unknown wilderness, the modern New Englander thereby adds glory to his or her quotidian pursuits. And this reenactment, this temporal collapse, works in the opposite direction as well: Leif Eriksson becomes a New Englander.

As Richard John has noted in his discussion of Eben Norton Horsford, "Horsford's archetypal American came to resemble no one so much as Horsford himself: a successful industrial entrepreneur who had turned nature to profit." In Horsford's version of the Vinland story, Eriksson and Karlsefni set up an ingenious timber-mining operation, complete with a series of dams whereby logs could be floated easily to the sea from inland. Indeed, in Horsford's account, Eriksson was not only a fellow entrepreneur; he was also a neighbor. From information in the Icelandic sagas, Horsford calculated the location where Eriksson had built his house. John writes: "[A]s luck would have it, . . . the site turned out to be a mere three blocks from Horsford's Craigie Street home."[14]

This neighborly connection to long-dead Vikings indicated not only that great men had lived in the area but also that they were, in reality, just men. Hero-making history tends to obliterate the prosy day-to-day lives of those eventually elevated to greatness, but contact with the physical remnants of their everyday activities functions to humanize them once more. Thus, even as sharing the space of the Vikings ennobles humdrum daily pursuits with the thrill of historical association, it also makes room for future greatness by concretizing the heroes of the past through the objects that they touched and the ground that they trod, thereby shrinking them from their mythic, disembodied immensity. It provides greatness by association, but also allows the possibility of greatness of one's own.

The Vinland craze, with its extensive and elaborate mapping of Viking sites, therefore illustrates the allure of history, especially history grounded in the landmarks of the local landscape. Such history fosters a sense of intimate connection between oneself and historical figures who once occupied the same physical space, a kind of contact zone that bridges temporal distance and allows the past and the present to coexist—in a more radically kinesthetic way than occurred with the imaginative contact zones created by texts such as narratives of imperial eclipse. Vinlanders took an active role in helping to construct this type of contact zone, bringing together eleventh-century Vikings and nineteenth-century New Englanders through the stories they told about the history of the landscape.

Seeing oneself as connected to the past and discovering one's potentialities through it can lead to an intense investment in particular historical accounts, because some histories will undermine the present instead of authorizing it. Eriksson's New England landing occasioned fierce and often bitter disputes in the nineteenth century because it enabled some historical legacies while it threatened others. Most obviously, Leif Eriksson represented competition for Christopher Columbus's right to the title of New World discoverer, and he thus posed a major challenge to deeply cherished historical priorities. Eriksson lent himself to national and regional pride by situating ground zero of European discovery of the Western Hemisphere in what would become the mainland territory of the United States rather than in the West Indies, as Columbus did. European discovery could thus more easily be claimed as a specifically national rather than simply a continental legacy, and the tradition of a New England city on a hill could stretch back even farther into history.

Opinions about the likelihood of a Viking New England did not always map neatly onto regional affiliations, however. John has noted that the Massachusetts Historical Society and the Harvard intelligentsia tended to denounce the Vinland hypothesis, in large part because they thought that it detracted from the region's Puritan legacy, of which these organizations regarded themselves as the "principal intellectual conservator."[15] These Vinland critics often descended from first-generation Puritan settlers and therefore had a familial investment in their primacy. Furthermore, some of them had written books about Columbus to coincide with the nation's centennial and the quatercentenary of Columbus's voyage and therefore had a professional and monetary investment in the standard story of discovery.

In contrast, the Rhode Island and Watertown historical societies were delighted by the Viking excitement.[16] Rhode Island could claim some of the most sensational Vinland relics, including the Newport Tower.[17] Watertown, Massachusetts, which had far fewer claims to historical greatness than its neighbors Cambridge and Boston, had been identified as the probable site of Norumbega, the main town of the Vinland settlement. Understandably, then, Watertown's historically oriented residents embraced the Vinland scholarship that emphasized the importance of what would become town land, even though many in the intellectual world judged this scholarship highly dubious.

Indeed, because the New England landing site has now been disproved, the created and imagined elements of this heritage (often owing their shape to personal investments in particular historical narratives) have become especially apparent.

Today, many of the most prominent reminders of the Vinland craze are not relics once thought to be Norse but artistic productions inspired by the idea of New England Norsemen. These include the statue of Leif Eriksson and the prows of Viking longboats that adorn the central piers of Longfellow Bridge (which stretches between Boston and Cambridge and was named to commemorate Longfellow's 1845 poem "The Bridge," set on an older bridge that had previously occupied that spot on the river). The Eriksson statue faces west in a bid to conjure up its original, facing west into the new land that he had discovered. The prows on the bridge, placed close down by the river's surface, reenact a time when Viking ships had supposedly navigated those same waters. By the positioning of the statue and the bridge carvings in space, their creators facilitated the visualization of a tangible, concrete Viking past.

This typified the approach to Viking sites taken by popularizers of the Vinland theory. They would reinscribe landmarks to corral them explicitly into the Vinland narrative in a way that worked to elicit visitors' embodied visualization of past events. On the putative site of Eriksson's house, for example, Horsford placed a stone tablet reading simply, "ON THIS SPOT / IN THE YEAR 1000 / LEIF ERIKSSON / BUILT HIS HOUSE IN / VINELAND." He included no indication of when or by whom the marker had been placed, and the statement on it carries such absolute declarative conviction that the assertion takes on the mantle of historical fact. Given the emphasis on exact place ("on this spot"), the domestic and humanizing nature of Eriksson's activity ("built his house" rather than "built a habitation" or something similar), and the avoidance of syntactical vagueness (the sentence could have used a passive rather than an active verb—"on this spot Leif Eriksson's house was located"), the tablet encourages an immediate sense of Eriksson's physical presence in the very place where passersby stand to read the marker.[18]

The Eriksson house marker encourages the sense of walking in an environment full of Viking landmarks, and a replica of a Norse tower that Horsford created at a site up the Charles River goes even further toward reconstructing Viking space.[19] Horsford built the tower where he had found what he thought to be archaeological evidence of a Norse fortification; its explanatory plaque does not indicate who wrote the text or placed the marker and does not explicitly acknowledge the tower as a re-creation. As they ascended the tower, then, visitors could imagine themselves moving through space formerly inhabited by Vikings, although the structure is in actuality a complete historical fabrication.[20]

Horsford saw what he wanted to see and marked the land in ways that allowed and in fact pushed others to accept his vision of the past. Horsford, Longfellow, and everyone else who advanced the Vinland theory practiced a kind of landscape architecture, as it may be called—an ideological analogue to conventional, botanical landscaping. Landscape architects materially and rhetorically shaped spaces into legible, storied landscapes, using features of the physical environment as anchors for telling particular histories of the community. Their use of specific local landmarks to ground these histories brought them to life in an embodied, concrete, and palpable way for present inhabitants of the reimagined sites, who were thereby invited into a contact zone with the past. The strategies of landscape architecture had obvious political import depending on what pasts were installed and why. Undesirable histories could be overwritten with communally sanctioned or politically useful pasts. Angela Miller has identified a kindred process in landscape painting of the same era, as artists "struggled to find a visual or narrative resolution to unresolved problems of cultural identity . . . to test alternative futures" or, in the case of Vinland, to test alternative pasts; "conflicts . . . could be rehearsed through spatial scenarios."[21]

One conflict that the landscape architects of Viking New England attempted to negotiate involved both emerging and chronic racial tensions in the area. As Janet Headley points out in her discussion of the Boston monument to Leif Eriksson, this statue could be understood as a reaction against the Italian Catholic Columbus at a time when Italian immigrants were flooding into Boston in record numbers.[22] The Vinland hypothesis gave Boston Brahmins like Longfellow a discoverer and settlers from one of the white races of the North to counter and predate the southern European Columbus.

In addition to mediating (and aggravating) the split between established Bostonians and immigrant outsiders, Eriksson and his crew allowed the Anglo-American community to engineer a solution to, or at least a distraction from, another troubling racial anxiety. In an era of national Indian removals, New England no longer had extensive, ongoing native land arbitration of its own, but reminders of the Indian inhabitation that predated European settlement necessarily put pressure on whites' uncomplicated and self-authorizing relationship to the land. As such, Native Americans proved less desirable as former occupants than Eriksson and his fellow explorers. In the map of Viking New England, Vinland proponents used the strategies of landscape architecture to set the scene for Scandinavia to edge out native America.

Skeletons

Despite the fact that Longfellow's "Skeleton in Armor" takes place in a local landscape and revolves around what would have been familiar landmarks to his New England audience, the poem's gothic atmosphere introduces an element of uncanny strangeness into these comfortable surroundings. In the bizarre premise of the poem, the narrator conducts a conversation with an animated version of the Fall River skeleton. The poem opens disorientingly, without a substantive explanatory frame narrative, dropping the reader abruptly into an agitated injunction by the narrator: "Speak! speak!" he cries to the skeleton; "Why dost thou haunt me?"[23] The narrator's obvious perturbation combines with the eerie intensity of the skeleton's subsequent discourse to unsettle the sense of familiarity aroused by the poem's local referents. The skeleton identifies himself as a Viking and recounts how he stole his bride away from her hostile father, sailing with her to the New World. After a period of happiness, she dies; he then takes his own life, falling on his spear while wearing his armor (which clearly associated him with the armored Fall River skeleton). The poem's foreboding atmospherics prompt the question: why would the Fall River skeleton haunt anyone?

Although the remains were initially assumed to belong to a Native American, some later claimed that its weapons of war ruled out the possibility of an Indian attribution: its breastplate and spear were pronounced inconsistent with the style and material of native armory. But as later archaeologists determined, the remains unearthed in Fall River did indeed belong to a Native American man, probably from the Narragansett people. The erroneous Viking provenance of the skeleton, whose accoutrements obviously indicated a warrior, had the effect of metaphorically disarming the threat of violent native opposition in an age of tense race relations between the white and Indian communities. Longfellow's narration of his death as a suicide, rather than as the result of a battle, also avoids the specter of aggression directed outward by imagining an impulse toward self-annihilation (akin to Hiawatha's self-imposed exile), further defusing the potential threat that the actual skeleton symbolized.[24] In addition, the very act of reascribing the skeleton's origin erased a reminder of native occupation from the landscape, further effacing the traces of native possession that would provide evidence for and emotional power to their prior ownership of the land.

The pictographs on Dighton Rock, first recorded by Europeans in 1680, underwent a similar reinscription. Commentators on the boulder in the seventeenth and eighteenth centuries assumed that its markings were of Native American origin. But just as many people abandoned the idea that the Fall River skeleton was a Native American when Carl Rafn published his Viking counterreading in his *Antiquitates Americanae*, Rafn's runic interpretation of the rock likewise caused many to view the carvings as ancient graffiti left behind by Viking explorers to record their passing. In 1854, Henry Rowe Schoolcraft—the U.S. Indian agent and collector of Ojibway stories from whom Longfellow drew much of his material for *The Song of Hiawatha*—published a corrective in which he attributed Dighton Rock's inscriptions to local Algonquin Indians, the theory that currently holds sway in the academic community.[25] To this day, though, popular historians continue to debate the petroglyphs' origins. For example, in the early twentieth century, Edmund Delabarre advanced the hypothesis that a Portuguese explorer in the 1500s made the marks, a theory that continues to be attractive to the Portuguese community in the Taunton/Fall River area. As Stephen Williams observes about this phenomenon, "The archaeological lesson the Rock does teach is that of perception: 'In every object there is inexhaustible meaning, the eye sees in it what the eye brings means of seeing.'"[26]

Indeed, all the signs of Viking possession hailed in the nineteenth century as proof of the New England Vinland settlement are now attributed to Native American or colonial settlement, or are in fact discounted as completely imaginary. This indicates a willful investment in the region's Norse ancestry all the more significant because it had no legitimacy. An 1839 book, *The Northmen in New England* by Joshua Toulmin Smith, illustrates the kind of rhetoric that fueled the reinscription of Native American artifacts as Norse. Smith writes that due to the remains of long-dead Vikings (like the Fall River skeleton) committed to the local soil, "NEW ENGLAND may be said to have become *classic ground*, since the discoveries of the Northmen have become generally known." The vestiges of Native American occupancy clearly could never confer this classic prestige on the landscape; according to Smith, the Vikings "discovered and explored the very same shores where a new race, of Anglo-Saxon blood has fixed its habitation, and made once savage and barbarous America assume an important station in the history of the world."[27] Although Native American inhabitants color the description of the continent as "savage and barbarous," Smith's rhetoric removes them from the history of the area as real, bodily presences.

Geraldine Barnes has argued that Longfellow's "Skeleton in Armor" participates in this kind of politically convenient erasure. "As a student of Amerindian languages, admirer of Amerindian culture, and author of *Song of Hiawatha*," Barnes writes, Longfellow should have known better than to perpetuate the "removal of the native presence" from the Vinland narrative during the very same era that forcible physical removals were displacing native populations from their lands.[28] But the fact that Longfellow's skeleton haunts and disturbs his interlocutor in the poem indicates that Longfellow could not cavalierly ignore the troubling implications of his Viking attribution. Renée Bergland, who has discussed the prevalence of Indian hauntings in American literature, argues that these ghosts are born from acts of dispossession; although Native Americans have been displaced, they still retain an unexorcisable hold over the New World's new inhabitants.[29] In Longfellow's poem, the "skeleton" not only haunts the narrator, he also co-opts the poem and Longfellow's pen in the service of his tale. The narrator is initially allowed two stanzas to introduce the story, but at the close of the poem, he adds only, "Thus the tale ended." The narrator's framing is lopsided, the poem ultimately overwhelmed and possessed by the skeleton's haunting voice.

Although Longfellow presents his "Skeleton in Armor" as a Viking, the very category of Viking cannot be cleanly separated from the category of Indian because the two were often yoked in a way that reveals the politics of the connection. Barnes has noted that the Viking encounter with Native Americans as retold in nineteenth-century essays and reviews differed according to the varying political views of the commentators. Specifically, a massacre of natives by Vikings, originally depicted in the Icelandic sagas without moral commentary, served as an opportunity for U.S. reviewers of the sagas to condone or condemn self-serving brutality toward native peoples; in one case that Barnes cites, it leads to a passionate denunciation of U.S. policies of Indian removal.[30] And for those who wished to excuse or overlook outrages perpetrated against Indian populations, the New England Vikings provided a perfect projection of contemporary actions and attitudes by which to deny wrongdoing. Vikings provided both the opportunity for and the means by which Anglo-Americans could exonerate themselves with regard to their treatment of Native Americans, whether because Viking violence provided a ratifying precedent for their own violence, or because the history of Vinland could be used to overwrite the history of Native American inhabitation and thus avoid the question altogether.

The Vinland fad, although most pronounced in New England and to a lesser extent in midwestern locations where large numbers of Scandinavian immigrants had settled, conformed to much broader historiographical impulses. The tendency to fixate on narratives of continental "discovery" by Europeans necessarily lessened mindfulness toward the inhabitants that had already been living on the continent. The nineteenth-century debate over the relative importance of Columbus and Leif Eriksson pitted their respective achievements and legacies against each other, and thus kept people from questioning whether either deserved so much attention in the context of a country struggling with its approach to its indigenous population.

The Anarchy of Landscape

Proponents of the New England landing theory tended to use Vinland, consciously or unconsciously, to distract and detract from the power of prior Native American occupation by prioritizing one history of the landscape over another. In "The Skeleton in Armor," Longfellow does participate in this prevailing cultural tendency to reinscribe the native landscape as a Viking one. However, in his other major simultaneous engagement with these two traditions—*The Song of Hiawatha*—the pattern is reversed: he arguably remakes a Scandinavian landscape into a Native American one.

Longfellow, in both *The Song of Hiawatha* and his earlier poem *Evangeline* (1847), represents the North American continent in terms borrowed from descriptions of the Swedish countryside.[31] Andrew Hilen has demonstrated that Longfellow's depiction of Acadia in *Evangeline* owes its tone and many of its particulars to contemporary depictions of Sweden.[32] Using travel accounts as well as his own memories of his 1835 visit to Sweden, Longfellow had written about its landscape in an 1837 *North American Review* essay and had published a slightly revised version of that essay with his 1841 translation of "Nattvardsbarnen," or "Children of the Last Supper," a poem by Esaias Tegnér, Sweden's premier poet.[33] As Hilen shows, the beginning of *Evangeline* clearly borrows from these representations of Sweden. Both have "primeval" forests with anthropomorphized trees that "sing" the area's history in mournful voices and that keen in tandem with the sounds of the nearby sea.

I would argue that this similarity with Longfellow's vision of Sweden extends beyond *Evangeline* and into the landscape of *The Song of Hiawatha*. The "groves of singing pine-trees" in this later poem bear a striking resemblance to the primeval forests of both his imagined Acadia and his idealized Swedish countryside.[34] Longfellow employs the same physical descriptors in *The Song of Hiawatha*—branches in the shape of fans, the blue cones of fir trees, vast dark reaches of gloomy forest—as he does when he describes the landscape of Sweden. In *Hiawatha*, the voices of the trees and the "sea" (the Big-Sea-Water of Lake Superior) speak in personified dialogue to register the losses of the community that dwells nearby, just as the voices of the forest and the ocean in *Evangeline* do. The trees by Gitche Gumee lament, just as those near the village of Grand Pré in Acadian Nova Scotia and those in the country around the Göta Canal in Sweden mourn.

It is impossible to say definitively whether or not Longfellow, as he began in 1855 to create yet another representation of huge pine forests standing by a vast body of water, was thinking specifically of his 1837 and 1841 writings on Sweden. It seems clear, though, that his work on Swedish and Nova Scotian landscapes contributed to his poetic repertoire; those earlier pieces furnished him with certain vocabulary and images that could be and were later employed in the delineation of *The Song of Hiawatha*'s setting. Sweden influenced and helped to shape Longfellow's description of the land of the Ojibway.

But Longfellow had no interest in replacing the map of Ojibway inhabitation with a Swedish one, in contrast to the way that the map of Vinland had been imposed over the map of Narragansett and Pequot and Mohegan territory. Longfellow's Swedish elements in *The Song of Hiawatha* jostle about with compositional ingredients drawn from many other languages and cultures, including that of the Ojibway, the English, the French, the Dacotah (Longfellow's spelling of "Dakota," which I will use throughout), the Yankee, and the Southron. Christoph Irmscher justifiably calls the poem's artistic influences "cheerfully eclectic."[35] Over the course of the poem, Longfellow presents a veritable salmagundi of claims on the land and frameworks for understanding it. The landscape that Longfellow imagines is in a state of constant, dynamic contention, and *The Song of Hiawatha*'s linguistic and cultural geography foregrounds the fact that multiple traditions have occupied the land and continue to exist within the space of the poem.

The Song of Hiawatha tells the story of the Indian leader Hiawatha from his birth through his heroic efforts to improve the lives of his people, ending with his willing self-exile after white men arrive among the Ojibway. The action of the poem takes place in what is now the Upper Peninsula of Michigan. Longfellow writes at the beginning of his "Notes" (a section of annotations placed just after the end of the main text) that "the scene of the poem is among the Ojibway on the southern shore of Lake Superior, in the region between the Pictured Rocks and the Grand Sable" (161).

The area that Longfellow describes is now known as the Pictured Rocks National Lakeshore, located between the towns of Munising and Grand Marais, Michigan.[36] In 1966, it became the first site ever designated as a "National Lakeshore" and it is maintained by the National Park Service. It has therefore been thoroughly inscribed as U.S. national property. But the area as depicted by Longfellow in *The Song of Hiawatha* certainly does not lend itself to such a clear sense of ownership.

In the notes, Longfellow explains the derivation of the English name for the Pictured Rocks, the dramatic sandstone cliffs that rim the southern side of Lake Superior: the seepage of mineral-laden groundwater has created bright, multicolored stains on the cliffs that sometimes appear to form pictures. But Longfellow also mentions the name that is "applied to them by the French voyageurs ('Les Portails')" (167). "Les Portails" means "The Gates" or "The Portals" (especially of a cathedral); the moniker comes from the dramatic erosions caused by lake water beating against the cliffs. "Voyageurs" were boatmen employed by French fur companies to transport supplies into the wilds of the interior and bring furs back out to trading centers like Québec; given the early operation of the French fur trade in this area, the French name would have predated the English one. Longfellow acknowledges here that landmarks can have multiple names used by the different populations that occupy an area, and that each of these names may be worth recording because they offer information that helps to illuminate the nature of the landmark.

The landscape often becomes a subject in and of itself in *The Song of Hiawatha*, as when Longfellow relates the myth of the origin of Grand Sable, an area of towering sand dunes that stretches for five miles along the lake. The name "Grand Sable," although now pronounced in a half-Anglicized manner ('grand 'sah-bull), is from the French, meaning "Big Sand." When Longfellow references it in the main text of the poem, however, he calls Grand Sable "Nagow Wudjoo" and, famously, he calls Lake Superior "Gitche Gumee," names used by the Ojibway, the traditional residents of the area.[37] According to an Ojibway creation story, as Longfellow records it in the poem, the trickster Pau-Puk-Keewis created the dunes by kicking up sand during a long, energetic dance at a communal celebration.

Longfellow clearly knew that his multilingual lexicon would pose a challenge to his English-speaking readers. In addition to the citations of pertinent source material provided in his notes, Longfellow appends a "Vocabulary" section to help his readers navigate the poem's many Ojibway terms; it contains entries like "Nagow Wudjoo, *the Sand Dunes of Lake Superior*" (170). *The Song of Hiawatha*'s exegetical apparatus, notably elaborate for a creative work, correlates Longfellow's approach with the dedication to research evinced by the other authors of imperial eclipse narratives. Furthermore, the "Vocabulary" indicates that Longfellow anticipated some reader confusion but chose to assist the reader in managing that linguistic confusion rather than eliminating the experience of confusion altogether (by purging the foreign vocabulary, for example). Even the placement of the "Vocabulary" at the end of the book prevents readers from settling comfortably into the story, because they must continually flip back and forth, juggling the two languages. This is in fact typical of Longfellow's willingness to leave cultural tensions unresolved in the poem. Irmscher notes that Longfellow, a talented linguist, approached his many works of translation with the philosophy that "[f]oreign texts needed to retain some of their strangeness even in English dress," and he resisted fully "assimilat[ing] a foreign text to American culture"; he expressed regret that a German translation of *The Song of Hiawatha* had cut out many of the Indian names.[38]

Contemporary records of reader response—parodies—indicate that Longfellow was successful in preserving a degree of linguistic otherness. Such a swarm of parodies was printed in the wake of *The Song of Hiawatha*'s publication that some claim it to be the most commonly burlesqued poem in the English language (a clear sign of its popularity).[39] In their mimicry, the parodies exaggerate peculiar or characteristic features of the original, idiosyncrasies that will readily identify the object of the parody for the reader. This quality of mimetic exaggeration means that parodies record what contemporary audiences found most striking about a given work of art. Furthermore, in their tendency to poke fun at perceived aesthetic flaws or weaknesses (which can sometimes be among the most salient features of a piece), parodies can also provide a guide to moments of reader estrangement from the original—moments when readers stumbled over and onto something that seemed especially unusual or awkward. The parodies nearly always mocked Longfellow's constant invocation of Ojibway words, indicating that wrestling with the foreign vocabulary—and, by association, the indigenous culture from which they came—made up a substantial part of the reading experience.

The poem and the "Vocabulary" thus do not encourage a straight, satisfied translation of the native context back into the Anglo-U.S. American context.[40] The place-names that Longfellow invokes reflect varying territorial claims, and typically no one particular claim is presented as outweighing the others. Undifferentiated by a chronological organization that would mark a place as now called such-and-such,[41] or then known as so-and-so, place-names in *The Song of Hiawatha* do not support a teleological narrative of the eclipse of one culture by another, of Native American names and peoples being supplanted by English, or even more broadly European, names and peoples. Longfellow creates a complicated linguistic and territorial picture in which the unsettled interplay between and among traditions leaves the reader with the sense of an epistemological anarchy rooted in shifting definitions of and competing claims on the land.

The eclipse of Native America by Euro-America is directly undermined by the tensions and competitions within Euro-America itself. The early French history of the area around Lake Superior troubles any direct presumption by the United States to the energy and spirit (and land) of Hiawatha and the Ojibway.[42] Place-names like Grand Sable or Sault Sainte Marie remain as a nagging reminder of the prior European claim to this land, once called New France (and, more to the point, Nouvelle-France).[43] In contrast to the neatness of cyclical history's rise and fall of empires, in which one empire succeeds the next and the falling empire leaves the field of dominance clear for the rising empire to occupy, Longfellow's landscape puts various empires into competitive coexistence.

An embodiment of interimperial rivalry in the poem comes in the form of the European figure who arrives at the end; often termed the "White Man" even though Longfellow never actually refers to him with that title, he should not be read as a synecdoche for all white men. He is described as "the Black-Robe chief, the Prophet, / He the Priest of Prayer, the Pale-face" (155). This "Black-Robe" (a fairly common native term for a Jesuit, inspired by the black robes that members of the Society of Jesus then wore) is to a certain extent an amalgam figure, but he is primarily modeled on Jacques Marquette, a French missionary to Native American communities in what would become Michigan and surrounding territories.[44] Marquette is credited with the first accurate European charting of the Mississippi

River; missionaries ultimately functioned as both religious ambassadors and political surveyors. "The Black-Robe chief" is heavily marked as Catholic; the theology he presents to Hiawatha and his people puts great emphasis on Mary, one of the characteristic features of Roman Catholicism. He hails Hiawatha with the salutation "Peace of Christ, and joy of Mary," and in narrating his creed, starts off by telling the people "of the Virgin Mary, / And her blessed Son, the Saviour" (156, 157). This obviously French Catholic figure, from a religious order that had long been hated and mistrusted by New World Protestants (as we saw with Motley and the Know-Nothings), represents the religious, economic, and political opposition. He therefore proves an odd choice if he is supposed to symbolize the passing of supremacy from Hiawatha and his people to the emerging, heavily Protestant—and, in 1855, increasingly anti-Catholic—United States in some straightforward sense.

An acceptance of the "Black-Robe" priest and his companions did not mean an acceptance of white Europeans in general, and certainly did not lead naturally and steadily to an acceptance of U.S. dominance. The Ojibway in fact fought with the French in the French and Indian wars and with the British in the War of 1812. Despite Hiawatha's parting counsel to the warriors of his village to listen to and accept the truth of the white "guests" (159), that resignation did not translate itself historically into a willing authorization of U.S. land control.

Furthermore, the "anarchy of empire" created when European and Euro-American powers vied for control of western lands only added to a history already rife with that kind of struggle before any white presence was ever felt.[45] Native American peoples warred so violently and unceasingly with each other that it is said that the Great Spirit, Gitche Manito, fashioned the first peace pipe from the rock of the "great Red Pipe-stone Quarry" to encourage them to put aside intertribal conflict (5, 7). This quarry, located in what is now Pipestone, Minnesota, enshrines in the landscape an overlap of cultures that sometimes resulted in violent conflict and the need to mediate among coexisting peoples.[46] Longfellow foregrounds this history and the push for peace by making the Ojibway story of the quarry's creation the first section after the prologue.

Longfellow continues to raise the specter of native discord throughout the poem. He implies that part of the danger inherent in the "fearless" Hiawatha's long journey west to confront his delinquent father, Mudjekeewis, lies in the necessity of crossing through "the land of Crows and Foxes"—territory defined by its status as the possession of foreign peoples—and passing by "the dwellings of the Blackfeet" (27, 28). The Fox—long-standing enemies of the Ojibway—lived traditionally in what would become Wisconsin; the Crow, who often warred with the Blackfeet and Dacotah, lived in parts of Minnesota and the Upper Missouri River area:

North Dakota, eastern Montana.[47] With the "land of Crows and Foxes" and the land of the dwellings of the Blackfeet (probably indicating Montana west to the Rockies),[48] Longfellow narrates what would become the continental United States as a series of Indian lands, potentially radical in the way that it establishes prior native ownership. In addition, though, he represents Hiawatha as traveling not through an undifferentiated swathe of Native American land but through substantively different domains, controlled by peoples not always united in confederation just because they could all be lumped together as Indians by Europeans and Euro-Americans. Despite the fact that many critics, reasonably, interpret Hiawatha as a symbol of all native peoples—his fate stands for the fate of all the supposedly vanishing Indians—the poem's implicit and explicit presentation of intertribal tension highlights the multiplicity and complexity of the many cultures that made up the Native American world. Indeed, despite the deliberately mythic explanation of Hiawatha's destination when he departs at the end of the poem—he seeks "the portals of the Sunset," "the regions of the home-wind, / Of the North-west wind, Keewaydin" (158)—the movement of his canoe "Westward! westward!" will actually take him straight back into hostile territory (159).

On the return trip from his father's home in the Rocky Mountains, Hiawatha travels through "the land of the Dacotahs," now Minnesota and Wisconsin (32). In the poem, the threat of discord simmers most threateningly in the conflict between the Ojibway and the Dacotah, their traditional enemies. Hiawatha marries Minnehaha, a Dacotah, in part to end this rivalry. When Nokomis, his grandmother, objects to "a stranger / from the land of the Dacotahs" because "Often is there war between us, / There are feuds yet unforgotten, / Wounds that ache and still may open," Hiawatha responds, "For that reason, if no other, / Would I wed the fair Dacotah, / That our tribes might be united, / That old feuds might be forgotten, / And old wounds be healed forever!" (69). Despite Hiawatha's optimism and relentlessly progressive vision, however, the feud continues. Chibiabos, one of Hiawatha's best friends, is drowned by "Unktahee, the god of water, / He the god of the Dacotahs" (108). And Hiawatha, just before the "White Man's Foot" arrives, prophesies that "our nations [will be] scattered, / All forgetful of my counsels, / Weakened, warring with each other," and that this will lead to the uprooting and eventual extinction of the native peoples (153).

The role of Europeans in uprooting and eliminating native peoples is noticeably and conveniently absent from this prophecy, in conformity with Hiawatha's general self-annihilating embrace of white dominance. Similarly blind, though, is the vision that accompanies this "darker, drearier" one: "I beheld the western marches / Of the unknown, crowded nations. / All the land was full of people, / Restless, struggling, toiling, striving, / Speaking many tongues, yet feeling / But one heart-beat in their bosoms. / In the woodlands rang their axes, / Smoked their towns in all the valleys, / Over all the lakes and rivers / Rushed their great canoes of thunder" (152–53). This fantasy of manifest destiny, powered by the industry and energy of immigrants speaking many different languages, posits a spiritual unification of U.S. Americans despite their obvious differences—an ideal contradicted, for example, by the ethnic tensions evident in Irving's treatment of the Dutch in *A History of New York*.

Furthermore, in 1855, the notion of "one heart-beat" animating the bosoms of everyone in the Union amounted to a sectional wish fulfillment. The danger of discord that looms over Hiawatha and his people was threatening the United States, too. Daniel Aaron, among others, has argued that Longfellow was becoming concerned at the time of the poem's composition with "the political implications of the growing acrimony between the paleface 'tribes' of North and South over slavery and his premonitions of civil strife. Given his apprehensions, it is not farfetched to hear him speaking in the voice of the Great Spirit warning his disunited children to stop their 'wranglings and dissensions' and in Hiawatha's prophecies of calamity."[49] As with the other narratives of imperial eclipse that we have seen, in this aspect of *The Song of Hiawatha*, the specter of intranational troubles is evoked by international history (and I do consider the territory depicted in the poem as international, because the contested nature of the landscape does not lend itself to a proto-national interpretation of its significance).

The competition of cultures in the poem takes place across and is embodied in the land. In Hiawatha's vision of the future, the transformation of the landscape indexes the shift in cultural power: he pictures the woodlands, the valleys, the lakes and rivers, and how they will be changed by European occupation. But each successive culture leaves its traces, especially in the form of place-names that reflect different linguistic traditions and different ways of interacting with and understanding the environment. Jared Farmer, in his analysis of the ideology of U.S. place-names, argues that white adoption of Indian names actually abetted the process of removal by facilitating resigned regret to native disappearance: "Indians die; only their names remain."[50] But in *The Song of Hiawatha*, Longfellow does not use Ojibway place-names as nostalgic grave markers; he envelops the reader in a dense cloud of Ojibway terms and re-creates a world in which they were actively used, alongside Dacotah and French and English words. He presents place-names to the reader without chronological or hierarchical differentiation, and the topography of the poem's landscape becomes layered with overlapping cultural domains. The various cultures he draws from stand in antagonistic relationship to one another—Ojibway versus Dacotah, Anglo versus Indian, English Protestant versus

French Catholic, North versus South—but Longfellow nonetheless allows them to remain together to trouble the reader's sense of order.

This contrasts starkly with the oversimplified clarity of the Vinland narrative as its adherents superimposed it on the landscape of prior Native American occupation. Analogously, in response to Longfellow's tolerance for cultural anarchy, early reviewers of the poem attempted to impose their own order on it. Their selective focus only on the Nordic elements of the poem's source history worked to neutralize the disturbing implications of its Native American subject matter.

The Politics of Plagiarism

In the months after its publication in 1855, *The Song of Hiawatha* itself became a contested site—this time in the literary landscape—around precisely this desire to manage the Scandinavian and Native American histories imbedded in it. Longfellow's material and methods in the poem drew from both North American Indian and Scandinavian sources, and despite the common critical belief that the poem is a massive racial wish fulfillment, he at the very least complicated the political expedience of his appropriation of native cultural material by dwelling on native myths and thus creating a poetics of nostalgia that undermined any triumphalism to Hiawatha being supplanted by white men. Longfellow also insisted on the primacy of native material to his sources.

His early reviewers, on the other hand, showed a tendency to de-emphasize native culture by isolating another of Longfellow's sources and exaggerating its significance. Whereas proponents of the Vinland theory, fleeing from the complications entailed by immigrant and Indian occupation, took refuge in the thought of ancient Icelandic explorers, *The Song of Hiawatha*'s reviewers seized on yet another Scandinavian diversion: the Finnish epic *Kalevala*, a collection of ancient Finnish poetry that was both an outgrowth of and an inspiration for the Finnish nationalist movement. Elias Lönnrot, *Kalevala*'s compiler, first published it in 1835–36; Longfellow read it in an 1852 German translation by Anton Schiefner.[51]

Much of the cultural energy that might have been devoted to confronting the prominent place of Native American sociology and myths in *The Song of Hiawatha* was deflected into a consideration of the poem's Finnish literary ancestry. From the very month of its publication, reviewers were arguing over the substance and significance of Longfellow's debt to *Kalevala*, creating an "unusually active" "din."[52] The controversy centered around an alleged similarity between Longfellow's poem and the Finnish one, so marked that some claimed it bordered on outright imitation.

Longfellow had long been dogged by the charge of imitation. The *Kalevala* controversy reignited charges of plagiarism that Edgar Allan Poe had leveled at him very publicly several years earlier.[53] Furthermore, Longfellow's deep and constant engagement with European literary forms and traditions, his respect for and emulation of such writers as Goethe, appeared suspect to some guardians of U.S. cultural independence. But this authorial history does not sufficiently explain the intensity of the hue and cry raised when Thomas Conrad Porter, Longfellow's main accuser, launched the attack in the *Daily National Intelligencer* on November 26, 1855. He declared that Longfellow had "transferred the entire form, spirit, and many of the most striking incidents of the old Finnish epic to the North American Indians."[54] He criticized the poet for failing to acknowledge his radical indebtedness to this Scandinavian source—and indeed, Longfellow's only conceivable admission in the original edition that he did borrow his meter from the German translation of *Kalevala* comes in the notes, when he cryptically calls the poem his "Indian Edda" ("Edda" being an Icelandic collection of ancient legendary poetry). Porter's accusation quickly sparked a heated debate that raged most intensely in the *Intelligencer* and the London *Athenaeum*.

The controversy, as it played itself out in U.S. papers, used the origins of the poem as a way to argue over the ethics of national writing (an important issue, although I will argue that this debate ultimately allowed reviewers to neglect even more substantial issues raised by the poem). Longfellow's reviewers focused their intellectual urgency on whether the poem was appropriately universalist or unscrupulously imitative. In his critique of *The Song of Hiawatha*, Thomas Conrad Porter aimed to rebut the praise earlier heaped on the poem by Moncure Daniel Conway, Longfellow's main apologist during the plagiarism controversy. In a review, to which Porter's piece on November 26 was a response, Conway had forcefully emphasized the strong nationalist promise of the poem: he called it "perhaps the only American Epic." Longfellow, he said, had managed to capitalize on "the only contribution that our country could give the muse" in setting to verse "our highly poetic Indian legends."[55]

Despite characterizing the poem as "purely original and proper," Conway actually admired its unoriginal elements, which it shared with other countries' epics. He marveled at "the unity of Man in the midst of his so great differences! There is not one of these Indian legends which is not native to every race of men. . . . Who is Hiawatha but Siegfried of the Norsemen, Hercules of the Greeks, Moses of the Jews, Haroun Al Raschid of the Arabs?" Because of this unity, similarity does not necessarily imply derivation. One culture does not copy its heroes from another, but all bear a family resemblance due to the universality of the human imagination. In Conway's sense of the poem's universality, it should be noted, the legacy of the "Norsemen" does not predominate; it takes its place in the field of other correspondences.

Porter tries to combat the leveling effect of this supposed "unity" on national expression. Obviously, an enfranchising human unity would undermine the claim of theft to which he was publicly committing himself. He rightly questions the suspect prerogatival power involved in declaring ideas and culturally specific expressions to be universal human property. The concept of imaginative unity can be easily marshaled toward the end of unscrupulous intellectual appropriation. To bring order to this nebulous and potentially predatory unity, he insists on a more hierarchically structured view of the fusion of traditions. He narrows the cultural focus to Finland and *Kalevala*, isolating them and giving them pride of place in his story of the poem's origins. He calls attention to Longfellow's only hint of credit to Scandinavian sources, which "is found in the beginning of his first note, where he says, 'This Indian *Edda*, if I may so call it.'" Porter adds italics that did not appear in the original, and in doing so emphasizes one part of the cultural equation that Longfellow left in ambiguous relation. Porter here works to separate out national traditions, structure them in a system of precedence, and thereby identify patterns of borrowing that a vision of human imaginative "unity" could erase.

Porter's attempt to argue for intellectual property prompts Conway to deny its applicability in this case. He argues that Longfellow owed no particular responsibility to *Kalevala*'s balladic structure or mythic spirit because both *The Song of Hiawatha* and *Kalevala* owed that style to much older bardic sources. He furthermore denied that Longfellow needed to acknowledge the debt that *The Song of Hiawatha*'s distinctive meter owed to *Kalevala*'s trochaic tetrameter rhythm, since poetic meters and forms do not belong to their creators (for example, a poet would not be expected to cite Petrarch when composing a Petrarchan sonnet). He reaffirms a global unity that undermines such individualistic notions of poetic property; to him, any similarity between Indian and Finnish legends "only shows that man has a common nature in every sense. And the real value of national epics is, that *there never was one written true to the legends and myths it celebrated which did not resemble in many respects all the rest.*" Far from endorsing a national poetics of originality, then, Conway claims that formal or stylistic similarities follow appropriately from analogous cultural enterprises: "[I]t was highly proper that Mr. Longfellow should have adopted" a style drawn from other traditions "in which so many legends are well told which bear the same relation to their nation as Hiawatha to ours."[56]

Both of the explanatory models that emerge from these early reviews—national distinctiveness and a common universal nature—speak to major issues in the process of national culture formation. The Finnish *Kalevala* offers Porter, Conway, and other reviewers an opportunity to theorize about the contours of a national literature in relationship to other countries' traditions. However, this debate drew attention away from domestic sources of the poem—the Native American cultural material that comprises the vast majority of *The Song of Hiawatha*. When Porter claims that Longfellow had "transferred the entire form, spirit, and many of the most striking incidents of the old Finnish epic to the North American Indians," he evacuates the significant native contribution to the poem and replaces it with his Finnish one. He empties out perhaps the most sophisticated and undoubtedly the most popular literary reconstruction of the Indian cultural imagination ever put before a white audience to that point.[57]

The controversy over Longfellow's potential plagiarism of *Kalevala* distracted attention away from the other, more obvious, more pressing cultural borrowing that had taken place. By the disputants' own admission, the alleged theft of Scandinavian materials could be suitably adjudicated only within the tiny community of intellectuals actually familiar with the Finnish text; the rhetoric of the reviews stayed self-consciously academic in tone.[58] The main import of the debate for the wider public was limited to Longfellow's personal credibility. But the appropriation of Native American culture for purposes that might include the artistic and monetary gain of a white poet and the implicit authorization of Indian displacement and Anglo-American manifest destiny—this was far from an academic issue. The entire country was party to the latter theft, and its ramifications were clearly more politically urgent than any debt to Finnish culture. But the brouhaha over plagiarism functioned to contain the problem of culpability to questions of proper authorial practice, to be decided by an elite group of specialists. Longfellow would be pronounced innocent or guilty of the charge; the country's guilt would not need to be addressed.

Thus U.S. reviewers concentrated on the charges of authorial theft, trying to establish the nature of plagiarism and what would actually constitute a cultural theft in the international arena, while avoiding the obvious domestic application of that question. In a different but similarly ideological move, English and other European reviewers, especially in the hot debate in the pages of the London *Athenaeum*, were predictably unconcerned with questions about Longfellow's wrongdoing and devoted their attention instead to determining which European country he had borrowed his meter from—an act to which none of them particularly objected—and which nation therefore deserved the cultural credit for his production.[59] In both of these controversies, American Indian culture becomes almost totally a foil and an afterthought.

The racist underpinnings of this shift in attention are clearly articulated in a review of *The Song of Hiawatha* published in the December 1855 issue of *Put-*

nam's Monthly. The writer expresses "doubts" as to "whether the Indian brain be really responsible for [all the poem's legends] . . . [some] are too finely and fancifully touched to be of Indian origin. We think we see the 'supreme Caucasian mind' in" certain elements; "[f]ancies like these, we cannot think came from our brethren who paint their faces in blue and bistre."[60] Operating within a paradigm of native barbarism, this reviewer decides Longfellow probably has lifted material from European sources—white races—rather than attribute a sophisticated cultural imagination to the savage "Red Man."

His characterization of Longfellow's method of composition reveals yet again the use of Scandinavian culture to absorb and contain the native material: Longfellow, he writes, has "constructed a sort of Edda of the Indian mythology. . . . This application of a Scandinavian form to receive the Indian fancies, this second discovery of America by the Northmen, is thoroughly characteristic of the author of the 'Skeleton in Armour.'"[61] He holds up the Norse discovery and settlement of the continent in the Vinland narrative as a conquest parallel to Longfellow's supposed seizure of raw native imaginings to be used as fuel in an ultimately Scandinavian work. But the impulse to deny agency in this seizure and depict the cultural transfer as willingly authorized by Native Americans can be seen in the contradiction between "application" and "receive." Longfellow is actively applying the Scandinavian form to Indian fancies but is somehow passively receiving those fancies, not taking them.

As the *Putnam's* reviewer indicates, the early reception history of *The Song of Hiawatha* follows the pattern of the Vinland craze; the reviewer explicitly correlates the two as analogous projects. The literal geographical remapping of territory, which redrew the history of native occupation as the history of Viking exploration, bequeaths a legacy of racial misdirection to the literary recasting of Longfellow's sources. In each case, the chicanery of race politics used Northmen, whether Leif Eriksson or the Finnish bards responsible for *Kalevala*, to distract attention away from the evident sophistication of Native American culture and civilization.

This problematic substitution did not go totally unchallenged by Longfellow's early reviewers.[62] In a January 1856 piece in the *North American Review*, a reviewer states that immediately after reading the poem, "then begins the questioning, 'Where did this come from?' and 'Where did that come from?' And one says, 'Edda,' and another says, 'Swedish,' and another, 'Goethe,' as if it were our first business to forget that we have been fascinated by the song, whatever it is, and that the scanty literature of aboriginal life has at last one poem."[63] This writer reflects on the critical controversy that had been raging since November 1855 and diagnoses what gets forgotten in the debate over foreign sources: the fact that the poem constitutes a long overdue, significant contribution to an undeservedly neglected subject of white writing, "the scanty literature of aboriginal life," even though that contribution is inadequate to the need (the emphasis on "one" in "has at last one poem" highlights the limited nature of the contribution).

The reviewer furthermore diagnoses the resolute nature of this turn away from the "aboriginal" issue in characterizing the impulse as "our *business* to forget." This phrasing suggests that by a willful mechanism of psychological response, reviewers were erasing the most salient aspect of Longfellow's poem—what they knew before they settled down to the business of forgetting—and replacing it with thoughts of Eddas and Swedishness and Goethe. Just as the Vinland theory had done for the landscape of New England, the *Kalevala* debate seemed determined to remove Native Americans from the landscape of *The Song of Hiawatha*.

Longfellow strenuously resisted the marginalization of the native influence in his reviewers' accounts of the poem's cultural scheme. He repeatedly stressed the centrality of ethnographer Henry Rowe Schoolcraft and his collections of native legends to any discussion of his sources and expressed some bewilderment over the attention paid to the importance of *Kalevala*.[64] Some of this can of course be attributed to Longfellow's defensiveness at being charged once again with plagiarism. He cited Schoolcraft and other authorities on native culture amply in his notes but did not mention the Finnish poem or its 1852 German translation by Anton Schiefner, although the latter did form the basis for *The Song of Hiawatha*'s meter.[65] He would therefore stay on more solid ethical ground by insisting on the relative insignificance of the poem's Finnish heritage. But he does maintain in a letter to his friend Charles Sumner that "I can give chapter and verse for these Legends. Their chief value is that they are Indian Legends."[66]

Similarly, when his longtime friend and German translator Ferdinand Freiligrath published a supportive statement in the *Athenaeum* on the origin of the poem's meter, stating its pivotal source as Schiefner's translation, Longfellow wrote him that although the piece was "excellent," "it needs only one paragraph more, to make it complete; and that is the statement that *parallelism* belongs to Indian poetry as well as to Finnish. . . . And this is my justification—if any be needed—for adopting it in 'Hiawatha.'"[67] Even with well-meaning friends, then, who rigorously defended him against the charge of plagiarism, Longfellow remained adamant in contesting the skewing of critical focus toward *Kalevala* and away from native culture.

He had no patience for the allegation that he had imported *The Song of Hiawatha*'s "striking incidents" from elsewhere: as he writes to Sumner, "I know 'Kalewala' very well; and that some of its legends resemble the Indian stories preserved by Schoolcraft, is very true; but the idea of making me responsible for that is too ludicrous!" He echoes Moncure Daniel Conway in arguing that any similarity of content in the thrusts of the stories could only be rightly attributed to the quirks of the universal mind in giving all peoples the same kind of mythic imaginings. He disavows authorial control—and therefore authorial culpability—over these similarities, arguing that "whatever resemblance . . . may be found between the poems of 'Kalevala' and mine . . . is not of my creating, but lies in the legends themselves."[68]

Not only was he innocent of forging these similarities but they also provided a justification for his most questionable citation decision. He did reuse the German-inflected Finnish meter of Schiefner without acknowledging that debt. But "resemblances" between the Finnish and the Native American literary traditions made that meter seem to him a natural choice for his own poem. He envisions that his poetic project parallels that of the Finnish rune writers, since "[i]n 'Hiawatha' I have tried to do for our old Indian legends what the unknown Finnish poets had done for theirs, and in doing this I have employed the same meter."[69] As an author, he believes he stands in the same relation to his national culture and its originary Indian material as the Finnish poets of *Kalevala* stood to their legends. Clearly this entails a problematic naturalizing of Indian culture as "ours," as the spiritual origins and rightful property of Anglo-American society. But in his declaration that *The Song of Hiawatha* and *Kalevala* constituted analogous national undertakings, he indicates that his primary concern lay with the Indian legends.

His linguistic sensibilities further explained his choice of meters. To his eye, the Finnish and German-inflected Finnish verse that formed the basis of Hiawatha's trochaic tetrameter shared their most salient metrical traits with native poetic utterance. As Schoolcraft justified his own use of trochaic tetrameter in *his* native-themed long narrative poem *Alhalla*, "The measure (tetrameter) is thought to be not ill adapted to the Indian mode of enunciation. Nothing is more characteristic of their harangues and public speeches, than the vehement, yet broken and continued strain of utterance. . . . It is not the less in accordance with these traits that nearly every initial syllable of the measure chosen is under accent."[70] As Wilbur Schramm has pointed out in a line of argument that has been almost completely buried by focus on *Kalevala* as Longfellow's main source, Schoolcraft's *Alhalla* and a series of other Anglo-American poems on Indian themes—which all predate *The Song of Hiawatha*—tended to employ tetrameter, especially trochaic tetrameter.[71] Thus Longfellow joined with a number of other poets in believing that trochaic tetrameter verse, taken in his case from a Finnish model, suited the native culture primarily under focus.

Longfellow's poem bears out his assertion that for him, the "chief value" of his primary source materials lies in their Indianness. Christoph Irmscher argues that while the striking and memorable native stories that Longfellow includes do not "make *Hiawatha* a 'native' poem, [they] also considerably complicat[e] the reader's attitude toward the arrival of the white colonizers at the end of a poem that has often been misconstrued as a more or less racist endorsement of Indian removal."[72] In cantos 1–17, Longfellow relates a series of tales that illuminate the daily life of the Ojibway, stories of hunting and planting and eating, of healing and fighting and celebrating: details that flesh out Ojibway culture in vital and compelling terms. Although the accommodationist prologue and final cantos somewhat undermine the effect of the stories presented in the middle, the reverse is also true: the middle undermines the effect of the beginning and the end of the poem. The reader grows to cherish the Ojibway worldview over the course of the poem in ways that don't vanish simply because Hiawatha in the end vanishes.

This process happens in part through a deep linguistic engagement with Ojibway words. By wrestling with Longfellow's Indian lexicon (difficult to process even given the assistance provided by his "Vocabulary"), readers could form an intellectual investment in the living language of the Ojibway. Longfellow intended for the experience of cultural engagement by means of translation to be profound. In his July 1837 *North American Review* article, "Tegnér's *Frithiof's Saga*," in which he reviewed existing English translations of Esaias Tegnér's poetry and provided one of his own, he wrote that translation should involve "transport[ing] ourselves over to [a foreign author], and adopt[ing] his situation, his mode of speaking, his peculiarities."[73] Longfellow reprinted large portions of the original Swedish to emphasize the need to enter deeply into the language and culture of the original work. As Thomas Conrad Porter warned, the adoption of a foreign mode of speaking could constitute a suspect cultural appropriation. But it also involves a substantial imaginative stretching, an effort to inhabit an alien position that does not tend to encourage the dismissal of that position as "vanished," because the act of translation initiates a fresh use of the alien language that brings it alive for the translator. In requiring his readers to be Ojibway translators, then, Longfellow disrupts the idea that the Ojibway culture's day is done.

Ojibway place-names have a dual function in resisting Indian eclipse: readers experience them in the linguistic vitality of translation, and they implicitly substantiate Ojibway land rights because names are both a form of and a record of ownership. Unlike words such as "Mississippi," names never adopted by whites, such as Nagow Wudjoo, Pauwating, and Gitche Gumee, consequently never lost their association with Indianness. Longfellow's poem depicts a landscape not only defined in Ojibway terms but also inhabited by the people who used those terms. The names, in their foreignness, conjure up foreign speakers to speak them, and Longfellow thereby stocks the landscape of northern Michigan with Native Americans rather than displacing them (and he does the same with the French). Furthermore, many of the poem's stories focus on the land and narrate its shape as the result of Ojibway occupation. The Taquamenaw River calls to mind the efforts of Hiawatha and his friend Kwasind to clear it and make it navigable; Nagow Wudjoo calls to mind Pau-Puk-Keewis literally dancing up a storm in the dunes (51, 79). With these stories, Longfellow practices landscape architecture, and just as proponents of the Vinland theory did, he helps to nurture a vivid, concrete sense of embodied history rooted in the local landscape. But unlike Vinlanders, he chooses to accentuate rather than to remove the native presence from Michigan's Upper Peninsula. His contact zone invites his readers to coexist with Native Americans.

Longfellow's writings often attempt to elicit a tangible sense of physical setting, with a resulting awareness of the profusion of historical associations that can occupy a single space. In Longfellow's kind of history writing, all current and former inhabitants of an area meet through the juxtaposition of their tangible remnants in the spaces that they all occupied.[74] This undermines the politics of progress that the poem supposedly espouses. Hiawatha's decampment makes room for European expansion, but in dwelling on and creating pleasure in the myths of a (theoretically) now eclipsed culture, Longfellow staves off that culture's eclipse in a way that fosters ambivalence about the eventual outcome.[75] *The Song of Hiawatha*'s removalist messages must battle against its sustained re-creation of the Ojibway world, its polyglot poetics, and the landscape architecture that inscribes the history of Ojibway inhabitation deep into the environment.

White writers during this period would never have dignified North American Indian groups with the title of "empire," because that would admit a level of civilizational sophistication and organization deeply disturbing to the manifestness of the United States' right to the continent. But clearly the fantasy of the vanishing Indian conformed to the imperial eclipse pattern. To the extent that *The Song of Hiawatha* reiterates this fantasy by concluding with "Hiawatha's Departure," Longfellow colludes in the eclipse of Native America. But to the extent that the poem's middle section undermines the fantasy, Longfellow resists the supersession of Hiawatha's community by whites, whether French Jesuits within the narrative or U.S. Americans in the era of the poem's publication. And in denying *Kalevala*'s centrality to his source material, Longfellow resisted the symbolic substitution of Scandinavia for Native America—another kind of eclipse, a cultural overshadowing that functioned to obscure the ongoing crime of Indian displacement. In contrast to those who embraced international Viking history as a vehicle for obfuscating intranational racial tensions, Longfellow's anarchic mixture of internationalism and intranationalism in his poetic landscapes challenged the inexorability of Indian eclipse.

Conclusion

The French would not retain possession of the land of the Ojibway for very long; New France stayed true to the domino pattern that had structured the course of so many early modern empires. For a century following Père Marquette's advent into Ojibwan territory, the French struggled with the British in a contest for imperial control over North America. They lost that contest in 1763, with their defeat in the Seven Years' War (the "French and Indian War," so called by the British and their allies, formed only a part of this larger conflict). At the conclusion of the Seven Years' War, Britain became the undisputed reigning empire in North America.

Francis Parkman, Boston historian and heir to the historiographical tradition of William Hickling Prescott and John Lothrop Motley, told the tale of New France and the battle for North American imperial supremacy.[1] Although Parkman produced his most significant historiography after the Civil War, and although his work reflected the continued development of the historical discipline in the latter half of the nineteenth century, his historical philosophy in many ways mirrored the approach of his colleagues who worked earlier in the century. He continued to imagine world history in cyclical terms and struggled to identify an exceptional historical destiny for the United States. His account of early modern North American history took the form of an extended narrative of imperial eclipse and depicted the next casualty in the rapid-fire succession of eclipsed empires in the early modern period.

Parkman's monumental seven-part work, *France and England in North America* (1865–92), proceeds chronologically through the story of New France except for the final two parts: *Montcalm and Wolfe*, published in 1884, and *A Half-Century of Conflict*, which came out in 1892. *Montcalm and Wolfe* actually chronicles the final phase of the conflict, but Parkman wrote and published it before *A Half-Century of Conflict* because he feared that he might die before he could tell the most important part of the epic story. *Montcalm and Wolfe*, the chronological climax of the imperial struggle between England and France over North America, ends with the 1763 Treaty of Paris, in which the French ceded control of their North American territories to the British.[2]

In the concluding chapter of *Montcalm and Wolfe*, Parkman reflects on the history he has recounted. He portrays 1763 as a moment of imperial eclipse. He writes of the "inevitable downfall" of France as it now entered a period of "decay," "moving swiftly and more swiftly towards the abyss of ruin."[3] France's "vast possessions" in North America had once "dwarfed those of every other nation," but "all this was now changed"; "of all her boundless territories in North America nothing was left but the two island rocks on the coast of Newfoundland that the victors had given her for drying her codfish. . . . as a world power her grand opportunities were gone" (1476). On the other hand, "All, and more than all, that France had lost England had won." England had no more rivals. Spain and Holland, specifically mentioned by Parkman, are described as in this era "sinking into . . . decay" and having "long ago fallen hopelessly behind," respectively. With the conquest of the French, then, the field of world domination lay totally open to the British: the "Peace of Paris secured the opportunities and set in action the forces that have planted English homes in every clime, and dotted the earth with English garrisons and posts of trade" (1477). Their last major source of competition humbled—eclipsed by the mighty and still-rising power of England—the British proceeded to cast an imperial net over the whole world.

But soon after 1763 came 1776. "Scarcely" had Britain subdued France "when the British provinces showed symptoms of revolt" (1478). At this point, Parkman, a U.S. historian, should be almost twitching with historical anticipation. One more small world historical step, in the form of a revolution, and the mantle of progress, the *translatio imperii*, would pass to the United States. And indeed he does produce some of the expected patriotic rhetoric, congratulating England on "the glory of giving birth to the United States" (1477). With "astonishing audacity," he writes, the British colonies in America "affronted the wrath of England in the hour of her triumph, forgot their jealousies and quarrels, joined hands in the common cause, fought, endured, and won. The disunited colonies became the United States" (1478).

But he does not end his story there, at that moment of national origin and victory. Each of Parkman's chapter titles provides the year-span covered in that particular chapter; the dates for the concluding chapter are "1763–1884," ending with the very year of *Montcalm and Wolfe*'s publication (1475). The arc of Parkman's reflections has carried him all the way to the present moment. (I will in fact be making a similar move in the latter half of this conclusion.)

From the perspective of 1884, rather than 1776, the place of the United States in world history seems somewhat less glorious. The Civil War obviously tarnished the sense of the United States as exceptional and blessed, but Parkman does argue that the war really "served only to compact and consolidate" the Union. Nonetheless, despite having "grown to a mighty people," the United States still occupies an unnervingly precarious position (1478). In the midst of his celebratory rhetoric, Parkman breaks out into the same anxiety for his nation that we have seen in each of the narratives of imperial eclipse already discussed:

> Those who in the weakness of their dissensions needed help from England [in the French and Indian War] against the savage on their borders have become a nation that may defy every foe but that most dangerous of all foes, herself, destined to a majestic future if she will shun the excess and perversion of the principles that made her great, prate less about the enemies of the past and strive more against the enemies of the present, resist the mob and the demagogue as she resisted Parliament and the King, rally her powers from the race for gold and the delirium of prosperity to make firm the foundations on which that prosperity rests, and turn some fair proportion of her vast mental forces to other objects than material progress and the game of party politics. (1478–79)

The United States, the culmination of human history's march of progress, is beset no longer by "the savage" but instead by a host of debilitating internal weaknesses. The enemy lies within; the nation is its own most dangerous foe. Having traced the deterioration of New France in exquisite detail, Parkman has been sensitized to all the potential missteps that an empire can make. He brings this perspective to bear on his assessment of his own culture in his own day: he argues that unless U.S. Americans tread very carefully, the relentless cyclical pattern of imperial eclipse that humbled Spain, the Netherlands, France, and England in rapid succession over the course of the early modern period will inevitably envelop them as well.

This fear manifested itself in all narratives of imperial eclipse. These narratives generally went to great lengths to bring the history of past civilizations to life for their readers; they thereby provided an intimate acquaintance with case studies that fleshed out and animated history's grim statistics on imperial survival. Blithe claims that the United States was an unprecedented and exceptional nation that would not suffer the same fate as past empires, would not succumb to their pattern of rise and fall, became more difficult to make after studying a past empire deeply enough to see the similarities between its problems and those of the United States.

Certainly, this chastening did not obviate all expectation of progress and exceptionalism—ideologies rightfully considered widespread and influential in this period. Parkman's mixture of self-congratulatory and self-censuring rhetoric about the nation illustrates that the progress mentality could and often did exist side by side with apprehensions that arose from familiarity with world history's cautionary tales. For example, the beginning of the quote above has an odd velocity to it: "Those who in the weakness of their dissensions needed help from England against the savage on their borders have become a nation that may defy every foe but that most dangerous of all foes, herself." Two ideas have been run together here in almost breathless fashion—first, that the once-weak colonies have now become strong, a reason for celebration; and second, that the nation's greatest foe is itself, a cause for concern. Parkman slides from the triumphalist into the jeremiadic mode without pause.

His syntax seems to signal an ambivalence about his introduction of this gloomy note. He buries the beginning of the jeremiad in the middle of the sentence, with the words "but that most dangerous of all foes." Then he packs the warning into one (long) sentence so that the next sentence can return to the triumphalist mode. He continues, "She [the United States] has tamed the savage continent, peopled the solitude, gathered wealth untold, waxed potent, imposing, redoubtable; and now it remains for her to prove, if she can," her superiority to previous forms of social and political organization (1479). His ominous "if she can" injects doubt into the situation, as does the conditional mode of his statement in the previous sentence: the United States is "destined to a majestic future *if*" it shuns Parkman's pitfalls. The triumphalist vision of the country's future depends on the extent to which his warning is heeded.

Success in establishing U.S. superiority over the rest of the world would come only if U.S. Americans took the lessons of the past to heart. As world history textbooks repeatedly emphasized, the histories of past empires displayed the range of possible snares to which the United States might fall prey. While not usually explicitly didactic, narratives of imperial eclipse nonetheless offered a valuable opportunity for learning what to avoid—or rather, what to eradicate, given that most of the dangers had already made an appearance in U.S. society.

The various imperial eclipse narratives discussed in this book explored a series of spatiotemporal contact zones. These contact zones linked the nineteenth-century United States back and out to eighteenth-century Venice, Incan Peru, conquistadorial Peru, the Netherlands in the sixteenth century, New Netherland in the seventeenth century, and the Ojibway homeland just before the arrival of the French. These linkages resulted from the authors' disturbing realization that "world" "history" actually looked very much like the national present; the spatial and temporal (and therefore psychological) distance between the nineteenth-century United States and the fallen empires of the past had collapsed. Through their research, they began to see Venetian senators, Incan agrarianists, Spanish abolitionists and inquisitors, New Netherland settlers, and Viking explorers (or the Hiawatha-era Ojibway themselves, in Longfellow's more culturally anarchic vision) cropping up in their own society. Whig politicians, utopian socialists, immediatist abolitionists, the Know-Nothing Party, the ethnic Dutch, and sectional North-South factions seemed to reincarnate the divisive elements of past imperial societies that had destabilized them and facilitated their eclipse by other empires.

International history thus could not be disentangled from the intranational problems to which people became sensitized as a result of their contact with the past's fallen empires. U.S. Americans in the nineteenth century generally anticipated a great future for the United States, which they regarded as a nation on the rise, but many unknowns still surrounded the destiny of this relatively young, still-developing country. The advocates of world historical literacy argued that clues about the future of the nation could potentially be extrapolated from the world's past and from the outcomes that had greeted analogous endeavors undertaken in previous eras. World history might be a map of things to come. But if the early modern period was in any way an accurate predictor of how the rest of the modern period would proceed, trouble lay ahead.

Apocalypse Now

Spatiotemporal contact zones create "adjacencies between what was and what will be."[4] Although seemingly disjunctive, they bring together moments in time that resonate with each other. It is fitting, then, that I jump from 1884 to 2006, from nineteenth-century narratives of imperial eclipse to a comparable narrative produced in the twenty-first century. The global position of the United States changed significantly from the nineteenth to the twenty-first century, but we have now returned to a moment in which the spectacle of world empires being eclipsed seems to hold renewed and portentous meaning for the prospects of the nation.

"A great civilization is not conquered from without until it has destroyed itself from within." With this epigraph from historian Will Durant, Mel Gibson places his 2006 film, *Apocalypto*, in the interpretive framework of overall world history.[5] The epigraph invites the viewer to interpret Gibson's story of excess and heroism, set in the Postclassic period of the Maya just prior to the arrival of Columbus, in a context of world historical laws that govern all civilizations. In doing so, and in depicting the richness and complexity of Mayan culture only to point toward its imminent destruction by European colonization, Gibson produces an archetypal narrative of imperial eclipse.

As a culture producer, Mel Gibson shares many aspects of the social and artistic position that the nineteenth-century imperial eclipse authors had occupied. Their writing careers had a popular orientation; similarly, Gibson makes films intended for popular audiences, designed to satisfy their desire for engrossing stories. At the same time, his directorial work in the mid-2000s showed a considerable dedication to historical research, most noticeably in his efforts to use linguistic authenticity as a method of re-creating and reembodying the past: the actors in his 2004 *The Passion of the Christ* speak Aramaic, Latin, and Hebrew, and the actors in *Apocalypto* speak Yucatec Maya (a parallel to Longfellow's approach in *The Song of Hiawatha*, even though Gibson's consistent subtitling arguably effaces linguistic otherness more completely than Longfellow's gestures of translation). Although detailed analogies between the sociopolitical perspectives of Gibson and the nineteenth-century authors break down given the vast differences between the sociopolitical landscapes of the nineteenth and twenty-first centuries, Gibson holds generally conservative views, as the imperial eclipse authors also did. His conservatism lends itself to a reactionary attitude toward the supposed declensions of the present moment, a mindset that fits well with the pessimistic implications of an imperial eclipse narrative.

Narratives of imperial eclipse seem to emerge at moments when the trajectory of the U.S. empire is an explicit topic of cultural discussion, whether on the upswing in the nineteenth century or the downslide in the twenty-first. Like the nineteenth-century works discussed in this book, *Apocalypto* stages the eclipse of a complicated civilization, one doomed to decline but nonetheless offering compelling spectacles of heroism and vice. And just as nineteenth-century narratives of imperial eclipse were a vehicle for reflecting on the contemporary state of U.S. culture, so, too, does *Apocalypto* provide Gibson with a forum for commentary on the state of the United States today.

As William Hickling Prescott did before him, Gibson draws inspiration from the indigenous history of the Americas and the epochal shift symbolized by the arrival of the Spanish. The film tells the story of Jaguar Paw, a Maya from a forest tribe whose village is attacked by raiders from the nearby Mayan city. The raiders take the villagers hostage and bring them to the city to serve as human sacrifices in rituals supposedly intended to address the environmental and social ills plaguing the Maya and manifestly on display in the city. Jaguar Paw escapes from his captors and is chased through the forest as he attempts to return to the wife and child he left hidden in the village—which he in the end successfully manages to do. The chase culminates on the beach, where Jaguar Paw and his final two pursuers find Columbus and his band disembarking from their ships. This scene, and its role within the film as a whole, is the key to understanding *Apocalypto* as a narrative of imperial eclipse.

In the DVD commentary on the film, Gibson discusses this scene with his co-writer, Farhad Safinia. Safinia remarks,

> "So this is where the story started really, isn't it?"
>
> "Yeah, it's the first thing I thought of," Gibson replies.
>
> "You said it as a joke. What if there's this guy, being chased by ten really bad guys, and he comes out onto this beach and he collapses and he's exhausted and he looks up—and there's Columbus. And we laughed and thought, that's really funny."[6]

The effect of this "joke" derives not so much from its humor (the onset of European colonization really isn't a laughing matter) as from its unexpected lurch from one kind of story to another. The internal narrative structure of the chase scene,[7] which focuses solely on whether or not the pursued can escape the pursuer, gives way to a sudden additional problem: to what is the pursued escaping? This broadening of narrative concern involves more than just the pursued leaping out of the frying pan and into the fire, more than just a continuation and intensification of the *individual*'s struggle with threatening forces. Columbus poses a challenge not only to the pursued but also to the pursuers. The latter are suddenly yanked from their position of narrative power into a position of vulnerability that they share with the former object of their chase. The chase—the reasons behind it, the outcome of it, the whole system of power in which the pursuers control and dominate the landscape from which the pursued must flee (the pursued runs because he or she does not have the power to stay and fight)—is narratively superseded when the locus of power shifts to a third party, and the main agon is revealed as a struggle taking place between the pursuer/pursued and the third party.

I say that the agon "is revealed" rather than "becomes" because the struggle was never *not* with Columbus. At the local level, the syntax of a joke dictates that the punch line be predetermined, and that the material preceding it exist solely to set up the punch line. Syntactically, then, Columbus was there the whole time. This message is reinforced by the staging and camera movement in the beach scene. The camera faces Jaguar Paw and his pursuers as they burst from the forest; in a 180-degree pan, the camera then turns to face the water—and the Spanish. They have dropped anchor and launched shore boats, so Columbus has clearly already been there for some time. His presence remained undetected simply because all focus was directed toward the chase. The camera movement therefore literalizes the broadening of vision and perspective that makes visible the wider historical context, always there but not recognized until then.

Gibson's "joke" itself becomes the punch line of the entire film; the entire film is designed to lead up to this moment and make it meaningful. The Columbus scene comes at the end of the movie, but according to Safinia, this is "where the story started." The ending is therefore a foregone conclusion (because it was in fact the starting point), especially since both the filmmakers and audience know that Columbus did come, and that any representation of a so-called pre-Columbian civilization necessarily presages his arrival.

Buttressing what we may call the historical joke syntax of the film is its constant emphasis on prophecy. The title immediately conveys this, because the primary meaning of *apocalypse* (from the Greek word for "uncover" or "disclose") is "prophecy" or "revelation." From its association with the biblical book of Revelation, which predicts the end of the world, *apocalypse* has also come to suggest a cataclysmic event. The film therefore is both a tale of the end of a world and a piece of prophecy continuously predicting that end. And, as Gibson suggests with his repeated extrafilmic comparisons between Mayan and contemporary U.S. culture, it might also be predicting similar ends for similar cultures.

In addition to presenting itself as prophecy, *Apocalypto* also thematizes prophecy within the story. Early in the film, before the raiders attack the village, the villagers hold a communal celebration at which a wizened elder relates "The Myth of the Man's Sadness."[8] In it, the creatures of the earth give many gifts to Man to alleviate his sadness but he remains unsatisfied. Though the villagers live in Edenic harmony with the natural world, this tale foreshadows the environmental depredation wreaked by the Mayan city dwellers' practices, an aspect of Mayan culture that Gibson, in interviews about the film, has equated with contemporary abuse of the environment. Though not explicitly presented as a prophecy, this tale thus functions to set up a predominant theme of the movie and make its later appearance a narrative inevitability.

A similar narrative inevitability flows from the film's explicit figure of prophecy: a dying girl whom the raiders meet as they cart the captives to the city. She asks for help and is callously pushed away by the raiders. She then transforms from the normal, sick child that she initially appears to be into an oracle with an apocalyptic prophecy (that this prophecy can be read as a curse in retaliation for the raiders' callousness supports the morally problematic argument of the film's epigraph: the internal evils of the Mayan civilization, symbolized here by the raiders' heartless indifference to the suffering of the poor and the sick, made it susceptible to outside attack and thus caused its downfall).[9] In a speech that elliptically but precisely lays out the events of the rest of the film, she says of the raiders' chase to recapture Jaguar Paw that "the one he takes you to will cancel the sky and scratch out the earth. Scratch you out. And end your world. He's with us now. Day will be like night and the man jaguar will lead you to your end." "Day will be like night" refers to the literal eclipse that occurs during the sacrifice scene but also points to the civilizational eclipse of the Maya, a broader meaning suggested by the centrality of eclipse imagery to the film's advertising. An eclipse figures prominently in the trailer and the one-sheet (the advertising poster) and is in fact worked into the "c" of *Apocalypto* in visual renderings of the title. The cataclysmic "apocalypse" of the title, the end of the Mayan world, comes in the form of an eclipse of the Maya by Europeans.

As the immediate agent of this civilizational eclipse, Columbus and his role in destroying the "pre-Columbian" world ("the one he takes you to will . . . end your world") are ever present in the film's worldview. The oracle's statement "He's with us now" refers both to Jaguar Paw, who is literally with the group when it meets this girl, and to Columbus. Given that the film's action covers only a few days, Columbus may well already be literally at the coast and therefore "with us now." But certainly the prophecy (along with our knowledge of world history and of his imminent arrival in the Americas) ensures his figurative presence as well. As the villagers return from their tapir hunt at the beginning of the film, a lingering shot of the empty beach framed by trees and vines foreshadows a similar shot at the end of the film, when the Spanish ships will be visible. Thus even when the beach is empty, its emptiness signifies that it will soon be otherwise.

The constant emphasis on prophecy and foreshadowing therefore ensures that the whole film proceeds from "where the story started"—that is, the end. As in a joke, the lead-up to the ending—in this case, the entire story—is shaped and given meaning by the narrative punch line. But the simplicity of this structure is complicated by a series of false prophecies in the story, symptoms of a counterimpulse in the narrative.

As he presides over the human sacrifice, the high priest acknowledges the scourges afflicting Mayan society (drought, crop failure, plagues) but proclaims, "Great people of the banner of the sun, I say we are strong. We are a people of destiny, destined to be the masters of time, destined to be nearest to the gods." Because the film characterizes the high priest as a political operator who manipulates the spectacle of sacrifice and the eclipse to control the crowd (similar to Cooper's corrupt Venetian politicians who pacify the restive masses by stoking their jingoism), we can dismiss his obviously false prophecy as political spin, lies designed to flatter the people's hubris and distract them from serious social problems. But not all of the film's false prophecies can be so easily dismissed, because they come from more virtuous characters.

Early in the film, Flint Sky, Jaguar Paw's father, introduces himself to the leader of a tribe fleeing through their area: "I am Flint Sky. I have hunted this forest from the day I came of age. My father hunted this forest with me and before me. . . . He [Jaguar Paw] hunts this forest with me. He will hunt it with his son after I am gone." He further emphasizes lineage as a source of comfort and guidance when he counsels Jaguar Paw to reject the fear emanating from the passing tribe: "At first light we will gather with the elders at the sacred hill of our fathers. There we will call on their spirits to guide us." The vision of an uninterrupted lineage and an unchanging relationship to the land is of course undermined by the raiders' attack, in which Flint Sky is killed and Jaguar Paw captured and separated from his son and pregnant wife. These statements could serve merely as a tragic commentary on the idyllic world that the iniquity of Mayan city life destroys, because Flint Sky makes them in ignorance of the impending calamity.

But Jaguar Paw repeats the sentiment when he escapes back to the forest. He jumps over a waterfall to avoid recapture and shouts up at his pursuers: "I am Jaguar Paw, son of Flint Sky. My father hunted this forest before me. . . . This is my forest. And my sons will hunt it with their sons after I am gone."[10] Certainly, this prophecy cannot be fulfilled in any straightforward way, because the village with its attendant way of life has been destroyed. Furthermore, European conquest will disrupt and largely extinguish indigenous modes of life. Jaguar Paw's boast therefore constitutes a false prophecy in the broad historical context announced by the film's epigraph.

In the narrower narrative context of the chase, however, the prophecy does prove true, at least to a certain extent. Jaguar Paw asserts his relationship to and effective ownership of the land by using his native knowledge of the forest to outwit his pursuers, especially when he kills his main pursuer with a tapir trap. Furthermore, the main sentimental plot of the film stresses the importance of lineage in Jaguar Paw's heroic and ultimately successful efforts to return and rescue his son and wife, who has in the meantime given birth to their second son. At the end of the film, the reunited family turns away from the Europeans on the beach and (vanishing west like Longfellow's Hiawatha) disappears into the forest, where perhaps the film would like to suggest that some semblance of the Edenic village life can be re-created on the strength of their familial bond.[11] So in the outcome of the chase and in the possible future that awaits Jaguar Paw and his sons, the film in some ways does authorize and ratify his prophecy. The emotional and narrative emphasis placed on his story creates a counterweight pulling against the joke structure of the film, because Jaguar Paw cannot be easily shrugged off as a mere vehicle of the world historical joke.

Certainly, though, the ability of one man and his family to elude pursuers and re-create a prelapsarian lifestyle is irrelevant in the broader historical context of the Spanish conquest. It would not have mattered to the primary agon of the narrative, which I have argued is the impending conflict between the Maya and Europeans, if Jaguar Paw had been captured and killed and his wife and son drowned in the cenote in which they were trapped. The "real story" only appears to be about these individuals.

The film's one-sheet demonstrates this (see figure 1). One might easily assume that the central figure in the image—who is backlit by a partial eclipse and the torches held by the figures behind him and whose face is therefore in shadow—is Jaguar Paw, ostensibly the main character. Because this figure occupies the foreground alone (as typically only a main character would) and has one foot lifted as if actively running away from those behind him, head tilted down and to one side as if checking how closely he is pursued, he naturally suggests Jaguar Paw. But the backlighting (perhaps intentionally) obscures the true identity of this figure, who can be correctly identified from his tattooing, hair style, and, symbolically, his bloody knife: this is one of the raiders, Middle Eye, the most vicious persecutor of Jaguar Paw. The choice to feature Middle Eye so prominently focuses attention primarily on the viciousness and brutality of Mayan society, which the epigraph argues will make it vulnerable to outside attack, a consequence implied by the visual impression that Middle Eye himself is being chased. He is a figure of historical vulnerability, whatever power he may have over Jaguar Paw within the narrative of the chase. In the visual argument of the one-sheet, then, Jaguar Paw's absence from the image manifests his irrelevance to the real story, even though the image and the wider story initially appear to center around him.

The poster's tagline—"No one can outrun their destiny"—functions similarly. It seems to describe Jaguar Paw, who spends much of the film attempting to outrun things. But because he does eventually outrun his pursuers, this phrase actually more aptly describes Middle Eye and the Maya more generally, who cannot escape their civilizational destiny: to be conquered. In this context, the grammatical error is felicitous, because no "one" individual can escape "their" (the Mayan) collective destiny. Despite the narrative investment in particular characters, they will all be subsumed en masse into the drama of Spanish imperialism.

Nonetheless, the film does devote the majority of its duration and emotional energy to the story of Jaguar Paw as an individual. This distracts from the real story and provides a counterweight to it, but in a way that nonetheless serves a crucial structural purpose for that real story. The whole film must set up the Columbus

punch line without becoming boringly obvious. The audience must therefore be diverted away from the message of the epigraph and the oracle's prophecy in order for the scene on the beach to have dramatic impact. The main chase sequence performs this pivotal narrative distraction.

The elaborate city sequence of the film fulfills a similar function. The intricately rendered urban landscape and city society absorb audience attention into its details and away from the broader perspective offered by the oracle just prior to the city scenes. The hemming in of perspective is echoed and effected by the crowded frames, in which bodies often press close to the camera and provide a visceral experience of urban claustrophobia with its accompanying limitation of vision. The city's energy, chaos, and profusion engross the viewer as they engross our proxies in the scene—Jaguar Paw and his fellow captives. In their experience and that of the viewer, class hierarchies dominate urban life. People from the upper classes recline languidly, eat to excess, treat servants rudely, and travel about in litters, while people from the lower classes steal food, desperately hawk cheap wares, or prostitute themselves. These cues direct the audience to consider the relationship between the rich and the poor within Mayan society, thereby tending to avert audience attention away from the place of the Maya within a wider world, a world in which Mayan rich and poor will suffer equally at the hands of the Spanish. In the same way, the captives experience the city as a manifestation of the power of the Mayan rulers, before which they are helpless. This again obscures the vulnerability of these rulers themselves to the outside threat that Columbus embodies. In dwelling on the details of Mayan city life, then, the film sets the audience up for its lurch back into the Columbus frame of reference, and in addition establishes the stakes of that frame of reference by illustrating the complexity and richness of the culture that Spanish colonization will largely destroy.

But this significant investment of narrative focus in Mayan society on its own terms does potentially endanger the punch line if the Mayan world ultimately proves more compelling or meaningful than the world of European colonization. If we become too invested in Jaguar Paw's individual story and heroism, then we will not condone the destruction of the Maya as the film's epigraph in effect encourages us to do.

Furthermore, we will also rebel against the epigraph if we become too invested in Mayan vices, a distinct possibility given Mel Gibson's efforts to draw parallels between Postclassic Mayan and contemporary U.S. society. In press for the film, Gibson repeatedly emphasized modern corollaries to Mayan sins. He told *Time Magazine*, "The fearmongering we depict in this film reminds me a little of President Bush and his guys."[12] In the DVD commentary on the film, Gibson refers to the high priest as a "politician": "Who does he remind you of? Which congressman?"[13] Safinia told *Time*, "The parallels between the environmental imbalance and corruption of values that doomed the Maya and what's happening to our own civilization are eerie."[14] In the most controversial of these statements, Gibson told the press, "The precursors to a civilization that's going under are the same, time and time again. . . . What's human sacrifice if not sending guys off to Iraq for no reason? . . . I don't mean to be a doomsday guy, but the Mayan calendar does end in 2012, boys and girls. Have fun!"[15]

In dwelling on the details of Mayan society, then, Gibson comes to a newly vivid awareness of the social and political ills affecting the United States today (just as the Venetians sensitized Cooper to the tyrannical tendencies of oligarchical government, the Peruvians sensitized Prescott to the dangers of socialism and abolitionism, the Spanish sensitized Motley's reviewers to the rise of religious intolerance, the New Netherland Dutch sensitized Irving to ethnic intractability, and the Ojibway and Dacotah sensitized Longfellow to sectional conflict). Although Gibson halfheartedly disavows "doomsday" thinking, the epigraph to his film clearly argues that civilizations as rotten as he depicts the Mayan one are susceptible to outside conquest. *Apocalypto* therefore participates in a currently widespread U.S. cultural anxiety:[16] that the country's days of global hegemony are over, and the self-delusive fantasy of U.S. power denies the reality of a world bristling with formidable economic and military threats and various empires poised to eclipse us.

Notes

Introduction

1. Willard, *Universal History in Perspective*, iii, 526, v; *Willard's Historic Guide*, 3.

2. David Levin similarly argues that the Romantic historians such as Prescott and Motley attempted to inculcate "contact with the life, the vital feeling of the Past" in their works (*History as Romantic Art*, 8).

3. Whelpley, *Historical Compend*, 1:157. This quotation is from the 1806–7 edition. In later editions, retitled *Compend of History*, a typo replaced the word *form* with *term* in this sentence.

4. Washington Irving even uses the label of "empire" to refer to a colony, New Netherland, which he satirically transforms into a great state. The only civilization to which I apply the term *empire* anachronistically is the Ojibway; nineteenth-century U.S. Americans bent over backward to avoid characterizing North American Indian societies as developed and stable in ways that would militate against removal policies, as the denomination "empire" surely would. But Longfellow's representation of the Ojibway conforms to the same narrative pattern followed by other chroniclers of great early modern states. On the ideological distinction made between North American Indians and the Incan and Aztec "empires," see Wertheimer, *Imagined Empires*, 13.

5. Callcott, *History in the United States, 1800–1860*, vii. In 1794, John Payne could write that "nothing upon the plan of" his *Epitome of History*, an overview of world history, "has yet been attempted" (iv). In contrast, T. M. Merriman admitted in 1860, "It would seem almost superfluous to make any addition to the numerous works already published on the great subject of Universal History" but justified his adding to this number by arguing that "the vastness of the subject is such, and its importance being equally great, we may rest assured that its merits have not yet been fully set forth" (*The Trail of History*, xxix). On the place of history in nineteenth-century U.S. culture, see Callcott; Baym, *American Women Writers and the Work of History, 1790–1860*; Cheng, *The Plain and Noble Garb of Truth*; Pfitzer, *Picturing the Past* and *Popular History and the Literary Marketplace, 1840–1920*; and Van Tassel, *Recording America's Past*.

6. Authors who mention in their prefaces that the rise and fall of empires constitutes a key component of world history's interest and value include Joseph Emerson Worcester in his widely used world history textbook, *Elements of History* (iv), and Samuel Griswold Goodrich, author of the popular Peter Parley books for children, in *Peter Parley's Common School History* (9). See also Barber, *Elements of General History*, 6; Pike, *Intellectual Chronology*, 5; and Robbins, *The World Displayed*, 7. This list does not mention any of the many authors who do not use the phrase explicitly in their prefaces but who organize their material according to the rise and fall of empires pattern and thereby conform to the standard format for books of this type, which proceed chronologically from the creation of the world forward through the rise and fall of each major world empire.

7. Choate and Brown, *The Works of Rufus Choate*, 2:422.

8. *The Gladiator* opened on September 26, 1831 (Bird completed it in April of that year as a submission to Forrest's annual playwriting competition). Nat Turner's rebellion began on August 22, 1831, and Turner remained at large until October. On the multiple aspects of the play's contemporary relevance, see Richards, headnote to *The Gladiator*, 167–68. All quotations from the play will refer to Bird, *The Gladiator* (hereafter cited parenthetically in the text).

9. Walt Whitman once observed that *The Gladiator* "is as full of 'Abolitionism' as an egg is of meat." On the other hand, Curtis Dahl argues that while Bird's "Thracian rebels are pictured as noble and generous," his correspondence indicates that he did not view slave revolt in the United States so favorably. See Whitman, "*The Gladiator*—Mr. Forrest—Acting," 69; Dahl, *Robert Montgomery Bird*, 59.

10. Edwin Forrest marked this speech to be cut from the script, so audiences may not have heard it, but Bird clearly did intend for the eventual decline of Rome to be part of the meaning of the play's conclusion.

11. In this vein, John Carlos Rowe has written of "the diverse inter- and intracultural areas of the new American Studies" (*The New American Studies*, 4).

12. This attempt frequently occurs in discussions of wealthy, white male writers, because separating the transnationalist practices of women and people of color from their intranational identities and domestic politics never seems feasible, as indeed it shouldn't for white men either. On "pluralism" and transnationalism as separate "branches" of scholarship, see Messmer, "Toward a Declaration of Interdependence," 50–51. Paul Giles calls these scholarly emphases "competing paradigms" ("Transnationalism and Classic American Literature," 63). For the critique of "multiculturalism" as a potentially simplistic and reactionary "pluralism"—which implies that true political progressiveness can more likely be pursued with transnationalist than with multiculturalist scholarship, which in turn implies a competitive division between the two—see Rowe, *The New American Studies*, 7–10; and Kadir, "Introduction: America and Its Studies," 13–14. Colleen Glenney Boggs refers to the "myopia of this multicultural turn" of late '70s and '80s criticism (*Transnationalism and American Litera-*

ture, 7). (Interestingly, Paul Giles, one of the major spokespeople for transnationalist literary studies, notes the opposite problem: that international scholars can lack sensitivity to aspects of U.S. multiculture such as class; see *Virtual Americas*, 3–4.) For a rejection of the bifurcation between transnationalism and multiculturalism, see, for example, Ngai, "Transnationalism and the Transformation of the 'Other,'" 59–60, 64. Emory Elliott acknowledges that "cultural diversity in the United States" and "the internationalization of U.S. Studies" are "two directions, often seen as being opposed," but he argues for their intertwining, especially given the long history of transnationalist methodologies in ethnic studies, and advocates "explor[ing] the transnational without undermining the political and institutional stakes of" African American, Latina/o, Chicana/o, and Native American studies ("Diversity in the United States and Abroad," 9, 9–10).

13. On "subnational," see Dimock, "Scales of Aggregation," 226.

14. I am therefore practicing what might be called "United States studies." Janice Radway suggested this as a possible new name for American studies in her 1998 American Studies Association Presidential Address, "with the proviso that analysis of the U.S. would have to foreground its relationships to the rest of the world as well as to non-national communities" ("What's in a Name?" 18). Similarly, Gregory Jay advocates teaching "Writing in the United States" in lieu of "American Literature" ("The End of 'American' Literature"). And John Carlos Rowe suggests "U.S. Studies" as a name for a field focused on the United States that nonetheless acknowledges the hemispheric scope of the term *American* (*The New American Studies*, 53). This sensibility motivates my use of "U.S. Americans" throughout this book to describe people living in the United States.

15. Bender, "Introduction: Historians, the Nation, and the Plenitude of Narratives," 12, 10. Wai Chee Dimock's notion of a "subset" within a "set" also describes the relationship that I envisage between U.S. studies and transnationalism studies ("Introduction: Planet and America, Set and Subset," 3).

16. Damrosch, *What Is World Literature?* 27. Donald Pease critiques Dimock's theory of planetary literature on just this point: that she fails to account accurately for the subject position of those whom she drafts into the matrix of planetary literature ("The Extraterritoriality of the Literature for Our Planet").

17. On this divide, see Rowe, "Nineteenth-Century United States Literary Culture and Transnationality," 78; and Dimock, "Introduction: Planet and America, Set and Subset," 1–2. Dimock herself tends very heavily toward the utopian reading of transnationalism, as evidenced by her many references to literature's impressive ability to exceed the jurisdictional boundaries of the nation-state. For the Marxist interpretation of globalization, see, for example, the work of Immanuel Wallerstein on world-systems. On the postnational, see, for example, Habermas, *The Postnational Constellation*. On critiques of the concept of postnationalism, see Giles, *Virtual Americas*, 9–10, 20–21; Giles, "Transnationalism and Classic American Literature," 64–65; and

Rowe, "Nineteenth-Century United States Literary Culture and Transnationality," 79–80, 88. On the planetary, see Spivak, *Death of a Discipline*, esp. 72, where she discusses her sense of the difference between globalization and planetarity.

18. Rowe, *The New American Studies*, 7, 10–16.

19. Pratt, *Imperial Eyes*, 7, 8. Although her theory makes room for a temporal application, Pratt herself usually uses "contact zone" in a purely spatial sense, as a synonym for "colonial frontier" (8). Dimock has rightly pointed out the spatial bias of most theories of globalization, which "is assumed to occur along one particular axis: space"; Dimock argues for "another axis of globalization, intersecting with the horizontal but not reducible to it": time ("Planetary Time and Global Translation," 489).

20. Colleen Glenney Boggs also argues for this interpretation of the contact zone (*Transnationalism and American Literature*, 30–31).

21. Dimock, *Through Other Continents*, 126; "Literature for the Planet," 179.

22. Damrosch, *What Is World Literature?* 283, 164.

23. My decision to treat early modern Dutch, Ojibwan, and French territory in North America as foreign to U.S. writers also arises from my reluctance to superimpose the United States' nineteenth- and twentieth-century boundaries anachronistically back onto a period in which the Americas were organized geographically according to very different frameworks. Many scholars of colonial American literature have critiqued such temporal imperialism; see, for example, Ralph Bauer citing William Spengemann's foundational *A New World of Words* to make this argument ("Toward a Cultural Geography of Colonial American Literatures," 38–39).

24. Ramsay, *Universal History Americanised*, vol. 1, front matter, unpaginated. Library catalogues, following the Shaw-Shoemaker bibliography and database, often erroneously state that Ramsay's *History of the United States* (1819) forms volumes 1–3 of *Universal History Americanised* and offer only volumes 4–9. In reality, the volumes of *Universal History Americanised* are numbered 1–9 and all deal with world history; the *History of the United States* has a separate volume series numbered 1–3. Together they form the twelve volumes mentioned on the title page of *Universal History Americanised*.

25. Ramsay writes, for instance, that the "obscure, broken and dubious annals of Abyssinia [now Ethiopia], an uncivilized nation, which has never had any influence on the politics, and scarcely any connexion to the commerce of the United States, cannot be very interesting to the American reader. Our view of it, therefore, will be short" (*Universal History Americanised*, 9:165).

26. Ramsay's engagement with world history occurs within a spatiotemporal contact zone structured by the "highly asymmetrical relations of domination and subordination" that so frequently characterize a contact zone, according to Mary Louise Pratt (*Imperial Eyes*, 7). On the topic of "temporal colonization," Wai Chee Dimock argues that "any domestication [of an alien segment of time] we undertake is bound to be limited, limited by the paradox of these texts being ours and not ours, both in

and not in our hands" (*Through Other Continents*, 132). But the degree of domestication will no doubt vary with the intensity of the effort made at domestication. Ramsay exerts a great deal of effort to make the world an ideological extension of home.

27. Damrosch, *What Is World Literature?* 133.

28. Lowenthal, *The Past Is a Foreign Country*. Lowenthal takes this phrase from L. P. Hartley's 1953 novel, *The Go-between*.

29. For the role of the classics and the classical world in U.S. culture, see, for example, Reinhold, *Classica Americana*; and more recently, Shields, *American Aeneas*; and Winterer, *The Culture of Classicism*.

30. Willard, *Universal History in Perspective*, 291, 291–92.

31. U.S. historians at this point knew little about China's lengthy history, and what they did know conflicted with the biblical dating of the world, and they therefore often explicitly discounted it. Textbook writer Elizabeth Palmer Peabody noted that Chinese historians' claims had been discredited by Western scholars, writing that the "history of China has very little relation with the general progress of the race. It has never been connected with the nations which are to us *the world*" (*The Polish-American System of Chronology*, 131). Although rarely so explicitly acknowledged, "*the world*" of nineteenth-century U.S. interest in world history always represented only a portion of the planet as a whole. On this dynamic, see Damrosch, *What Is World Literature?* 12–13.

32. Willard, *Universal History in Perspective*, 292.

33. DeGuzmán, *Spain's Long Shadow*. DeGuzmán argues that in playing itself off against the idea of Spain, "Anglo-American culture, despite its fragmentation and fragility, ascends toward a seemingly unified and coherent imperial identity" (xvii). In contrast, I argue that the idea of Spain and other failed empires often convinced U.S. Americans precisely of their nation's "fragmentation and fragility."

34. For examples of one-nation studies with a substantial nineteenth-century emphasis, see DeGuzmán, *Spain's Long Shadow*; Martin and Person, *Roman Holidays*; Thurin, *The American Discovery of the Norse*; Trafton, *Egypt Land*; and Wasserman, *Exotic Nations*. This list does not include the many works that deal with the connections between American literature and England, France, or Germany, countries long understood to be key cultural interlocutors of the United States. Studies that have attempted to address broader swathes of cultural engagement and interlocution have often adopted the rubric of a particular geographic and imaginative region, for example, the Americas, the Orient, or the Pacific Rim; see, among others, Brickhouse, *Transamerican Literary Relations and the Nineteenth-Century Public Sphere*; Schueller, *U.S. Orientalisms*; and Huang, *Transpacific Imaginations*. Aside from the Pacific Rim scholarship, these regions tend to create critical divisions between the Eastern and Western Hemisphere, or white Europe and racialized non-Europe, divisions that this book works across. The various foreign spaces that I discuss in this book don't fit neatly into a regional model: they are neither physically contiguous nor imagina-

tively unified into a cohesive "region" by the U.S. writers who represent these spaces. Although certainly a place like Peru should really be understood in the context of the Pacific world, many of this book's foreign spaces could be categorized as members of the Atlantic world (a top-heavy Atlantic world, to be sure, with no African representation: my focus on historiography precludes sub-Saharan Africa and most of Asia, given nineteenth-century U.S. ignorance about the history of those areas). And they all occupy the "Western world," broadly understood, reflecting the Euro-American biases of most nineteenth-century U.S. Americans.

35. Callcott, *History in the United States, 1800–1860*, 92.

36. Although Peter Novick in a foundational account focuses on the late nineteenth century to discuss the origins of historiography in its modern form, I agree with Eileen Ka-May Cheng in locating the emergence of certain aspects of modern historiographical practice in early nineteenth-century U.S. writers. See Novick, *That Noble Dream*; Cheng, *The Plain and Noble Garb of Truth*, esp. 13–51.

37. On the blurring of generic boundaries in historiography of this period, see Cheng, *The Plain and Noble Garb of Truth*, 64–75.

38. Levin, *History as Romantic Art*, 3–7.

39. On the jeremiad, see Bercovitch, *The American Jeremiad*. Bercovitch analyzes discourses of national decline similar to imperial eclipse narratives but he does not focus on the role that world history played in U.S. representations of decline. He also emphasizes the consensus-building function of jeremiads, which in his analysis stress a shared, providential mission in the process of criticizing any straying from that original mission. Although I agree that sometimes "Anxiety functions . . . to excite and fortify expectations. Divisions and conflicts serve as prelude to the assertion of continuity," I would argue that Bercovitch's Fourth of July speeches hinge on nationalist consensus more fundamentally than representations of early modern world history do (146).

40. See Baym, *American Women Writers and the Work of History, 1790–1860*. See also Cheng, *The Plain and Noble Garb of Truth*, 48–51, 60–64, 111–15; and Winterer, *The Mirror of Antiquity*, esp. 138–41, 173–75.

41. Baym's chapter on world history, "History from the Divine Point of View," mainly discusses textbooks (see *American Women Writers and the Work of History, 1790–1860*, 9, 46–66). Baym writes that in this period, "there were distinctions between levels of history, whereby pietistic, didactic history was allotted to women and children, while a more secular historicism was associated with men" (66). Eileen Ka-May Cheng discusses the cultural obstacles—personal diffidence, disapprobation from male historians, the improbability of work by women being reviewed and therefore advertised—to women's production of original, scholarly historiography (*The Plain and Noble Garb of Truth*, 48–49).

42. Peabody, *First Steps to the Study of History*, 9, 2. She argues for the particular importance of female historical education: "[A]s history is the department of human knowledge which is more within the sphere of woman's attainment than any other, so

the study of it is the most important to women, and has the most direct influence in forming them for the duties peculiar to their relation in life" (12–13). Peabody here seems to be acceding to traditional gender roles, given that history can "enlighten the retirement and freedom of home" and lend "character" and "influence" to women's "conversation" (12, 13). But in a later textbook she makes an ambiguous but provocative statement about the potential for a more substantial civic role for women: "It is obvious to common sense, that where every man in the community—we had almost said every woman—has a direct influence upon the measures of government, as in our country, a general knowledge of history is absolutely necessary to the common weal" (*The Polish-American System of Chronology*, 3).

43. Peabody, *First Steps to the Study of History*, 9, 10.

44. Rowson, *Exercises in History, Chronology, and Biography, in Question and Answer*, 170.

45. See, for example, the conclusion of Emma Willard's *Universal History in Perspective*, already quoted at the beginning of this introduction; Butler, *Sketches of Universal History, Sacred and Profane*, 275; Whelpley, *Compend of History*, 2:209–10; and the ending of Francis Parkman's *Montcalm and Wolfe*, which I discuss in the conclusion. Samuel Griswold Goodrich tended to be more optimistic in his conclusions, but his 1837 *Peter Parley's Universal History, on the Basis of Geography* contains a delightfully anxiety-ridden extended metaphor comparing the U.S. government to a crumbling house (2:285–86). Nathaniel Hawthorne may have actually authored this text, although Goodrich held the copyright.

46. See Cheng, *The Plain and Noble Garb of Truth*, 36–37.

47. On the conservatism of the Whig party, see Howe, *The Political Culture of the American Whigs*, 210–37. Howe argues that Whigs embraced the economic changes wrought by the progress of capitalism but rejected attendant social changes like the decline of deference (219). As we shall see in chapter 2, Whigs certainly rejected economic innovations that challenged capitalism's hegemony.

48. See Buell, *New England Literary Culture*, 195–96; Callcott, *History in the United States, 1800–1860*, 68; and Cheng, *The Plain and Noble Garb of Truth*, 21.

49. O'Connor, *The Athens of America*; Widmer, *Young America*. O'Connor, a historian, does not produce a particularly sensitive account of nineteenth-century literature (98–110); Lawrence Buell's *New England Literary Culture* provides a more reliable regional literary history.

50. Widmer, *Young America*, 10, 12. On newness and the Whig New England/Democratic New York antagonism, see also 3–4, 10–13, 23–25, 35–44, 54–62, 90–92, 102, 110–11, 120–21. On the Whig philosophy of history, especially its combination of optimistic progressiveness and gloomy meditations on cyclical history, see Howe, *The Political Culture of the American Whigs*, 74–75. Although heavily focused on the idea of U.S. American history, J. V. Matthews's analysis of Whig attitudes toward history is also useful ("'Whig History'").

51. Widmer calls the *Knickerbocker Magazine* "the pride of New York Whiggery," on the other side of the "ideological fence [from the *Democratic Review*] within the microcosmic world of the New York literary scene" (*Young America*, 34, 121). On the Knickerbocker group, see Callow, *Kindred Spirits*; and Taft, *Minor Knickerbockers*, xiii–cx. On the contention between the Knickerbocker and Young America groups, see Bender, *New York Intellect*, 130–56; and Perry Miller, *The Raven and the Whale*, 11–117.

52. The dueling New York and New England forms of nationalism in the nineteenth century can be helpfully categorized in terms of what Julia Wright, in her analysis of Irish nationalism, labels the "inaugural" and the "antiquarian" strains. According to Wright, both forms of nationalism were "radically temporal," but inauguralists sought "to transcend the past and move forward in a new track" while antiquarians steeped themselves in the past (*Ireland, India, and Nationalism in Nineteenth-Century Literature*, 30, 31).

53. Lewis, *American Adam*, 5, 159, 160. Although he doesn't actually name Lewis, David Levin criticizes Lewis's claim that Prescott tried to "put the Past safely away in a separate place" (*History as Romantic Art*, ix).

54. On Irving's, Cooper's, Longfellow's, and Prescott's financial success—an indication of their broad regional, national, and international readerships—see Charvat, *Literary Publishing in America, 1790–1850*, 38, 44, 51–55, 66–72, 74–80. Charvat notes that history proved the most lucrative genre during this period.

55. See Bender, "Introduction: Historians, the Nation, and the Plenitude of Narratives," 5.

56. I resist the classification "antebellum" in this book because although the majority of my material originates before the Civil War, Parkman clearly partakes of the same worldview that characterized pre–Civil War world historiography. The careers of many of the authors that I discuss continue in the postbellum period; for example, Motley produces scholarship on the Dutch Republic well into the 1860s and '70s. In addition, inexorable focus on the Civil War as watershed has been critiqued as having anti-globalist intellectual underpinnings, and therefore seems particularly inappropriate for this project. See Giles, "Transnationalism and Classic American Literature," 74.

Chapter 1

1. On *The Bravo* as a Gothic novel, see Ringe, "*The Bravo*."

2. Dekker and McWilliams, *Fenimore Cooper*, 6.

3. Cooper, *A Letter to His Countrymen*, 98 (hereafter cited parenthetically in the text).

4. On the European trilogy, see Nattermann, "Ahistorical Histories." Nattermann writes that in all three novels of the trilogy, "America is the *telos* of the his-

torical process"; the books argue that "the abusive systems of Europe are eventually supplanted by the positive model of America." But although Nattermann recognizes that this "propagandistic" project does not entirely succeed, he does not discuss Cooper's doubts over whether the United States itself lived up to the "positive model of America" (275).

5. Although scholars tend to pair *The Bravo* with the other novels of the European trilogy, George Dekker characterizes *The Bravo* as *The Water-Witch*'s "companion-piece and peer" (*James Fenimore Cooper*, 134).

6. Cooper called his 1830s travelogue series *Gleanings in Europe*. On this series, see Kennedy, "Cooper's Europe and His Quarrel with America." On Cooper's Europe trip, see Spiller, *Fenimore Cooper*, 99–204.

7. James Grossman writes that although "Cooper's aim was 'a series of tales, in which American opinion should be brought to bear on European facts,'" he nonetheless sometimes "glanced at American facts to note that they were startlingly like the European" (*James Fenimore Cooper*, 77).

8. On the possibility that Cooper may have planned some carryover from *The Water-Witch* into *The Bravo*, see Schachterle, "A Long False Start."

9. Cooper, *J. Fenimore Cooper's Works*, 30. All subsequent in-text parenthetical citations for *The Bravo* refer to this edition. No up-to-date scholarly edition of *The Bravo* has yet been published, but one is forthcoming from the "Writings of James Fenimore Cooper" project (Lance Schachterle, series editor).

10. On Venice in this period, see Laven, *Venice and Venetia Under the Habsburgs, 1815–1835*.

11. On the importance of the cyclical history concept for Cooper, see Axelrad, *History and Utopia*; Kelly, *Plotting America's Past*, 45–84; and Levine, *Conspiracy and Romance*, 69–85.

12. Cooper, *The Water-Witch*, 10 (hereafter cited parenthetically in the text).

13. Cooper offers another comparison of the Naples and New York bays in his Italian travelogue. On the subject of this by-then conventional topic, Cooper wonders "[w]hat dunce first thought of instituting a comparison" between the two bays. He labels New York Bay "barely pretty," while he describes the Bay of Naples as "glorious and sublime." See Cooper and Denne, *Gleanings in Europe, Italy*, 93, 94.

14. On the Tasso villa, see Spiller, *Fenimore Cooper*, 156–57.

15. Philbrick, *James Fenimore Cooper and the Development of American Sea Fiction*, 258. For Philbrick's reading of *The Water-Witch*, see 68–83, 257–258. For a good nonmaritime reading of the novel, see Dekker, *James Fenimore Cooper*, 118–26.

16. Grossman, *James Fenimore Cooper*, 72.

17. Cole produced several paintings in 1826–27 illustrating scenes from Cooper's *Last of the Mohicans*, indicating the painter and the author's mutual engagement with each other's work.

18. Wallach, "Thomas Cole," 92–94. For the Andrew Jackson argument, see

Angela Miller, *The Empire of the Eye*, 21–64; and her "Thomas Cole and Jacksonian America." Cooper, as a committed Democrat, supported Jackson and would not have accepted the specific political message of the canvases, though he clearly respected the artistic strategy that Cole uses.

19. Quoted in Noble, *The Life and Works of Thomas Cole*, 167, 168. Cooper wrote this assessment of *The Course of Empire* in 1849; his worldview gets progressively darker in the 1830s and '40s.

20. On millennialist philosophy as the foundation of American exceptionalism, see Tuveson, *Redeemer Nation*.

21. Wood, *The Creation of the American Republic, 1776–1787*, 98, 613, 614. See also J. G. A. Pocock, who interprets republican theory as a particular "form of historicism" (*The Machiavellian Moment*, 3). On the size of U.S. territory and its relationship to republicanism, see Wood, 499–506; and Pocock, 524–45.

22. On this myth, see Pocock, *The Machiavellian Moment*, 99–102, 112–13.

23. Cooper's knowledge of eighteenth-century Venice derived largely from Pierre Daru's seven-volume 1819 *Histoire de la république de Venise*. His other sources for *The Bravo* were mainly literary. This makes *The Bravo* the least well researched of the narratives of imperial eclipse discussed in this book, given the more intensive archival approach employed by most of the other authors. However, Cooper explicitly cites Daru in *The Bravo*'s preface, indicating that he desired his readers to understand the novel as based on real historical research.

24. For a consideration of the symbolic function of setting in *The Bravo*, see Denne, "Cooper's Use of Setting in the European Trilogy."

25. On Venetian masking in the eighteenth century, see Johnson, *Venice Incognito*.

26. Cooper believed a similar form of manipulation to be at work in the censorship culture of nineteenth-century Italy. When Roman censors refused to publish *The Water-Witch* because of the line about Rome's "fallen temples and buried columns" in his cyclical history articulation, he wrote a friend, "The rogues wish to make their people think Rome is still Rome." Quoted in Philbrick and Philbrick, "Historical Introduction," xviii. See also Susan Fenimore Cooper's account of this incident in *Pages and Pictures from the Writings of James Fenimore Cooper* (230–31).

27. On this obliviousness, see also Levine, *Conspiracy and Romance*, 76.

28. For more on Cooper's often paradoxical, aristocratical Democratic politics, see Grossman, *James Fenimore Cooper*; and Parrington, *Main Currents in American Thought*, 2:222–37. Another useful biographical source is Wayne Franklin's *James Fenimore Cooper: The Early Years*. The second installment of Franklin's Cooper biography, which will cover the years discussed in this chapter, is still forthcoming.

29. On U.S.-Venetian parallels, see Levine, *Conspiracy and Romance*, 82–89, 97.

30. Bewley, "Fenimore Cooper and the Economic Age," 181, 179. Lance Schachterle concurs: "Cooper set *The Bravo* in the ancient Venetian republic, in decline in the early

eighteenth century, as a clear warning to the young American republic" ("A Long False Start," 85).

31. Bewley, "Fenimore Cooper and the Economic Age," 182.

32. See Waples, *The Whig Myth of James Fenimore Cooper*. For more on Cooper's troubled relationship to the press, see Outland, *The "Effingham" Libels on Cooper*.

33. Cooper, *The Letters and Journals of James Fenimore Cooper*, 4:461 (hereafter cited parenthetically in the text). See also Clavel, *Fenimore Cooper and His Critics*, 389–94.

34. The boldness of this assertion is somewhat undercut by the fact that Cooper made this claim for at least one other of his novels—*Home As Found*: Cooper "considered *Home As Found* to be 'the most thoroughly American in spirit' of anything he had written." See Adams, "*The Guardian of the Law,*" 122.

35. His recollection of *The Bravo*'s reception apparently upset Cooper enough to halt his autobiographical attempt; the letter fragment breaks off abruptly with this excoriation on the misconceptions of the masses.

36. For an analysis of how Cooper's narrative strategies in *The Bravo* help paint him into this corner, see Levine, *Conspiracy and Romance*, 98–101.

37. Gould, "The Man in the Claret-Coloured Coat to His Countrymen." All quotations from Gould's text are drawn from this online edition.

38. Waples, *The Whig Myth of James Fenimore Cooper*, 56–57.

39. Cooper also draws epigraphs from the Jack Cade episode of *Henry VI* for his chapters in *The Bravo* on the mob of fishermen; the epigraphs emphasize the fickleness of mobs (246, 253). Cooper had always entertained suspicions about the virtue of common people en masse, but his cynicism had grown much stronger between 1831 and 1851.

40. On Cooper's beliefs about the benefits of aristocracy, see Winters, "Fenimore Cooper or the Ruins of Time," 16–24. For an analysis of what Cooper meant by "aristocracy" and how he reconciled the seeming contradictions of his philosophy, see Axelrad, "Cooper, Aristocracy, and Capitalism."

Chapter 2

1. James Ely's description of Supreme Court chief justice John Marshall also applies to Prescott, who shared Marshall's overall political outlook: "To Marshall, property ownership both preserved individual liberty and encouraged the productive use of resources. Security of private property promoted the public interest by quickening commercial activity and thereby increasing national wealth" (*The Guardian of Every Other Right*, 63).

2. Whigs generally "attached a great deal of importance to protecting property." See Howe, *The Political Culture of the American Whigs*, 210.

3. On the centrality of Prescott's text to the culture of the conflict with Mexico, see Johanssen, *To the Halls of the Montezumas*, 150. Prescott in fact opposed the war. See Johanssen, 245–47; and Eipper, "The Canonizer De-Canonized," 420–21.

4. Critics who find Prescott complicit in the conquistadorial mentality include Aguirre, "Annihilating the Distance"; Alemán, "The Other Country"; Brading, *The First America*, 630–34; Buell, *New England Literary Culture*, 203; Clendinnen, "'Fierce and Unnatural Cruelty'"; DeGuzmán, *Spain's Long Shadow*, 76–90; Keen, *The Aztec Image in Western Thought*, 310–11, 354–63; Leask, "'The Ghost in Chapultepec'"; and Poole, "Landscape and the Imperial Subject," 112–13. Those who defend Prescott in whole or in part include Alarcón, *The Aztec Palimpsest*, 52–57; Ernest, "Reading the Romantic Past"; Gladsky, "Revolution and Renewal in Prescott's *The Conquest of Peru*"; Pearce, "Prescott's Conquests"; and Wertheimer, *Imagined Empires*, 91–132.

5. Spanish imperial action was replicated in similar forms in both locations; Prescott remarks several times that Francisco Pizarro modeled his strategies against the Incas on what Hernàn Cortés had done against the Aztecs, as when he writes in book 3 that Pizarro consciously followed the "model" and "example of his great predecessor," Cortés. See Prescott, *History of the Conquest of Mexico; and History of the Conquest of Peru*, 897. All subsequent in-text parenthetical citations, for either history, refer to this edition. For examples of critics who arguably treat Prescott's representation of Peru as identical to or as a mere extension of his representation of Mexico, see Pearce, "Prescott's Conquests"; Wertheimer, *Imagined Empires*; and Jaksić, *The Hispanic World and American Intellectual Life, 1820–1880*, 155–60. Even Prescott himself sometimes espoused this interpretation, especially when he marketed *The Conquest of Peru* to potential publishers, whom he assured that "all who have the one work may be expected to become purchasers of the other, as a pendant to it." See Prescott, *The Correspondence of William Hickling Prescott, 1833–1847*, 614.

6. When Prescott was writing *The Conquest of Peru*, the United States did have one major economic interest in a Peruvian resource: guano (bird droppings)—a wondrously efficacious fertilizer in abundant supply on islands off Peru's west coast. See Gootenberg, *Imagining Development*; and Skaggs, *The Great Guano Rush*. Prescott remarks in *The Conquest of Peru* that the accomplished farmers of Incan Peru "made great use of *guano*, the valuable deposit of sea-fowl, that has attracted so much attention, of late, from the agriculturalists both of Europe and of our own country" (800).

7. Manthorne, *Tropical Renaissance*, 4. For the Monroe Doctrine and U.S. attitudes toward the newly formed Latin American republics, see 34–35; and Gretchen Murphy, *Hemispheric Imaginings*.

8. For articulations of a northerly focus in two seminal works of Americas criticism, see Brickhouse, *Transamerican Literary Relations and the Nineteenth-Century Public Sphere*, 8; and Gruesz, *Ambassadors of Culture*, xi. Other important contributions to Americas studies include Chevigny and Laguardia, *Reinventing the Americas*;

Belknap and Fernández, *José Martí's "Our America"*; and Levander and Levine, *Hemispheric American Studies.*

9. Prescott's representation of Incan Peru corresponds with modern scholarly consensus in some respects but not others. For example, María Rostworowski de Diez Canseco labels the various preconquest Peruvian economic systems "redistributive" but also argues that although "Inca organization was admired by Europeans and praised as a kind of utopia," Incan stockpiling of goods did not generally serve "humanitarian ends" (*History of the Inca Realm*, 202). Some of Prescott's sources expressed the utopian economic interpretation, and he reacts strongly against it, criticizing the "expressions of admiration" of early European visitors and later commentators such as Gian Rinaldo Carli, an eighteenth-century Italian economist whose "fancy had colored" his sense of "public prosperity and private happiness under the rule of the Incas" (818, 819). But Prescott also clearly believed his sources' basic assertion about the Incan government's effective provision for the people's welfare.

10. According to William Charvat, Prescott "believed that the indigence and distress of the poor, the handicapped, and the unfit were best ameliorated by private charity," but he also "protested against the kind of private charity which robs the individual of his sense of personal dignity" ("Prescott's Political and Social Attitudes," 330). For U.S. philanthropic practices in the nineteenth century, and literary representations of them, see Bergman and Bernardi, *Our Sisters' Keepers*; Bremner, *From the Depths*; Jones, *American Hungers*; McCarthy, *American Creed*; Rothman, *The Discovery of the Asylum*; and Ryan, *The Grammar of Good Intentions.*

11. Charvat, "Prescott's Political and Social Attitudes," 330.

12. In discussions of Poor Law reform, many in the United States expressed the fear that certain forms of state-sponsored charity could encourage dependence and permanent pauperism in people who would otherwise have the incentive to work hard and remain self-sufficient. For the ways in which this attitude buttressed capitalist free-market labor ideologies, see Glickstein, "Pressures from Below."

13. Kagan, "Prescott's Paradigm," 429; Charvat, "Prescott's Political and Social Attitudes," 329.

14. For this aspect of biographical information, see Charvat and Kraus, *William Hickling Prescott*, xv. For other biographical accounts of Prescott, see Darnell, *William Hickling Prescott*; Gardiner, *William Hickling Prescott*; Ogden, *William Hickling Prescott*; Peck, *William Hickling Prescott*; Ticknor, *Life of William Hickling Prescott*; and Stanley T. Williams, *The Spanish Background of American Literature*, 78–121.

15. Levin, *History as Romantic Art*, 41. See also Howe, *The Political Culture of the American Whigs*, 191–92.

16. Of course, Prescott also notes that the Incas "allow[ed] no man, however humble, to act for himself. . . . No Peruvian was too low for the fostering vigilance of the government" (790). For Prescott, Incan despotism effectively negated Incan benevolence.

17. William Hickling Prescott's father, William Prescott, did face some economic hardship in his youth due to inherited indebtedness. Through advantageous marriage, career choice, and investments, William Prescott secured a place in the wealthy elite, and his son the historian may well have had his example in mind when extolling the possibilities of advancement in U.S. society, although William Prescott (a Harvard graduate and son of a Revolutionary War hero) certainly hadn't begun on the lowest rung of society. See Gardiner, *William Hickling Prescott*, 9–10.

18. Prescott, "Transcribed Correspondence, 1834–1850," letter dated December 28, 1848. On Whig respect for the lessons of the past, see Howe, *The Political Culture of the American Whigs*, 75.

19. The state of his eyes (Prescott was mostly blind for the purposes of reading and writing) prevented him from traveling to the archives of Europe and Mexico to study the manuscripts that he regarded as essential to writing his histories. He therefore cultivated a network of diplomats and scholars who obtained material for him, Gayangos foremost among them. See Charvat and Kraus, *William Hickling Prescott*, xxxiv–xxxvi, lvii–lviii. Most of the Prescott biographies, as well as much of the Prescott textual criticism, discuss at length Prescott's visual disability and his compensations for it, especially his use of a noctograph, a writing aid for the blind.

20. Prescott, *Unpublished Letters to Gayangos in the Library of the Hispanic Society of America*, 78.

21. Prescott, *The Correspondence of William Hickling Prescott, 1833–1847*, 519, 513.

22. In contrast to Karl Marx's reaction to the European revolutions, as expressed in his 1848 *Communist Manifesto*, the threat of class warfare—of the "millions" rising up to force a change on the wealthy, propertied community—seems not to loom large on Prescott's horizons.

23. Lause, *Young America*, 3.

24. Scott, *In Pursuit of Happiness*, 58. Other forms of property did gain much more importance in this period, but "land remained an extremely important form of property," and thus stayed for northerners conceptually yoked with "property"; see Alexander, *Commodity and Propriety*, 130.

25. In a later section dealing with Peruvian agriculture, Prescott remarks again on the Incas' "remarkable provisions for distributing the land in equal shares among the people" (798).

26. Hazewell, "Agrarianism as a Term of Reproach," 25.

27. Ibid.

28. For the relationship between the National Reform Association and utopian socialists, see Lause, *Young America*, 29–33. Marx created the now-standard label "utopian socialism," but nineteenth-century adherents to this philosophy tended to label it "Associationism," because of its emphasis on small "associations" of people living communally and laboring collectively.

29. Matthiessen, *American Renaissance*, viii.

30. On Brook Farm, see Delano, *Brook Farm*; and Francis, *Transcendental Utopias*. See also Nathaniel Hawthorne's *The Blithedale Romance*, based loosely on his experiences at Brook Farm; he discusses the relationship between his novel and the Brook Farm "Socialist Community" in his preface (38). David Levin notes that "Parkman scorned 'the she-philosophers' of Brook Farm and Prescott and Motley had little more respect for them" (*History as Romantic Art*, 26).

31. Guarneri, *The Utopian Alternative*, 63, 5. Utopian socialists like Fourier did not propose such radical critiques of capitalism as communists did. Their communities often retained a system of personal property but endeavored to allow all their members to own some portion of the means of production (see 9–10, 107, 127, 139).

32. Hobsbawm, *The Age of Revolution*, 304.

33. Guarneri, *The Utopian Alternative*, 61, 67.

34. Gardiner, *William Hickling Prescott*, 145–46.

35. A letter Prescott wrote on October 28, 1836, worries over the popular spirit of "speculation" (10–11). But in letters on January 6 and March 30 of 1837, he blames the crisis on Jackson and Van Buren's economic policies, a typical Whig move. On May 13, 1837, he describes being in the financial "hurricane," as the banks suspend payment and some begin to fail (19–20). A letter of April 21, 1838, mentions the continuing economic "terror" (28). During a brief period of economic recovery in 1838–39, Prescott writes hopefully of the upturn: "Everything promises, and many things pay well. . . . The fact is we are so young and healthy that we soon throw off the troubles and diseases that would prostrate an old and debilitated state" (48). But on April 4, 1839, he writes to the same correspondent of the country having been left "a little impaired" by the recent "rough times" (63). In April 1840, he discusses the failure of the United States Bank, the worthlessness of some of his own stock, and stocks being down and spirits being low in Boston. On July 29, 1840, he bemoans the "rotten state" of the U.S. economic system (144). Prescott in his penchant for economic optimism claims on January 1, 1841, that "[t]imes are brightening here very much" (191), but four months later he writes that "the wheels of business stick fast again in the old slough of despond" (219). On November 30, 1843, he more accurately diagnosed that the "country seems to be reviving rapidly from [its economic] prostration" (412). Buoyed by this state of affairs, Prescott begins work on *The Conquest of Peru* in 1844. All citations in this note are taken from Prescott, *The Correspondence of William Hickling Prescott, 1833–1847*.

36. On Panic fiction, see Fabian, "Speculation on Distress"; Fichtelberg, *Critical Fictions*, 117–59; Jones, *American Hungers*, 21–61; and Templin, "'Dedicated to Works of Beneficence'" and "Panic Fiction."

37. In a letter very similar to his May 30, 1848, "communist philosophers" letter, Prescott writes to Comte Adolphe de Circourt on April 3, 1848, that "we [in the

United States] have had a good share of common sense to keep us right—generally—against political dreamers & theorists, who would long since have converted this land into a laboratory for working out their own crazy experiments. But there is fortunately a strong basis of plain, practical common sense at the bottom of the Yankee character" ("Transcribed Correspondence, 1834–1850").

38. In this vein, Prescott concedes that Incan limitations on commerce ensured that in proto-communist Peru "[n]o adventurous schemer could impoverish his family by the spirit of speculation" (762).

39. Guarneri, *The Utopian Alternative*, 37; Glickstein, "Pressures from Below," 117.

40. Meyers, *The Jacksonian Persuasion*, 14.

41. Guarneri, *The Utopian Alternative*, 38.

42. Prescott, "Transcribed Correspondence, 1834–1850," letter dated September 28, 1848.

43. Jones, *American Hungers*, 24. See also Rothman, *The Discovery of the Asylum*, 158–59; and Lang, *The Syntax of Class*, 1–2. Fourierists, among others, "repudiat[ed] the widespread contemporary belief that American social and economic forms differed so drastically from European" (Guarneri, *The Utopian Alternative*, 99).

44. Prescott, "Transcribed Correspondence, 1834–1850," letter dated September 28, 1848.

45. In addition to the West, Whigs also looked to national economic development to rectify social inequalities, on the theory that a rising tide lifts all ships: "By increasing total wealth, the Whigs hoped to avoid having to equalize its distribution" (Howe, *The Political Culture of the American Whigs*, 9).

46. Guarneri, *The Utopian Alternative*, 107–8; Scott, *In Pursuit of Happiness*, 61–62.

47. Fichtelberg also uses this term, but seemingly only as a chronological delineation rather than to describe a distinct socioliterary mode of thought (*Critical Fictions*, 153).

48. Prescott, *The Correspondence of William Hickling Prescott, 1833–1847*, 60–61.

49. Prescott, *The Literary Memoranda of William Hickling Prescott*, 2:113, 119. For Prescott's research and composition process with the introduction, see 2:113–40. For more on Prescott's research process generally, see the biographies (n14 above) and Jaksić, *The Hispanic World and American Intellectual Life, 1820–1880*, 128–72. Prescott had the time and money to cater to his high standards for documentary evidence and accumulated a considerable archive of works on Peru's history, as his extensive footnotes attest.

50. Similarly, Bruce Harvey writes that "the sheer palpability of foreign topographies and peoples may quite likely, if not exactly pull the national subject out of the orbit of his or her nationality, at least highlight tensions within the national order" (*American Geographics*, 18).

51. For example, "It matters little what was the ostensible ground of collision between persons placed by circumstances in so false a position in regard to one another,

that collision must, at some time or other, inevitably occur" (902); "For the free, sanguine, and confiding temper of Almagro was no match for the cool and crafty policy of Pizarro; and he was invariably circumvented by his companion, whenever their respective interests came in collision" (1060); "But Almagro and his followers shrunk from this open collision with the Crown" (1101); "Valdivia, the famous conqueror of Chili, who, having returned to Peru to gather recruits for his expedition, had learned the state of the country, and had thrown himself, without hesitation, into the same scale with the president, though it brought him into collision with his old friend and comrade, Gonzalo Pizarro" (1197). See also 832, 887, 902, 1025, 1100.

52. [Whipple], review of *History of the Conquest of Peru*, by William Hickling Prescott, 276.

53. Levin, *History as Romantic Art*, 43; Howe, *The Political Culture of the American Whigs*, 101.

54. Prescott, *The Correspondence of William Hickling Prescott, 1833–1847*, 513; *The Literary Memoranda of William Hickling Prescott*, 2:151. Prescott also wrote that he wished Pizarro "was more of a gentleman and less of a bandit" (*Correspondence*, 553).

55. Alexander, *Commodity and Propriety*, 100. See also Howe, *The Political Culture of the American Whigs*, 299.

56. For a similar argument, see Gladsky, "Revolution and Renewal in Prescott's *The Conquest of Peru*," 315.

57. Gladsky argues that as William Henry Harrison, John Tyler, and James Polk "represented to Prescott the decline of the role of the natural aristocrat, so too Pizarro does in the history of Spain in the New World. . . . Like his American counterparts of the 1840s, Pizarro had neither breeding nor greatness" (ibid., 316).

58. For Prescott's disparaging remarks on the Specie Circular and his comments on the suspension of specie payments by U.S. banks, see *The Correspondence of William Hickling Prescott, 1833–1847*, 12, 15, 20.

59. On the gold humbug, see Shell, *Money, Language and Thought*, 5–23; and his *Art and Money*, 74–79.

60. For more on the encomienda system, see Ramírez, *Provincial Patriarchs*, 15–41. Colonists didn't actually own their indigenous laborers per se, but they had total control over their labor, and Prescott writes about them as "slaves."

61. On Las Casas, see Brading, *The First America*, 58–78. On the New Laws and the response to them in Peru, see 67–68.

62. Ibid., 68.

63. Prescott, *The Correspondence of William Hickling Prescott, 1833–1847*, 420. For more on Adams's fight against slavery in the context of Whig politics, see Howe, *The Political Culture of the American Whigs*, 60–67.

64. Huston, *Calculating the Value of the Union*, 105. In contrast, a few proslavery advocates such as George Fitzhugh represented plantations as socialist utopias; see his 1854 *Sociology for the South*.

65. Charvat, "Prescott's Political and Social Attitudes," 324. On Prescott's views regarding slavery, see also Charvat and Kraus, *William Hickling Prescott*, civ–cviii.

66. Prescott, "Transcribed Correspondence, 1834–1850," letter dated April 3, 1848.

67. Charvat and Kraus, *William Hickling Prescott*, ciii.

68. Prescott, *The Correspondence of William Hickling Prescott, 1833–1847*, 464, 487. See also Gladsky, "Revolution and Renewal in Prescott's *The Conquest of Peru*," 317. Prescott characterizes La Gasca as "a Spanish Washington" and "the best image—if there be an image—of the Deity on earth" (*The Literary Memoranda of William Hickling Prescott*, 2:165, 166).

69. Prescott, too, feared this aspect of the war's repercussions: "The question of Slavery . . . which must arise on the settlement of the new conquests, is a formidable one, more formidable than the war itself." He had earlier characterized the acquisition of Texas as "a mischief to our own confederacy, to open to it such an unlimited market for slaves, and to throw such a black preponderating weight into the political balance. *Horresco*!" (*The Correspondence of William Hickling Prescott, 1833–1847*, 656, 520). But he also recognized the catalytic effect of these developments on antislavery sentiment, "which gathers strength in all quarters of the free states, and the extension of slavery and the new territories widens the ground to a degree, that men of all parties, as well as the professed abolitionists, may meet on it" ("Transcribed Correspondence, 1834–1850," letter dated August 21, 1848).

70. Scott, *In Pursuit of Happiness*, 101.

71. Darling, *Political Changes in Massachusetts, 1824–1848*, 312. For more on the Whig party breakdown and the split between Cotton and Conscience Whigs, see 316–59.

72. Prescott signed a public statement supporting Webster's work with the Compromise. See Charvat, "Prescott's Political and Social Attitudes," 326; and Gardiner, *William Hickling Prescott*, 295–96.

73. Howe, *The Political Culture of the American Whigs*, 224, 217.

74. Quoted in Ely, *The Guardian of Every Other Right*, 78. For more on *West River Bridge v. Dix* and other antebellum cases involving the conflict between private property rights and the exigencies of the public good, especially the prerogatives of national economic development, see Alexander, *Commodity and Propriety*, 97–240; Ely, *The Guardian of Every Other Right*, 59–82, and his *Property Rights in the Colonial Era and Early Republic*; and Scott, *In Pursuit of Happiness*, 114–32.

75. For connections between the anti-rent movement and the agrarianist National Reform Association, see Lause, *Young America*, 23–24, 28–29, 39–41. For connections between the National Reform Association and abolitionism, see 43–45, 72–76, 78, 80–84. For ideological overlaps between anti-rentism and abolitionism, see Hecht, "Nature's 'Cunning Alphabet,'" esp. 28–32.

76. In fact, James Ely argues that, with the possible exception of bankruptcy laws, most antebellum legislation that cited the "general public interest" to justify inter-

fering with property owners was not "designed to transfer wealth from one portion of the population to another, and thus . . . produced little redistributive effect" (*The Guardian of Every Other Right*, 62, 66, 71). He characterizes antebellum jurisprudence as generally "property-conscious" (82).

77. Scott, *In Pursuit of Happiness*, 53–113.

78. In the early 1850s, Prescott himself, disgusted at the increasing aggression of the South, would join those ranks. See Charvat, "Prescott's Political and Social Attitudes," 326; and Charvat and Kraus, *William Hickling Prescott*, cvii–cviii.

Chapter 3

1. Prescott, *History of the Reign of Philip the Second, King of Spain*, 1–2.

2. Motley, *The Rise of the Dutch Republic*, 1:292, 293 (hereafter cited parenthetically in the text).

3. On the use of representative figures by Motley and his fellow Romantic historians, see Levin, *History as Romantic Art*, 49–73.

4. As David Levin points out, the facts of history fail to cooperate with Motley in this narrative agenda; in *The Rise of the Dutch Republic*, "progressive forces decline, rise, and finally decline," culminating with the assassination of Motley's hero (ibid., 188).

5. Brooks uses Motley's *Dutch Republic* as an example of a historian creating a usable past for his country. See Brooks, *Van Wyck Brooks, the Early Years*, 223.

6. Guberman, *The Life of John Lothrop Motley*, 47. On Motley's sales and other manifestations of his work's popularity, see also Edwards, "John Lothrop Motley and the Netherlands," 173; Wheaton, "Motley and the Dutch Historians," 324; and Wish, *The American Historian*, 70.

7. "Motley's *Dutch Republic*," *Southern Quarterly Review*, February 1857, 427.

8. Critics have frequently noted the tendency of Motley and the Romantic historians to conflate the exploits of the Anglo-Saxon race with the onward march of human progress. See Buell, *New England Literary Culture*, 45; Callcott, *History in the United States, 1800–1860*, 166–73; Kraus, *The Writing of American History*, 191; Van Tassel, *Recording America's Past*, 172; and especially Levin, *History as Romantic Art*, 74–92.

9. Quoted in Wheaton, "Motley and the Dutch Historians," 336.

10. The Batavian leader's actual name was Gaius Julius Civilis. I have used Motley's names and spellings throughout, even in those instances when he is now considered incorrect.

11. Sargent, "The Conservative Covenant," 249.

12. Motley strengthens this impression even when rejecting comparisons between the Dutch and U.S. situations on the basis of dissimilar historical particulars. He writes that the Compromise of 1556, a declaration signed by a number of Dutch no-

bles asserting the Netherlands' autonomy, did not get ratified in "any solemn scene like that of the declaration of American Independence," where all affixed their signatures at once (1:494). Motley may have wanted to downplay the Compromise's significance because his hero, William, did not sign it. But of course because Motley brings up this association, the reader begins to think of the two documents as similar in scope and consequence. Later in the history, Motley describes the literary style of the 1581 Act of Abjuration, the true Dutch "declaration of independence," in these terms: "[L]ike the American patriots of the eighteenth century, they on most occasions preferred punctilious precision to florid declamation" (3:508, 509).

13. See Howe, *The Political Culture of the American Whigs*, 74.

14. Motley, *John Lothrop Motley and His Family*, 36. For Motley's correspondence, see also Motley, *The Correspondence of John Lothrop Motley.*

15. David Levin remarks that "the most damaging fault in Motley's history is his repetitiousness" (*History as Romantic Art*, 196).

16. O. D. Edwards writes that the "*Dutch Republic* is famous or infamous for its obsessiveness about the utter goodness of William the Silent and the utter badness of Philip II" ("John Lothrop Motley and the Netherlands," 175). On Motley's use of stock villains and heroes, see Callcott, *History in the United States, 1800–1860*, 145–46, 159.

17. A contemporary reviewer commented on the *Dutch Republic*'s "hundreds of pages of hideous and too authentic detail." See "*The Rise of the Dutch Republic*," *Littell's Living Age*, May 24, 1856, 456. Strangely, the *Ladies Repository* reprinted a large portion of this Inquisition chapter, without commentary, in between a description of how Roman ladies wore their hair and a piece called "Pleasures of Home." See "Revolt of the Netherlands."

18. Motley, *The Correspondence of John Lothrop Motley*, 146; *John Lothrop Motley and His Family*, 42. Motley writes in *The Rise of the Dutch Republic* that the crimes of Spanish tyranny "will not make us love popular liberty the less" (2:424). See also 2:314.

19. See also Motley, *The Rise of the Dutch Republic*, 1:262. O. D. Edwards argues that with statements like these, which undercut the exceptionalism of heroic Pilgrim suffering, Motley sought "to fight the parochialism of his fellow countrymen" ("John Lothrop Motley and the Netherlands," 180).

20. Bradford, *Of Plymouth Plantation, 1620–1647*, 10.

21. "Bradford's *History of Plymouth Plantation*."

22. Keith Sprunger depicts a constant flow of people and ideas between England and the Netherlands in the sixteenth and seventeenth centuries. The Protestant refugees from Mary's Catholic persecutions, the communities of English merchants and traders operating in the Netherlands, and the outposts of English soldiers sent to fight with the Dutch against Spain—all these groups laid the groundwork for the exodus of whole Separatist congregations from England. The Netherlands became an active site

of English religious life in exile, influencing the shape of domestic religious debates. Sprunger argues that because of the United Provinces' policy of religious liberty, the makeup of its society was especially cosmopolitan: it drew persecuted peoples from everywhere in Europe, and this influx added to the diversity already encouraged by the global prominence of the Dutch in the arena of maritime commerce. See Sprunger, *Dutch Puritanism*, esp. 3–12.

23. Perhaps because of the markedly cosmopolitan nature of Dutch society, some members of the emigrating church feared a loss of their English nationality with continued residence in Leyden. According to Sprunger, "the tolerant Dutch environment encouraged mingling and assimilation," and he quotes Edward Winslow's fear expressed in *Hypocrisie Unmasked* of "how likely we were to lose our language, and our name of English" (ibid., 7). For a comprehensive summary of the Pilgrim time in the Netherlands, including a chapter on their reasons for leaving, see Kardux and van de Bilt, *Newcomers in an Old City*.

24. Bradford, *Of Plymouth Plantation, 1620–1647*, 28. Their emigration with an English patent to settle in England's New World territory was not foreordained. When word spread of their intention to sail to the Americas, various Dutch companies attempting to populate the New Netherland colony entered into negotiations with the Puritans to settle there. This plan fell through for financial reasons. See 22, 38, 44.

25. McWilliams, "Fictions of Merry Mount," 20. On Motley's representations of the Puritans in *Merry-Mount* and his 1849 *North American Review* essay entitled "Polity of the Puritans," see also Bell, *Hawthorne and the Historical Romance of New England*, 17–19, 157–59; Cheng, *The Plain and Noble Garb of Truth*, 170–75; McWilliams, *New England's Crises and Cultural Memory*, 58–65; and Sargent, "The Conservative Covenant," 248–49.

26. On Unitarianism's importance for nineteenth-century New England letters, see Buell, *New England Literary Culture*, 38–49; Howe, *The Unitarian Conscience*; and Levin, *History as Romantic Art*, 4–7. On Motley as a Unitarian and its effect on his historiography, see Levin, 4–5, 96–98. On the split between liberal Arminian-Unitarians and orthodox Calvinists, see Howe, and Conrad Edick Wright, *American Unitarianism, 1805–1865*, 2–50.

27. On Unitarian versus orthodox Calvinist attitudes toward the Puritans, see Buell, *New England Literary Culture*, 214–32. On the increasingly ambivalent attitudes toward the Puritans during this period in general, see also Bell, *Hawthorne and the Historical Romance of New England*, 8–104; and Cheng, *The Plain and Noble Garb of Truth*, 153–54, 164–65, 169–79, 182–85, 190–91, 204–7.

28. Bell, *Hawthorne and the Historical Romance of New England*, 86.

29. "*The Rise of the Dutch Republic*," *Democratic Review*, August 1856, 78. This attitude may have sprung in part from regional rivalry. The Boston-based *North American Review* discussed the Pilgrim connection to Motley's story reverently; see "Motley's *Rise of the Dutch Republic*," *North American Review*, July 1856, 184–85. In contrast,

the reviewer for the New York *Democratic Review* criticizes the Pilgrims as part of his effort to elevate the United States' Dutch heritage over its English one, a reinterpretation of U.S. ideological lineage that foregrounds New York, originally a Dutch colony, at the expense of New England and its English beginnings. He refutes the claim that the United States owes its republicanism and religious liberty "exclusively to our English ancestry. . . . We must ask the partisans of the purely English theory to read [*The Rise of the Dutch Republic*] and learn how much more of our system we owe to our Dutch than to our English ancestors" (71). On a similar, turn-of-the-century trend of denying the supremacy of English influence on U.S. history in favor of the Dutch, see Stott, *Holland Mania*.

30. "*The Rise of the Dutch Republic*," *Democratic Review*, August 1856, 75, 73, 78.

31. Ibid., 78.

32. In an example of the accusations directed at Catholics about their supposed Inquisitorial aspirations, *The Princess of Viarna; or, The Spanish Inquisition in the Reign of the Emperor Charles the Fifth* (1857) warned Protestants that "although the Spanish Inquisition is nominally extinct, the religious spirit which created it, not only lives among us, but ardently struggles to re-erect, in every quarter of the globe, its blasphemous tribunal"—closely echoing the rhetoric employed by the *Democratic Review* writer. Quoted in Griffin, *Anti-Catholicism and Nineteenth-Century Fiction*, 111.

33. On the Know-Nothings, see Anbinder, *Nativism and Slavery*; Mulkern, *The Know-Nothing Party in Massachusetts*; and Voss-Hubbard, *Beyond Party*.

34. Billington, *The Protestant Crusade, 1800–1860*, 86, 309–11.

35. Quoted in Anbinder, *Nativism and Slavery*, 23, 24.

36. Mulkern, *The Know-Nothing Party in Massachusetts*, 104, 102.

37. Anbinder, *Nativism and Slavery*, 139–40.

38. Ibid., 87.

39. "Motley's *Dutch Republic*," *Southern Quarterly Review*, February 1857, 440. Democrats dominated the South, so partisanship may play a role in the reviewer's critical reference to the Know-Nothings, as it did with the *Democratic Review* writer.

40. Ibid., 441.

41. Mulkern, *The Know-Nothing Party in Massachusetts*, 131.

42. Billington, *The Protestant Crusade, 1800—1860*, 375n66, 359. On the prevalence of references to the Inquisition in anti-Catholic discourse, see also Fenton, *Religious Liberties*, esp. 25–35.

43. Griffin, *Anti-Catholicism and Nineteenth-Century Fiction*, 180, 56. Motley's portrayal of the way that inquisitorial spies infiltrate into private "firesides" and induce wives to turn on their husbands recalls anti-Catholic rhetoric warning that nineteenth-century Jesuits sought to penetrate U.S. homes in order to seduce and convert American women. On the Catholic threat to Protestant homes, see 8–10.

44. Jenny Franchot notes, "Disease, death, and decomposition were frequently identified with a faith continually pathologized as dead" (*Roads to Rome*, 23).

45. Levin, *History as Romantic Art*, 112–13. For example, see 1:78.

46. "Motley's *Dutch Republic*," *Southern Quarterly Review*, February 1857, 448.

47. On "Romanism" as a term for Roman Catholicism, and what it signifies, see Franchot, *Roads to Rome*, xviii.

48. "*The Rise of the Dutch Republic*," *Littell's Living Age*, May 24, 1856, 451. The charge of anti-Catholicism carries all the more weight given that this reviewer (J. A. Froude) later describes Catholicism in the sixteenth century as a "destroying fiend" about which there should be no "bastard sentimentalism" (456). On the character of *Littell's Living Age* as a publication, see McGill, *American Literature and the Culture of Reprinting, 1834–1853*, 23–27.

49. Bassett, *The Middle Group of American Historians*, 229; Callcott, *History in the United States, 1800–1860*, 170; Levin, *History as Romantic Art*, 102. On the anti-Catholicism of romantic historiography, see Levin, 93–125; and Franchot, *Roads to Rome*, 35–82.

50. Motley, *The Correspondence of John Lothrop Motley*, 147.

51. Quoted in Hirsh and Motley, "John Lothrop Motley on the American Republic, 1846," 62. See also Motley, *The Correspondence of John Lothrop Motley*, 181. On the image of the Irish "Paddy" in antebellum discourse, see Knobel, *Paddy and the Republic*.

52. Edwards, "John Lothrop Motley and the Netherlands," 189, 190. Edwards also argues that the Gauls were "the future Confederates" (190). He says that Motley expresses a "crypto-disunionism" in *The Rise of the Dutch Republic* by presenting the dissolution of the 1581 confederation of Dutch provinces as inevitable; "Motley's overriding motivation was a concern to find European precursors less for the creation of the American union, than for its impending dissolution" over the issue of slavery (194, 190). Motley, though possessed of some racist attitudes, disapproved of slavery and felt that northern secession from the Union might be a viable solution (189–92). See also Motley, *The Correspondence of John Lothrop Motley*, 148. A review in *Harper's* picks up on this issue: "The story of the seven United Provinces of Holland is full of warning and instruction for the two-and-thirty United States of America. Sectional jealousy, and disunion of States that had stood side by side in the great agony, left half complete the noble work that had begun in Holland. May the gods avert the omen!" See "*The Rise of the Dutch Republic*," *Harper's New Monthly Magazine*, May 1856, 769.

53. "Motley's *Dutch Republic*," *Southern Quarterly Review*, February 1857, 449.

54. See Cheng, *The Plain and Noble Garb of Truth*, 2–11. Cheng revises Peter Novick's long-standard assessment that objectivity did not become a historiographical priority in the United States until the late nineteenth century. She instead dates a concern with impartiality back to the 1820s (5). See also Novick, *That Noble Dream*.

55. "*The Dutch Republic*," 248.

56. For a description of Motley's time at Göttingen, see Trent, *The Cambridge History of American Literature*, 133. For a general description of this experience for

young U.S. American students, see Novick, *That Noble Dream*, 21–23. On the significance of figures such as Ranke, Bacon, Flaubert, and Niebuhr to U.S. historians, see Novick, 21; Cheng, *The Plain and Noble Garb of Truth*, 23–29; and Higby and Schantz, introduction to *John Lothrop Motley*, lxxii–lxxvii.

57. Motley, *The Correspondence of John Lothrop Motley*, 191, 203. On Motley's archival credentials, see Bassett, *The Middle Group of American Historians*, 229; Callcott, *History in the United States, 1800–1860*, 126–27; Cheng, *The Plain and Noble Garb of Truth*, 128–38; Edwards, "John Lothrop Motley and the Netherlands," 174, 183, 196; and Higby and Schantz, introduction to *John Lothrop Motley*, lxxxviii–xcviii. Motley describes archival work with a variety of striking metaphors, reporting "the digging out of raw material out of the subterranean depths of black-letter folios in half a dozen different languages," and being "buried in the deep bosom of the Dutch Archives." To Oliver Wendell Holmes, he writes that he goes to the archives every day, "studying the old letters and documents of the sixteenth century. Here I remain among my fellow worms, feeding on those musty mulberry leaves of which we are afterwards to spin our silk. How can you expect anything interesting from such a cocoon? It is, however, not without its amusement in a mouldy sort of way, this reading of dead letters. . . . It gives a 'realising sense,' as the Americans have it." See Motley, *The Correspondence of John Lothrop Motley*, 146, 158, 163. On his friendship with Holmes, see Tilton, "Holmes and His Critic Motley."

58. Edwards notes that Motley's "work stood strangely between pre-scientific partisanship and archivally dominated modernity of approach" ("John Lothrop Motley and the Netherlands," 178).

59. On Motley's use of "what might be called the Catholic sources," see Higby and Schantz, introduction to *John Lothrop Motley*, xcii–xciv.

60. Motley, *The Correspondence of John Lothrop Motley*, 209.

61. On the way that "[a]nti-Catholicism traditionally takes the honesty of Catholics as its target," see Griffin, *Anti-Catholicism and Nineteenth-Century Fiction*, 44–45.

62. Reviewers argued that Motley "is too apt to needlessly assert his principles, and to inveigh against tyranny," that he "is sometimes too fierce in his moral wrath," and that he "hates" and "lashes with all his heart" at Philip and the other villains of his story. See "Motley's History of the Dutch Republic," 175; "Philip II. and His Times," 602; "Motley's *Dutch Republic*," *Littell's Living Age*, June 26, 1858, 1018. The *North American Review* essay actually lauds Motley's "great fairness and moderation" and denies that he "ever indulge[s] in violent invective," but this does not reflect the general contemporary consensus on *The Rise of the Dutch Republic*; see "Motley's *Rise of the Dutch Republic*," *North American Review*, July 1856, 186.

63. "*The Rise of the Dutch Republic*," *Harper's New Monthly Magazine*, April 1856, 695.

64. "Motley's *Rise of the Dutch Republic*," *Littell's Living Age*, June 14, 1856, 692.

65. Ibid. In this self-contradiction, Motley resembles the nineteenth-century Anglo-Protestants who "could simultaneously tout their commitment to egalitarianism and mount campaigns to disenfranchise their Catholic neighbors" because they believed Catholicism to be an inherently despotic religion at odds with American liberal democracy, in Elizabeth Fenton's analysis (*Religious Liberties*, 9). Or, as Franchot argues, "Americans, by indulging in their taste for the pornographic, the inquisitional, and the violent, were practicing the very vices they ascribed to their enemy" (*Roads to Rome*, 107).

66. Howe, *The Unitarian Conscience*, 216, 215.

67. Griffin, *Anti-Catholicism and Nineteenth-Century Fiction*, 110.

68. Fenton writes that in nineteenth-century U.S. anti-Catholic rhetoric, "to be Catholic is to be a 'foreigner'" (*Religious Liberties*, 95).

Chapter 4

1. "Motley's *Dutch Republic*," *Southern Quarterly Review*, February 1857, 430–31.

2. Motley continued the story of Dutch independence in his later works, *History of the United Netherlands* (1860–67) and *The Life and Death of John of Barneveld* (1874).

3. Kenney, *Stubborn for Liberty*, 4.

4. On Sunnyside, see Anderson, "A Quaint, Picturesque Little Pile"; Faherty, *Remodeling the Nation*, 100–108; and Manca, "Erasing the Dutch," 83–84.

5. On the Dutch colonial period in North America, see Kenney, *Stubborn for Liberty*; Bonomi, *A Factious People*; Goodfriend, *Revisiting New Netherland*; and Rink, *Holland on the Hudson*.

6. Kupperman, "International at the Creation," 108, 110.

7. Dimock, "Scales of Aggregation," 225, 225–26. See also Dimock, "Introduction: Planet and America, Set and Subset," 7.

8. Kupperman writes that it "is symptomatic of the problem that we have no term by which to refer to the region that would become the United States" ("International at the Creation," 105).

9. For a related point about the way that Irving casts doubt on manifest destiny in his 1836 history of John Jacob Astor's fur empire, *Astoria*, see LeMenager, "Trading Stories," esp. 691.

10. See Insko, "Diedrich Knickerbocker, Regular Bred Historian," 609–14.

11. Irving, *Washington Irving: History, Tales and Sketches*, 503, 644; see also 583. All subsequent in-text parenthetical citations for the 1809 version of *A History of New York* refer to this edition.

12. White, "History as Literature," 573, 583.

13. Most critics treat Irving's New Netherland as within a U.S. national frame-

work. See, for example, Hedges, *Washington Irving*, 82; Insko, "Diedrich Knickerbocker, Regular Bred Historian," 608, 612–13, 618; and Roth, *Comedy and America*, 113, 133.

14. On "infancy" as a trope in *A History of New York* and nineteenth-century U.S. culture more generally, see Burstein, *The Original Knickerbocker*, 86.

15. Irving, *A History of New York*, 3.

16. Roth, *Comedy and America*, 157.

17. Many critics discuss Kieft as a satire on Jefferson. See, among others, Black and Black, introduction to *A History of New York*, xxvi–xxix; Burstein, *The Original Knickerbocker*, 76–81; Ferguson, "'Hunting Down a Nation,'" 28–30; Hagensick, "Irving: A Littérateur in Politics," 182–84; and Stanley T. Williams, *The Life of Washington Irving*, 1:117–18.

18. In later versions of *A History of New York*, Irving excised or moderated many passages like these. See Black and Black, introduction to *A History of New York*, lii–liii, lvi–lvii. Irving's habit of diluting his social and political mockery when making revisions explains why most critics consider the 1848 edition a watered-down version of the 1809 *History*.

19. Some critics believe that "[d]espite Irving's reservations about Jeffersonian America, the *History* was not meant to be aggressive, or even half serious" (Burstein, *The Original Knickerbocker*, 81). William Hedges asks, "[A]re we not subject to the author's posthumous laughter for our willingness to discuss such matters so seriously?" ("*The Knickerbocker History* as Knickerbocker's 'History,'" 161). But I agree with Robert Ferguson when he argues that Irving's absurd humor "allow[s] his tense fellow republicans to laugh away their anger and anxieties" but does not negate the underlying, very real causes for concern ("'Hunting Down a Nation,'" 39).

20. Ferguson, "'Hunting Down a Nation,'" 32–33. For examples of apocalyptic Federalist rhetoric, see Fox, *The Decline of Aristocracy in the Politics of New York*, 6–7.

21. For these critiques, see, respectively, Bowden, "Knickerbocker's History and the 'Enlightened' Men of New York City"; Insko, "Diedrich Knickerbocker, Regular Bred Historian," 612–21; and Ringe, "New York and New England." Stanley T. Williams writes, "It is dangerous to speak of the book as a burlesque on a single theme" (*The Life of Washington Irving*, 1:116).

22. On the Knickerbocker surname, see Kenney, *Stubborn for Liberty*, 198–99; and Bradley, *Knickerbocker*, 28, 156.

23. On the transition in the judicial system, see Kammen, *Colonial New York*, esp. 128–33. On efforts to Anglicize the Dutch, see Balmer, *A Perfect Babel of Confusion*, 72–98; Goodfriend, *Before the Melting Pot*, 188–205; and Murrin, "English Rights as Ethnic Aggression."

24. Goodfriend, *Before the Melting Pot*, 103, 106. On the history of Dutch language usage in New York and New Jersey, see also Balmer, *A Perfect Babel of Con-*

fusion, 72–153; and Narrett, "Dutch Customs of Inheritance, Women, and the Law in Colonial New York City," 34, 40–41. Anglicization altered even the structures of Dutch family life. Narrett discusses the eighteenth-century decline of Dutch inheritance customs, such as equal division of property among children of both sexes, a practice that Irving mentions in an editorial footnote (672).

25. Fabend, *Zion on the Hudson*, 32. Randall Balmer also states, "With so few reasons for remaining Dutch in eighteenth-century New York, the Dutch Reformed Church . . . languished as a fiduciary of Batavian traditions and culture" (*A Perfect Babel of Confusion*, 156). On the Dutch Reformed Church in this period, see also De Jong, *The Dutch Reformed Church in the American Colonies*.

26. Bruins, "Americanization in Reformed Religious Life," 176. On how this decline in church attendance encouraged people to disregard the deterioration of Dutch church buildings, see Manca, "Erasing the Dutch," 71–72.

27. On the history of Dutch festivals into the nineteenth century, see Cohen, *The Dutch-American Farm*, 158–66; and Fabend, *Zion on the Hudson*, 106–13. For the significance of festivals to ethnic identity, see Schoone-Jongen, *The Dutch American Identity*. Cohen notes that Pinkster in fact persisted in the black community after it had been abandoned by the Dutch; many Dutch kept slaves, who incorporated various aspects of Dutch cultural life into their carnival customs. Irving does mention the "dutch negroes" in a New Jersey community who wear "their holliday clothes" on Sundays (437).

28. On the ideology of "generations," see Sollors, *Beyond Ethnicity*, 208–36. For a list of other works on generational theory, see Schoone-Jongen, *The Dutch American Identity*, 49. Sollors argues that ethnic jeremiads like Knickerbocker's actually often functioned to strengthen ethnic ties: "[B]y scolding different people as a degenerate second generation one may in fact be molding a family" (222). On jeremiads as a tool for building consensus, see also Bercovitch, *The American Jeremiad*.

29. Bradley, *Knickerbocker*, 20.

30. Ibid., 35.

31. On the representation of the settlement period as a golden age in *A History of New York*, see Roth, *Comedy and America*, 122–29.

32. On the figure of the feeling historian, see Goode, *Sentimental Masculinity and the Rise of History, 1790–1890*.

33. Roth, *Comedy and America*, 154.

34. Antelyes, *Tales of Adventurous Enterprise*, 47–48, 211n1. On the feeling of homelessness in Irving's life and work, see Rubin-Dorsky, *Adrift in the Old World*, xiv–xvi, 2–8, 26–28. Of course, Antelyes argues that the overblown, pseudo-biblical rhetoric of "a stranger and a weary pilgrim in thy native land" "underscores Irving's satire of that pose," which fits with the mockery that Irving aims at the Dutch and his Dutch narrator (211n1).

35. Giles, *Transatlantic Insurrections*, 147.

36. Irving, *A History of New York*, 6.

37. Murray, *Forked Tongues*, 37. On the vanishing Indian, Indian melancholy, and farewell speeches, see also Sollors, *Beyond Ethnicity*, 102–30.

38. Secor, "Ethnic Humor in Early American Jest Books," 165, 163. Secor elaborates: "[H]umor functions to police a group's or a nation's boundaries, whether social, geographic, or moral. The values of the dominant group are reinforced by ascribing to the outsider those values that it rejects, mocking them as ludicrous through laughter. James Sulley called laughter 'a prophylactic against contamination from outside peoples'" (164).

39. Purvis, "The European Ancestry of the United States Population, 1790," 98; Casey, "The Limits of Equality," 43.

40. For this argument, see De Jong, *The Dutch Reformed Church in the American Colonies*, 219. On the persistence of the Dutch language into the nineteenth and twentieth centuries, see Bradley, *Knickerbocker*, 160n18; Cohen, *The Dutch-American Farm*, 150–52; De Jong, *The Dutch in America, 1609–1974*, 105–6; Fabend, *Zion on the Hudson*, 5, 12, 70–72, 81, 212–14, 238n11, 264n9; and Wermuth, *Rip Van Winkle's Neighbors*, 15.

41. Cohen, *The Dutch-American Farm*, 152.

42. Fabend, *Zion on the Hudson*, 70–72. Irving must have assumed that at least some of his readers would understand a bit of Dutch, given his use of a Dutch epigraph and his inclusion of Dutch swear words (363, 525). On the latter, see Webster, "Irving's Expurgation of the 1809 History of New York."

43. Fabend, *Zion on the Hudson*, 72–74. Similarly, Elton Bruins writes that after a new church constitution was adopted in 1792, the Dutch Reformed Church "was now an American church—but an American church which had reluctantly adapted to the American scene in order to survive. It was still very much the Dutch Reformed Church with emphasis on the Dutch even though its congregants now worshipped in English" ("Americanization in Reformed Religious Life," 180).

44. On Batavianization, see Fabend, *Zion on the Hudson*, 11–13. On Batavianizing in the immediate postconquest era, see Murrin, "English Rights as Ethnic Aggression," esp. 64.

45. See Cohen, *The Dutch-American Farm*, 33–132, 160–68; Fabend, *Zion on the Hudson*, 213–14; and Blackburn and Piwonka, *Remembrance of Patria*, 91, 117–18, 127–37, 170, 257–61.

46. Fabend writes that the Dutch in this period "still regarded themselves in many ways as 'apart,' a people with a particular historical past struggling for identity and integrity in an increasingly populous and pluralistic society" (*Zion on the Hudson*, 2).

47. Robert Swierenga observes that the idea that the "the Dutch in America are clannish . . . is a truism" (introduction to *The Dutch in America*, 8). Similarly, Joseph

Manca writes of the "growing distaste for the persistent clannishness and perceived peculiarity of the Dutch Americans," an "odd and separatist people" "who seemed to set themselves off from other Americans" ("Erasing the Dutch," 59).

48. See also 436, where "low dutch" speech is used as a torture device against Indians. Robert Secor argues, "One way of laughing at ethnic groups who are outside a bonded society is to make fun of their way of talking" ("Ethnic Humor in Early American Jest Books," 165).

49. On the Knickerbocker group, see Callow, *Kindred Spirits*; and Taft, *Minor Knickerbockers*, xiii–cx.

50. Cooper, *The Water-Witch*, v.

51. For the argument that the Dutch experience parallels the experience of other ethnic groups, see Balmer, *A Perfect Babel of Confusion*, x; De Jong, *The Dutch Reformed Church in the American Colonies*, 230–31; and Fabend, *Zion on the Hudson*, 228. J. Hector St. John de Crèvecoeur, in his famous "What Is an American?" section of *Letters from an American Farmer*, lists the Dutch as a constituent element in the American "new race of men" (70).

52. On Dutch support for the Revolution, see Balmer, *A Perfect Babel of Confusion*, 149–52; De Jong, *The Dutch in America, 1609–1974*, 109–25; and Kenney, *Stubborn for Liberty*, 153–72.

53. On anachronism and Irving, see Insko, "Diedrich Knickerbocker, Regular Bred Historian"; and McLamore, "The Dutchman in the Attic," 31–32.

54. Sollors, *Beyond Ethnicity*, 224. David Cohen similarly critiques "Irving's image of a static folk tradition" in his writings on U.S. Dutch cultural life (*The Dutch-American Farm*, 150).

55. Cohen, *The Dutch-American Farm*, 151. See also Goodfriend, *Before the Melting Pot*, 196.

56. Fabend, *Zion on the Hudson*, 228. David Cohen's reconstruction of a hybridized Dutch American "regional subculture" that emerged by the nineteenth century corroborates Fabend's assertion (*The Dutch-American Farm*).

57. See Black and Black, introduction to *A History of New York*, xix–xxiv; and Bradley, *Knickerbocker*, 15, 20–30, 40.

58. Irving's 1839 pieces "Communipaw" and "The Conspiracy of the Cocked Hats" also provide good illustrations of these alienating and anachronizing tactics. In "Communipaw," Irving writes that the Dutch village "is, to the ancient province of the New Netherlands . . . what Herculaneum and Pompeii are to ancient Rome." With its archaic fashions and tools, "Communipaw, at the present day, is a picture of what New Amsterdam was before the conquest." "The Conspiracy of the Cocked Hats" reveals, albeit humorously, that the ethnic Dutch as a whole are engaged in "a settled, secret, and determined conspiracy [that] has been going on for generations among this indomitable people . . . the object of which is, to redeem their ancient seat

of empire, and to drive the losel [worthless] Yankees out of the land." Irving, *Miscellaneous Writings, 1803–1859*, 123, 124, 130.

59. See Cohen, *The Dutch-American Farm*, 7, 149–50; DeJong, *The Dutch in America, 1609–1974*, 259; Fabend, *Zion on the Hudson*, 69; and Kenney, *Stubborn for Liberty*, 191–99.

60. See Black and Black, introduction to *A History of New York*, xxxii–xxxiii, xxxix, l–li; Burstein, *The Original Knickerbocker*, 74–75, 121; Fabend, *Zion on the Hudson*, 69; and Stanley T. Williams, *The Life of Washington Irving*, 2:274–76. See also Homer F. Barnes, *Charles Fenno Hoffman*, 214.

61. Quoted in Black and Black, introduction to *A History of New York*, xxxiii.

62. Irving, *A History of New York*, 4–5, 4.

63. Black and Black, introduction to *A History of New York*, liv–lv.

64. Sharp, *American Politics in the Early Republic*, 41.

65. Jefferson, *The Portable Thomas Jefferson*, 217.

66. On the commercial aspects of Jefferson's vision and how they disprove the supposedly nostalgic nature of his economic ideologies, see Appleby, "Economics."

67. See, for example, Balmer, *A Perfect Babel of Confusion*, 61, 102; Blackburn and Piwonka, *Remembrance of Patria*, esp. 40; Manca, "Erasing the Dutch," 75; and Narrett, "Dutch Customs of Inheritance, Women, and the Law in Colonial New York City," 28–29. Alice Kenney argues that by the time Irving wrote *A History of New York*, "the difference was becoming marked between the cosmopolitan burghers, who adjusted to the dominant culture of the new nation in the interests of commerce, and the boers, who clung to the dialect and folkways of their ancestors," a conflict that she sees as informing Irving's text and the Dutch response to it (*Stubborn for Liberty*, 193).

68. New Brunswick and perhaps Albany might be considered exceptions to this phenomenon, because these cities continued to have a Dutch flavor in the nineteenth century; see Fabend, *Zion on the Hudson*, 80.

69. On the market revolution in the early nineteenth-century Hudson River Valley, see Wermuth, *Rip Van Winkle's Neighbors*.

70. Morse, *The American Geography*, 289, 251, 252.

71. For other examples of rhetoric, both verbal and visual, that presents the Dutch as archaic relics rendered obsolete by the march of progress, see Bradley, *Knickerbocker*, 23–24; Manca, "Erasing the Dutch," 69–71, 79–82; and Stott, "Inventing Memory." Manca argues that negative stereotypes about the Dutch explain public apathy toward the preservation of Dutch architecture, resulting in its low survival rate as compared to other styles of colonial architecture; Dutch buildings, like Dutch people, had to make way for Anglo-American modernity.

72. On the later life of the Knickerbocker name, see Irving, *A History of New York*, 5; Black and Black, introduction to *A History of New York*, li; and Bradley, *Knickerbocker*.

Chapter 5

1. Aaron, introduction to *The Song of Hiawatha*, xi; Buell, introduction to *Selected Poems*, xxix. For a rehearsal of the damning case against *The Song of Hiawatha*'s racial politics, see Carr, *Inventing the American Primitive*, 101–46.

2. On *The Song of Hiawatha*'s popular reception, see Trachtenberg, *Shades of Hiawatha*.

3. On this kind of literary removal in general, see Maddox, *Removals*.

4. Case in point, Longfellow's violinist in *Tales of a Wayside Inn*, modeled on the Norwegian Ole Bull and identified as being of the "Norwegian race," is also identified as a "Norseman." See Longfellow, *The Poetical Works of Longfellow*, 207, 218.

5. Dimock, "Literature for the Planet," 174.

6. For comprehensive considerations of Viking exploration in the New World, see Fitzhugh and Ward, *Vikings*; and Geraldine Barnes, *Viking America*. Annette Kolodny's *In Search of First Contact*, which came out as this book was going to press, also provides a smart and thorough examination of Viking exploration in the Americas, the Vinland theory, and Longfellow's "The Skeleton in Armor," among other topics related to my analysis in this chapter.

7. In 1838, an abstract of Rafn's text, originally written in Latin, Danish, and Icelandic, was published in English as *America Discovered in the Tenth Century*. Longfellow owned an 1845 French reissue of the original edition, which he kept on the "Scandinavian" bookshelves in his study. On Rafn and the U.S. reception of *Antiquitates Americanae*, see Geraldine Barnes, *Viking America*, 44–50.

8. John, "Eben Norton Horsford, the Northmen, and the Founding of Massachusetts," 119, 130.

9. Horsford was the Rumford Chair of the Application of Science to the Useful Arts at Harvard, and the company that he formed to market his baking powder still bears the name of his professorship.

10. On Horsford's Vinland obsession, see Fitzhugh and Ward, *Vikings*, 374–84; Fleming, "Picturesque History and the Medieval in Nineteenth-Century America"; and Stephen Williams, *Fantastic Archaeology*, 206–9.

11. Shepard, *A Guide-book to Norumbega and Vineland*.

12. Quoted in John, "Eben Norton Horsford, the Northmen, and the Founding of Massachusetts," 132.

13. Quoted in ibid., 129.

14. Ibid., 138, 123. Craigie Street, incidentally, is a block away from Longfellow's Craigie House, which is located on Brattle Street in what is now known as the Old Cambridge Historic District (Longfellow and other famous residents have sanctified the area for us as the Vikings sanctified it for him and Horsford). Horsford and Longfellow were friends and worked together to bring about the Boston Leif Eriksson statue, a project finally completed several years after Longfellow died.

15. Ibid., 120, 128–29. For a summary of the ways in which the Pilgrims were subsumed into the teleology of the Viking settlement and legacy, see Geraldine Barnes, *Viking America*, 60–62. Certainly some Harvardians, like Longfellow and especially Horsford, embraced the theory. In fact, to this day, the carving of a Viking prow hangs over the door of Harvard's Weld boathouse, because whatever doubts the Harvard establishment had about the idea that Vikings had once sailed the Charles River, its crews were not above trying to evoke some of that celebrated Norse seamanship for themselves.

16. Geraldine Barnes, *Viking America*, 46; John, "Eben Norton Horsford, the Northmen, and the Founding of Massachusetts," 124, 130.

17. Businesses like Newport's Hotel Viking still trade on the old Vinland story.

18. The tablet still lies at the intersection of Memorial Drive and Gerry's Landing Road (which becomes Fresh Pond Parkway) behind Mount Auburn Hospital in Cambridge, Massachusetts.

19. The tower still stands in Weston, Massachusetts, across the Charles River Estuary from Norumbega Park.

20. Although my role as a critic generally precludes autobiographical meditations, one personal digression seems warranted here. In 1968, my parents moved from Salt Lake City, Utah, where they had each been born and bred, to Massachusetts. My father, an army captain, was stationed there and would later be deployed from there to Vietnam. My parents rented an apartment in West Newton, Massachusetts. Early in their stay, they were taking a walk along the Charles River when they came across a tower on the banks. My mother read the plaque on the tower, which told the story of the Norse settlement that had flourished there nearly a millennium before. My mother said to herself, "Huh. I didn't know there were Vikings here. How about that." She related this incident to me as we scouted out the tower as part of my research for this chapter. She later denied that she had ever believed the story on the plaque and did not recall telling me that she had. Her memory may be faulty, or mine may be. Willful historical fantasies seem common among those interested in the Viking heritage of New England. Whatever the truth may be, the nature of historical memory tied to physical spaces allows for the accretion of infinite layers upon layers of new associations. The tower now calls to mind for me my intellectual interest in Vinland relics, my parents' entry in the 1960s into the brave new world of their adulthood, and Horsford digging up rocks that in turn called to mind for him a bustling Viking settlement on that spot.

21. Angela Miller, *The Empire of the Eye*, 14. Martha Norkunas, in her study of formal and informal monuments in Lowell, Massachusetts, also notes, "Like the battlefields where Americans of various ideologies come to compete for ownership of powerful national stories . . . there are key sites in every city where citizens compete for the right to assert their identity and power" (*Monuments and Memory*, 181). Her

attention to these spaces and the histories they are made to hold informs my approach to the landscape architecture of Vinland.

22. Headley, "Anne Whitney's *Leif Eriksson*," esp. 51–53.

23. Hollander, *American Poetry*, 377.

24. Jared Farmer writes in a discussion of Lovers' Leaps that "legends about suicidal Indians may have assuaged [the] pangs" of guilt about Indian removal "by allowing an exercise in empathy for Indian characters; and by shifting attention from white-on-Indian violence to self-inflicted Indian violence" (*On Zion's Mount*, 312).

25. See Geraldine Barnes, *Viking America*, 53; Schoolcraft, *Inquiries Respecting the History, Present Condition, and Future Prospects of the Indian Tribes of the United States*.

26. Stephen Williams, *Fantastic Archaeology*, 216–17.

27. Smith, *The Northmen of New England*, vii, vi. Longfellow owned this book and kept it in the "Scandinavian" section of his study. Smith, an Englishman, published this work simultaneously in Boston (through Hilliard, Gray) and London (through Charles Tilt). In England, it went by the title *The Discovery of America by the Northmen in the Tenth Century*. In the U.S. edition, Smith apparently made some changes to the title and the preface (from which my quotations are taken), which seem to have been an effort to pander to New Englanders' particular investment in the Vinland narrative. Longfellow's copy may have been pirated, given the lack of a listed publisher, but his preface matches the Hilliard, Gray version.

28. Geraldine Barnes, *Viking America*, 120.

29. Bergland, *The National Uncanny*.

30. Geraldine Barnes, *Viking America*, 83–84, 86–87. The diatribe against Cherokee dispossession is in Smith's *Northmen of New England*, which, ironically, participates in the rhetoric of removal, as demonstrated above. Again, Longfellow owned this title.

31. For other similarities between the two poems, see Gruesz, "*El Gran Poeta* Longfellow and a Psalm of Exile," 413–14.

32. Hilen, *Longfellow and Scandinavia*, 32–37.

33. Longfellow actually found his time in Sweden intellectually unproductive and personally uncomfortable. But later, in the course of translating Tegnér's work, he conceived the more positive image of Sweden that colors his descriptions in *Evangeline* and *The Song of Hiawatha*. For accounts of Longfellow's trip to Sweden, see Hilen, *Longfellow and Scandinavia*, 11–27; and the most recent biography of the poet: Calhoun, *Longfellow*, 106–12.

34. Longfellow, *The Song of Hiawatha*, 2 (hereafter cited parenthetically in the text).

35. Irmscher, *Longfellow Redux*, 107.

36. Munising means "Place of the Great Island" in Ojibway, and Grand Marais means "Big Swamp" in French.

37. Longfellow did sometimes take poetic liberties with native words, as when he changed the name of his hero from the Ojibway Manabozho to the Iroquois Hiawatha simply for "euphony"; see Irmscher, *Longfellow Redux*, 107. And according to William Cowan, Longfellow's Ojibway orthography did not necessarily reflect standard spelling, although his main source, Henry Rowe Schoolcraft, was often inconsistent in this respect, so "given such a wide variety of spellings to choose from, Longfellow seems to have selected one and either stuck to it, or changed it to something else and stuck to that" ("Ojibwa Vocabulary in Longfellow's *Hiawatha*," 62). For example, Schoolcraft's *gitchiguma* became Longfellow's Gitche Gumee. For clarity, I have adopted Longfellow's spelling of Ojibway terms used in the poem.

38. Irmscher, *Longfellow Redux*, 240, 218, 242. Irmscher writes that "*Hiawatha* often reads like a draft of a translation abandoned halfway through, something that is neither 'Indian' nor English"; he argues that "Longfellow is asking the mid-nineteenth-century white American reader to perform more than just an act of retrospective historical empathy": the poem requires a significant and simultaneous temporal, cultural, and linguistic adjustment (113).

39. See Ernest Moyne, "Parodies of Longfellow's *Song of Hiawatha*," 93. On the parodies, see also Irmscher, *Longfellow Redux*, 117–24. For Lewis Carroll's parody of the poem, see Carroll, "Hiawatha's Photographing."

40. In contrast to my interpretation of the Ojibway terms' effect, Alan Trachtenberg argues that "Ojibway words pass fluently into English" for the reader due to Longfellow's habit of providing the Ojibway term and its English equivalent in the same breath: "Called Waywassimo, the lightning, / And the thunder, Annemmekee" (*Shades of Hiawatha*, 67). But I would argue that this superficial ease of translation is deceptive, at least for the reader committed to precise understanding of the poetry. The frequent juxtaposition of Ojibway and English terms creates an expectation of translational ease that causes frustration when Longfellow blocks the fluency of translation. He sometimes introduces an Ojibway term without an in-text translation, forcing the reader to pause and flip to the "Vocabulary" for illumination: e.g., "Yenadizze" (45), "Nushka" (99), "Medas" and "Wabenos" (101), and "Wahonowin" (145). Other Ojibway terms previously introduced with an in-text translation are reintroduced later without one, so that the reader must fumble in his or her memory for the meaning or once again flip back to the "Vocabulary": e.g., "Mishe-Nahma" (60), "Wawonaissa" (96), and the names of the various winds discussed in canto 2. In at least one instance, the in-text translation conflicts with the definition in the "Vocabulary": "Kenozha," which is translated as "pike" in the poem and "pickerel" in the "Vocabulary" (54, 169). Some Ojibway terms have in-text translations but do not appear in the "Vocabulary": e.g., "Sebowisha" (39), "Wagemin" and "Paimosaid" (95, 100), "Ojeeg" (113, 114), and "Waywassimo" (129). This causes confusion because the in-text poetic renderings do not always provide particularly clear definitions and the reader is furthermore denied the pronunciation assistance of the "Vocabulary,"

in which the most strongly stressed syllable of each term is marked. All of these moments of disjuncture between the poem proper and the "Vocabulary" create friction in the movement between Ojibway and English, forcing the detail-oriented reader to wrestle within the intellectual space of translation and discouraging a "fluent" resolution of Ojibway linguistic otherness into the familiarity of English.

41. Longfellow employs this technique in the first of his notes, where he glosses "the Vale of Tawasentha" (mentioned in the prologue) as "now called Norman's Kill" (161). Longfellow's notes, with their discursive, scholarly tone, tend to provide a hierarchically organized presentation of cultural encounters. They explain and bring order to people, places, and ideas that the poem itself invokes only ambiguously and ambivalently. Even this example, though, involves a muddle of multiple cultural traditions. Longfellow translates a half-Anglicized, half-Indian name, "the Vale of Tawasentha," into a half-Anglicized, half-Dutch name, "Norman's Kill." The term "kill" is from the old Dutch word *kil*, meaning riverbed or channel. Many rivers and streams in areas first colonized by the Dutch are still called kills, including Norman's Kill, a tributary of the Hudson River located near Albany, New York.

42. Longfellow's nationalist agenda in the poem is a critical standard: Eric Sundquist writes that "by combining European and Native American mythologies and yoking Native American mysticism to the principles of Christianity, Longfellow creates a god-hero whose exploits belong to legend but whose purpose is to sanctify the rise of a Western Christian agricultural empire in the United States" (*Empire and Slavery in American Literature, 1820–1865*, 111). Daniel Aaron, editor of the Everyman *Hiawatha*, quotes Robert Penn Warren as saying that Longfellow makes Hiawatha "a sort of culture spirit floating vaguely and edifyingly in the background of the by then not-so-young Republic" (introduction to *The Song of Hiawatha*, xvii).

43. Longfellow glosses "Pauwating" as "Saut [*sic*] Sainte Marie" (170).

44. In a footnote to the description of the Black-Robe priest's arrival, Longfellow writes, "In this manner, and with such salutations, was Father Marquette received by the Illinois" (168). He directs the reader's attention to this episode in Père Marquette's account of his travels. Longfellow worked with a French edition of *Voyages et découvertes* published in Albany in 1855; for a list of Longfellow's sources, see Earnest J. Moyne, *"Hiawatha" and "Kalevala,"* 58–60.

45. I take this term from Kaplan, *The Anarchy of Empire in the Making of U.S. Culture*.

46. Pipestone, Minnesota, sits atop a huge plateau called Coteau des Prairies that stretches across northeast South Dakota and southwest Minnesota. Longfellow refers to this landform as the "Mountains of the Prairie" in the main text of the poem (5, 7, 27), but in the notes he calls it by its French name, Côteau des Prairies (161). English speakers kept the name but dropped the accent. Various tribes of Plains Indians have used the quarry at Pipestone for centuries to obtain soft red stone for making pipes. The stone is now called Catlinite after the first Euro-American visitor

to the quarry: the artist George Catlin. Maintained by the National Park Service since its designation as the Pipestone National Monument in 1937, the quarry still serves as an active Native American sacred space, and therefore the site allows visitor access only in certain circumscribed areas. The park rangers there disavow any connection to Pipestone's annual Song of Hiawatha Pageant, a reenactment of Longfellow's poem, given the pageant's problematically stereotypical representation of Native Americans.

47. The Fox later in their history moved to Iowa, and the Crow relocated further west toward the Rockies. In the anarchy of the cultural mix, individual cultures themselves do not remain fixed and stable but rather change over time and thereby add still other sets of variables. For information on the groups that Longfellow discusses, see Pritzker, *A Native American Encyclopedia*, 302–5 (Blackfeet), 313–16 (Crow), 316–19 (Dakota), 406–12 (Anishinaabe, also known as the Ojibway), and 415–17 (Fox).

48. The Blackfeet also controlled territory well up into what is now Canada. That these native designations of the land function independently not only of geopolitical boundaries within the United States but also of international geopolitical boundaries offers yet another challenge to a U.S.-centered episteme.

49. Aaron, introduction to *The Song of Hiawatha*, xix. Robert Ferguson explores the generally ignored darkness of the poem and how that darkness reflects Longfellow's growing fears over sectional division (he was fast friends with Charles Sumner, who was caned in the Senate just months after *Hiawatha*'s publication). See Ferguson, "Longfellow's Political Fears."

50. Farmer, *On Zion's Mount*, 254. Sometimes place-names were merely "Indianist": Farmer notes the stupendous number of places named after characters from *The Song of Hiawatha* (252–53). The poem, due to its widespread popularity, influenced as well as recorded the cultural anarchy of the U.S. landscape.

51. See *Kalewala, das National-Epos der Finnen*.

52. Letter from Longfellow to George Bancroft, in Longfellow, *The Letters of Henry Wadsworth Longfellow*, 3:504 (letter dated December 1, 1855). For various accounts of the role of *Kalevala* in *Hiawatha*, see Hilen, *Longfellow and Scandinavia*; Nyland, "*Kalevala* as a Reputed Source of Longfellow's *Song of Hiawatha*"; and especially Earnest J. Moyne, *"Hiawatha" and "Kalevala."*

53. For an account of the "Little Longfellow War" that Poe waged, see McGill, "Poe, Literary Nationalism, and Authorial Identity."

54. T.C.P., "To the Editors."

55. M.D.C., "*The Song of Hiawatha*."

56. M.D.C., "'Hiawatha' and 'Kalewala.'"

57. This despite justified criticisms of the Victorian inaccuracies in his representation of native peoples and culture. For more on these criticisms, see Ferguson, "Longfellow's Political Fears," 197–98.

58. For example, Porter writes in his opening salvo, "Few of your readers, I imagine,

have ever heard of, much less read, the 'Kalewala,' the great national epic of the Finns." T.C.P., "To the Editors."

59. One British commentator, William Howitt, suggested that a consideration of the merits and characteristics of Finnish poetry was especially worthwhile at that moment given Britain's recent military involvement with Finland: specifically, the violence occasioned by the Crimean War. Russia had annexed Finland early in the nineteenth century and would be in control there until the early twentieth century. When Russia and Britain came into conflict during the Crimean War, Finland became a British target, because Sveaborg (now called Suomenlinna), the fortress island guarding Helsingfors (now known as Helsinki; Helsingfors is its Swedish name), functioned strategically as the gateway to St. Petersburg along the arm of the Baltic Sea south of Finland. In August of 1855, British warships attacked Sveaborg, and several months later, Howitt pointed to Helsingfors/Helsinki as the cradle of Finnish literary production. In reasoning strikingly similar to U.S. calls for the preservation and appreciation of the Indian culture threatened by U.S. expansion, Howitt encouraged British awareness of the Finnish literary tradition that naval attacks might soon destroy in the ongoing siege of military targets in southern Finland. Howitt, "Longfellow's *Hiawatha*," 1337.

60. "Longfellow's *Song of Hiawatha*," 586–87. The phrase "supreme Caucasian mind" comes from Tennyson's "Palace of Art," in which the narrator builds a grand palace of the imagination for his soul, filled with "every legend fair / Which the supreme Caucasian mind / Carved out of Nature for itself." While Tennyson clearly meant "Caucasian" to imply the whole of the Indo-European imagination, the *Putnam's* reviewer mobilizes the phrase to discredit the possibility of artistic "supremacy" in other races.

61. Ibid., 584.

62. For an example of an early review that did focus on *The Song of Hiawatha* as "aboriginal all over," see Trachtenberg, *Shades of Hiawatha*, 53.

63. "*The Song of Hiawatha*," 272–73.

64. Helen Carr gives a brief account of Schoolcraft and his attitudes toward his Indian subjects (*Inventing the American Primitive*, 121–24). More extensive but more dated biographical information and textual analysis can be found in Osborn and Osborn, *Schoolcraft, Longfellow, Hiawatha*; and Mentor Williams, *Schoolcraft's Indian Legends*. The former includes excerpts from Schoolcraft's works that formed the basis of Longfellow's legends, while the latter reprints the main source, *Algic Researches*, in its entirety. On Longfellow's written responses to the controversy, see Earnest J. Moyne, *"Hiawatha" and "Kalevala,"* 32–35.

65. See the potentially defensive letter to Schoolcraft, dated December 14, 1855, in which Longfellow writes "an acknowledgement of my obligations to you," declares that he has "adhered very faithfully to the old myths," and mentions the charges of Porter slightingly. Longfellow, *The Letters of Henry Wadsworth Longfellow*, 3:509.

66. Ibid., 3:507 (letter dated December 3, 1855).

67. Ibid., 3:517 (letter dated January 11, 1856). See also letter dated January 14, 1856, to Sumner: Freiligrath "did not know, or did not remember that the *parallelism* he speaks of, is quite the essence of Indian, as of Finnish song" (3:522). Fanny Longfellow writes in a letter to Mary Longfellow Greenleaf, again on January 14, 1856, that "it was a pity [Freiligrath] could not know that it was the similarity of Indian song with Finnish which suggested that metre,—making it the true one to use." Quoted in Earnest J. Moyne, *"Hiawatha" and "Kalevala,"* 34. On features of Indian poetry that caused Longfellow to make this claim, see Schoolcraft's observations in *Alhalla*, quoted in Mentor Williams, *Schoolcraft's Indian Legends*, 302.

68. Longfellow, *The Letters of Henry Wadsworth Longfellow*, 3:507 (letter dated December 3, 1855), 3:503 (letter dated November 29, 1855).

69. Ibid., 3:503 (letter dated November 29, 1855).

70. Quoted in Mentor Williams, *Schoolcraft's Indian Legends*, 302; and in Schramm, "*Hiawatha* and Its Predecessors," 340.

71. Schramm, "*Hiawatha* and Its Predecessors," 338–40. In his protestations of innocence, Longfellow never turns to this internal tradition to counter the plagiarism charges. He defends the linguistic appropriateness of his metrical choice without calling attention to the fact that similar choices had been made before, although by less capable and prominent poets. One might speculate that an investment in the appearance of authorial originality would have discouraged Longfellow from invoking these earlier poems, although his refusal to issue a public rebuttal himself (people like Conway and Freiligrath spoke for him) may also be to blame for the incomplete explanation of the poem's origins.

72. Irmscher, *Longfellow Redux*, 116.

73. Longfellow, "Tegnér's *Frithiof's Saga*," 159.

74. This same sensibility shows up in Longfellow's anthologies of verse from various traditions and in his *Tales of a Wayside Inn*, in which a Sicilian, a Spanish Jew, and a Norwegian, among others, exchange tales with an innkeeper, the grandson of a soldier who fought at the battle of Lexington and Concord. Their convergence at this inn mirrors the collection of their tales, drawn from their varying cultural traditions, into the shared space of the volume *Tales of a Wayside Inn*. The landlord's "Paul Revere's Ride" ("Listen, my children, and you shall hear / of the midnight ride of Paul Revere") occupies the same textual space as the Norwegian violinist's *Saga of King Olaf*, which chronicles the battle between Norse and Christian cosmology during the conversion of Norway in the years just before Leif Eriksson set off on his New World explorations. These histories exist together, brought into connection by physical proximity and thereby coming to occupy a shared imaginative space as well.

75. It should be noted that, unlike many other Native American nations, the Ojibway, although ultimately marshaled onto reservations, were not removed from their lands and displaced further west.

Conclusion

1. On Parkman, see Kraus, *The Writing of American History*, 145–56; Levin, *History as Romantic Art*; Van Tassel, *Recording America's Past*, 111–20; and Wish, *The American Historian*, 88–108.

2. On *Montcalm and Wolfe*, see Levin, *History as Romantic Art*, 210–17.

3. Parkman, *France and England in North America*, 2:1476 (hereafter cited parenthetically in the text).

4. Dimock, *Through Other Continents*, 126.

5. Durant was referring to Rome.

6. Gibson and Safinia, *Apocalypto* DVD commentary.

7. Gibson has repeatedly emphasized that he wanted to make a "chase" movie, that he was interested in the chase as a genre and how he could strip it to its bare essentials.

8. Gibson gives the title in the accompanying commentary and claims that it is an actual Mayan tale, though "modified a bit."

9. This shifting of moral blame for the end of the Mayan world from Europeans back onto the Mayans themselves is exacerbated by placing prophecies in the mouths of Mayan characters, which naturalizes the outcome. Gibson and Safinia claim that this prophecy was inspired by the Popol Vuh, among other sources, and that the Mayans were "obsessed with predicting and prophesizing the rise and fall of their times" (Gibson and Safinia, *Apocalypto* DVD commentary). Gibson speculates that this may have been a "self-fulfilling" prophecy, which echoes the film's tendency to blame the Maya for their devastation by the Spanish.

10. The film mocks him lightly because he clearly does not expect his pursuers to follow, and when they jump, too, he is taken aback and hurriedly begins to run again. But the bravery of his sentiment is still endorsed, especially when he later repeats, in a totally unsatirized moment, "I am Jaguar Paw. This is my forest. And I am not afraid" (it is perhaps telling that this statement merely asserts present ownership of the forest rather than predicting future ownership).

11. Even the possible hope of seeking a "new beginning," as Jaguar Paw expresses it, is undermined by the fact that the leader of the fear-filled tribe expresses the same goal but ends up captured anyway.

12. Padgett, "*Apocalypto* Now."

13. Gibson and Safinia, *Apocalypto* DVD commentary.

14. Padgett, "*Apocalypto* Now."

15. "US Is Like Doomed Mayans."

16. On this anxiety, see, for example, books like Cullen Murphy, *Are We Rome?*

Bibliography

Aaron, Daniel. Introduction to *The Song of Hiawatha*, by Henry Wadsworth Longfellow, xi–xix. London: Everyman, 1992.

Adams, Charles Hansford. *"The Guardian of the Law": Authority and Identity in James Fenimore Cooper*. University Park: Pennsylvania State University Press, 1990.

Aguirre, Robert. "Annihilating the Distance: Panoramas and the Conquest of Mexico, 1822–1848." *Genre* 35.1 (2002): 25–54.

Alarcón, Daniel Cooper. *The Aztec Palimpsest: Mexico in the Modern Imagination*. Tucson: University of Arizona Press, 1997.

Alemán, Jesse. "The Other Country: Mexico, the United States, and the Gothic History of Conquest." *American Literary History* 18.3 (2006): 406–26.

Alexander, Gregory S. *Commodity and Propriety: Competing Visions of Property in American Legal Thought, 1776–1970*. Chicago: University of Chicago Press, 1997.

America Discovered in the Tenth Century. New York: William Jackson, 1838.

"American Literature and Reprints." *Putnam's Monthly Magazine*, July 1856, 95–96.

Anbinder, Tyler. *Nativism and Slavery: The Northern Know Nothings and the Politics of the 1850s*. Oxford: Oxford University Press, 1992.

Anderson, David R. "A Quaint, Picturesque Little Pile: Architecture and the Past in Washington Irving." In *The Old and New World Romanticism of Washington Irving*, edited by Stanley Brodwin, 139–49. New York: Greenwood, 1986.

Antelyes, Peter. *Tales of Adventurous Enterprise: Washington Irving and the Poetics of Western Expansion*. New York: Columbia University Press, 1990.

Apocalypto. Directed by Mel Gibson. Burbank, CA: Touchstone Pictures in association with Icon Productions, 2006.

Appleby, Joyce. "Economics: The Agrarian Republic." In *Thomas Jefferson and the Politics of Nature*, edited by Thomas S. Engeman, 143–63. Notre Dame, IN: University of Notre Dame Press, 2000.

Axelrad, Allan M. "Cooper, Aristocracy, and Capitalism." In *James Fenimore Cooper Society Website*, edited by Hugh C. MacDougall. http://external.oneonta.edu/cooper/articles/ala/1996ala-axelrad.html (accessed January 6, 2013).

———. *History and Utopia: A Study of the World View of James Fenimore Cooper*. Norwood, PA: Norwood, 1978.

Balmer, Randall. *A Perfect Babel of Confusion: Dutch Religion and English Culture in the Middle Colonies*. New York: Oxford University Press, 1989.

Barber, John W. *Elements of General History*. 4th ed. New Haven, CT: Durrie & Peck, 1849.

Barnes, Geraldine. *Viking America: The First Millennium*. Cambridge: D. S. Brewer, 2001.

Barnes, Homer F. *Charles Fenno Hoffman*. New York: AMS, 1966.

Bassett, John Spencer. *The Middle Group of American Historians*. New York: Macmillan, 1917.

Bauer, Ralph. "Toward a Cultural Geography of Colonial American Literatures: Empire, Location, Creolization." In *A Companion to the Literatures of Colonial America*, edited by Susan Castillo and Ivy Schweitzer, 38–59. Malden, MA: Blackwell, 2005.

Baym, Nina. *American Women Writers and the Work of History, 1790–1860*. New Brunswick, NJ: Rutgers University Press, 1995.

Belknap, Jeffrey, and Raúl Fernández, eds. *José Martí's "Our America": From National to Hemispheric Cultural Studies*. Durham, NC: Duke University Press, 1998.

Bell, Michael Davitt. *Hawthorne and the Historical Romance of New England*. Princeton, NJ: Princeton University Press, 1971.

Bender, Thomas. "Introduction: Historians, the Nation, and the Plenitude of Narratives." In *Rethinking American History in a Global Age*, edited by Thomas Bender, 1–21. Berkeley: University of California Press, 2002.

———. *New York Intellect: A History of Intellectual Life in New York City, from 1750 to the Beginnings of Our Own Time*. New York: Knopf, 1987.

Bercovitch, Sacvan. *The American Jeremiad*. 1978. Anniversary ed. Madison: University of Wisconsin Press, 2012.

Bergland, Renée. *The National Uncanny: Indian Ghosts and American Subjects*. Hanover, NH: University Press of New England, 2000.

Bergman, Jill, and Debra Bernardi, eds. *Our Sisters' Keepers: Nineteenth-Century Benevolence Literature by American Women*. Tuscaloosa: University of Alabama Press, 2005.

Bérubé, Michael. "American Studies without Exceptions." Special issue, *PMLA* 118 (2003): 103–13.

Bewley, Marius. "Fenimore Cooper and the Economic Age." *American Literature* 26.2 (1954): 166–95.

Billington, Ray. *The Protestant Crusade, 1800—1860: A Study of the Origins of American Nativism*. New York: Macmillan, 1938.

Bird, Robert Montgomery. *The Gladiator*. In *Early American Drama*, edited by Jeffrey H. Richards. New York: Penguin Classics, 1997.

Black, Michael L., and Nancy B. Black. Introduction to *A History of New York*, by Washington Irving, xv–lxviii. Boston: Twayne, 1984.

Blackburn, Roderic H., and Ruth Piwonka, eds. *Remembrance of Patria: Dutch Arts and Culture in Colonial America, 1609–1776*. New York: Albany Institute of History and Art, 1988.

Blair's Outline of Chronology, Ancient and Modern. Boston: Richardson & Lord, 1826.

Boggs, Colleen Glenney. *Transnationalism and American Literature: Literary Translation, 1773–1892*. New York: Routledge, 2007.

Bonomi, Patricia, ed. *Colonial Dutch Studies: An Interdisciplinary Approach*. New York: New York University Press, 1988.

———. *A Factious People: Politics and Society in Colonial New York*. New York: Columbia University Press, 1971.

Bowden, Mary Weatherspoon. "Knickerbocker's History and the 'Enlightened' Men of New York City." *American Literature* 47.2 (1975): 159–72.

"Bradford's *History of Plymouth Plantation*." Review of *History of Plymouth Plantation*, by William Bradford. *North American Review*, July 1856, 269–70.

Bradford, William. *Of Plymouth Plantation, 1620–1647*. New York: Modern Library, 1981.

Brading, D. A. *The First America: The Spanish Monarchy, Creole Patriots, and the Liberal State, 1492–1867.* Cambridge: Cambridge University Press, 1991.

Bradley, Elizabeth L. *Knickerbocker: The Myth behind New York.* New Brunswick, NJ: Rivergate Books, 2009.

Bremner, Robert H. *From the Depths: The Discovery of Poverty in the United States.* New York: New York University Press, 1956.

Brickhouse, Anna. *Transamerican Literary Relations and the Nineteenth-Century Public Sphere.* Cambridge: Cambridge University Press, 2004.

Brooks, Van Wyck. *Van Wyck Brooks, the Early Years: A Selection from His Works, 1908–1925.* Boston: Northeastern University Press, 1993.

Bruins, Elton J. "Americanization in Reformed Religious Life." In *The Dutch in America: Immigration, Settlement and Cultural Change*, edited by Robert P. Swierenga, 175–90. New Brunswick, NJ: Rutgers University Press, 1985.

Buell, Lawrence. Introduction to *Selected Poems*, by Henry Wadsworth Longfellow, vii–xxxv. New York: Penguin Books, 1988.

———. *New England Literary Culture: From Revolution through Renaissance.* Cambridge: Cambridge University Press, 1986.

Burstein, Andrew. *The Original Knickerbocker: The Life of Washington Irving.* New York: Basic Books, 2007.

Butler, Frederick. *Sketches of Universal History, Sacred and Profane: From the Creation of the World, to the Year 1818, of the Christian Era.* 3rd ed. Hartford, CT: Oliver D. Cooke, 1820.

Calhoun, Charles C. *Longfellow: A Rediscovered Life.* Boston: Beacon, 2004.

Callcott, George H. *History in the United States, 1800–1860: Its Practice and Purpose.* Baltimore: Johns Hopkins University Press, 1970.

Callow, James T. *Kindred Spirits: Knickerbocker Writers and American Artists.* Chapel Hill: University of North Carolina Press, 1967.

Carpenter, Charles. *History of American Schoolbooks.* Philadelphia: University of Pennsylvania Press, 1963.

Carr, Helen. *Inventing the American Primitive: Politics, Gender, and the Representation of Native American Literary Traditions, 1789–1936.* New York: New York University Press, 1996.

Carroll, Lewis. "Hiawatha's Photographing." In *Evangeline and Selected Tales and Poems*, edited by Horace Gregory, 283–86. New York: Signet Classic, 1990.

Casey, Marion R. "The Limits of Equality: Racial and Ethnic Tensions in the New Republic, 1789–1836." In *Race and Ethnicity in America: A Concise History*, edited by Ronald H. Bayor, 41–62. New York: Columbia University Press, 2003.

Charvat, William. *Literary Publishing in America, 1790–1850.* Philadelphia: University of Pennsylvania Press, 1959.

———. "Prescott's Political and Social Attitudes." *American Literature* 13.4 (1942): 320–30.

Charvat, William, and Michael Kraus. *William Hickling Prescott: Representative Selections.* New York: American Book, 1943.

Cheng, Eileen Ka-May. *The Plain and Noble Garb of Truth: Nationalism and Impartiality in American Historical Writing, 1784–1860.* Athens: University of Georgia Press, 2008.

Chevigny, Bell Gale, and Gari Laguardia, eds. *Reinventing the Americas: Comparative Studies of Literature in the United States and Spanish America.* Cambridge: Cambridge University Press, 1986.

Choate, Rufus, and Samuel Gilman Brown. *The Works of Rufus Choate, with a Memoir of His Life.* 2 vols. Boston: Little, Brown, 1862.

Clavel, Marcel. *Fenimore Cooper and His Critics: American, British and French Criticisms of the Novelist's Early Work*. Aix-en-Provence: Imprimerie Universitaire de Provence, E. Fourcine, 1938.

Clendinnen, Inga. "'Fierce and Unnatural *Cruelty*': Cortés and the Conquest of Mexico." *Representations* 33 (1991): 65–100.

Cohen, David Steven. *The Dutch-American Farm*. New York: New York University Press, 1992.

Cooper, James Fenimore. *J. Fenimore Cooper's Works*. Vol. 1 (*The Bravo, Mercedes of Castile*). New York: n.p., n.d.

———. *A Letter to His Countrymen*. New York: J. Wiley, 1834.

———. *The Letters and Journals of James Fenimore Cooper*. 6 vols. Edited by James Franklin Beard. Cambridge, MA: Harvard University Press, 1960–68.

———. *The Water-Witch; or, The Skimmer of the Seas*. Ed. Thomas Philbrick and Marianne Philbrick. New York: AMS, 2010.

Cooper, James Fenimore, and Constance Ayers Denne. *Gleanings in Europe, Italy*. Albany: State University of New York Press, 1980.

Cooper, Susan Fenimore. *Pages and Pictures from the Writings of James Fenimore Cooper, with Notes by Susan Fenimore Cooper*. New York: W. A. Townsend, 1861.

Cowan, William. "Ojibwa Vocabulary in Longfellow's *Hiawatha*." In *Papers of the Eighteenth Algonquin Conference*, edited by William Cowan, 59–67. Ottawa: Carleton University, 1987.

Dahl, Curtis. *Robert Montgomery Bird*. New York: Twayne, 1963.

Damrosch, David. *What Is World Literature?* Princeton, NJ: Princeton University Press, 2003.

Darling, Arthur. *Political Changes in Massachusetts, 1824–1848*. New Haven, CT: Yale University Press, 1925.

Darnell, Donald G. *William Hickling Prescott*. Boston: Twayne, 1975.

DeGuzmán, María. *Spain's Long Shadow: The Black Legend, Off-Whiteness and the Anglo-American Empire*. Minneapolis: University of Minnesota Press, 2005.

De Jong, Gerald F. *The Dutch in America, 1609–1974*. Boston: Twayne, 1975.

———. *The Dutch Reformed Church in the American Colonies*. Grand Rapids, MI: Wm. B. Eerdmans, 1978.

Dekker, George. *James Fenimore Cooper: The Novelist*. London: Routledge & Kegan Paul, 1967.

Dekker, George, and John P. McWilliams, eds. *Fenimore Cooper: The Critical Heritage*. London: Routledge & Kegan Paul, 1973.

Delano, Sterling. *Brook Farm: The Dark Side of Utopia*. Cambridge, MA: Harvard University Press, 2004.

Denne, Constance Ayers. "Cooper's Use of Setting in the European Trilogy." *James Fenimore Cooper: His Country and His Art* (1981): 52–70.

Dimock, Wai Chee. "Introduction: Planet and America, Set and Subset." In *Shades of the Planet: American Literature as World Literature*, edited by Wai Chee Dimock and Lawrence Buell, 1–16. Princeton, NJ: Princeton University Press, 2007.

———. "Literature for the Planet." *PMLA* 116.1 (2001): 173–88.

———. "Planetary Time and Global Translation: 'Context' in Literary Studies." *Common Knowledge* 9.3 (2003): 488–507.

———. "Scales of Aggregation: Prenational, Subnational, Transnational." *American Literary History* 18 (2006): 219–28.

———. *Through Other Continents: American Literature across Deep Time*. Princeton, NJ: Princeton University Press, 2006.

Durant, David. "Aeolism in Knickerbocker's *A History of New York*." *American Literature* 41.4 (1970): 493–506.

"*The Dutch Republic.*" Review of *The Rise of the Dutch Republic*, by John Lothrop Motley. *Southern Literary Messenger*, October 1858, 241–49.

Edwards, [Owen Dudley]. "John Lothrop Motley and the Netherlands." In *A Bilateral Bicentennial: A History of Dutch-American Relations, 1782–1982*, edited by J. W. Schulte Nordholt and Robert P. Swierenga, 171–98. [New York]: Octagon Books; Amsterdam: Meulenhoff International, 1982.

Eipper, John. "The Canonizer De-Canonized: The Case of William H. *Prescott.*" *Hispania* 83.3 (2000): 416–27.

Elliott, Emory. "Diversity in the United States and Abroad: What Does It Mean When American Studies Is Transnational?" *American Quarterly* 59.1 (2007): 1–22.

Elson, Ruth Miller. *Guardians of Tradition: American Schoolbooks in the Nineteenth Century.* Lincoln: University of Nebraska Press, 1964.

Ely, James W. *The Guardian of Every Other Right: A Constitutional History of Property Rights.* 3rd ed. New York: Oxford University Press, 2008.

———, ed. *Property Rights in the Colonial Era and Early Republic.* Property Rights in American History 1. New York: Garland, 1997.

Ernest, John. "Reading the Romantic Past: William H. Prescott's *History of the Conquest of Mexico.*" *American Literary History* 5.2 (1993): 231–49.

Fabend, Firth Haring. *Zion on the Hudson: Dutch New York and New Jersey in the Age of Revivals.* New Brunswick, NJ: Rutgers University Press, 2000.

Fabian, Ann. "Speculation on Distress: The Popular Discourse of the Panics of 1837 and 1857." *Yale Journal of Criticism* 3.1 (1989): 127–42.

Faherty, Duncan. *Remodeling the Nation: The Architecture of American Identity, 1776–1858.* Durham: University of New Hampshire Press, 2007.

Farmer, Jared. *On Zion's Mount: Mormons, Indians, and the American Landscape.* Cambridge, MA: Harvard University Press, 2008.

Fenton, Elizabeth. *Religious Liberties: Anti-Catholicism and Liberal Democracy in Nineteenth-Century U.S. Literature and Culture.* Oxford: Oxford University Press, 2011.

Ferguson, Robert. "'Hunting Down a Nation': Irving's *A History of New York.*" *Nineteenth-Century Fiction* 36.1 (1981): 22–46.

———. "Longfellow's Political Fears: Civic Authority and the Role of the Artist in *Hiawatha* and *Miles Standish.*" *American Literature* 50.2 (1978): 187–215.

Fichtelberg, Joseph. *Critical Fictions: Sentiment and the American Market, 1780–1870.* Athens: University of Georgia Press, 2003.

Fitzhugh, George. *Sociology for the South; or, The Failure of Free Society.* Richmond, VA: A. Morris, 1854.

Fitzhugh, William F., and Elisabeth Ward, eds. *Vikings: The North Atlantic Saga.* Washington, DC: Smithsonian Press, 2000.

Fleming, Robin. "Picturesque History and the Medieval in Nineteenth-Century America." *American Historical Review* 100 (1995): 1079–84.

Fox, Dixon Ryan. *The Decline of Aristocracy in the Politics of New York.* New York: Columbia University Press, 1919.

Franchot, Jenny. *Roads to Rome: The Antebellum Protestant Encounter with Catholicism.* Berkeley: University of California Press, 1994.

Francis, Richard. *Transcendental Utopias: Individual and Community at Brook Farm, Fruitlands, and Walden.* Ithaca, NY: Cornell University Press, 1997.

Franklin, Wayne. *James Fenimore Cooper: The Early Years.* New Haven, CT: Yale University Press, 2007.

Gardiner, C. Harvey. *William Hickling Prescott: A Biography.* Austin: University of Texas Press, 1969.

Gibson, Mel, and Farhad Safinia. DVD commentary. *Apocalypto.* Burbank, CA: Buena Vista Home Entertainment, 2007.

Giles, Paul. *Transatlantic Insurrections: British Culture and the Formation of American Literature, 1730–1860.* Philadelphia: University of Pennsylvania Press, 2001.

———. "Transnationalism and Classic American Literature." Special issue, *PMLA* 118 (2003): 62–77.

———. *Virtual Americas: Transnational Fictions and the Transatlantic Imaginary.* Durham, NC: Duke University Press, 2002.

Gladsky, Thomas. "Revolution and Renewal in Prescott's *The Conquest of Peru.*" *Modern Age* 29.4 (1985): 314–18.

Glickstein, Jonathan A. "Pressures from Below: Pauperism, Chattel Slavery, and the Ideological Construction of Free Market Labor Incentives in Antebellum America." *Radical History Review* 69 (1997): 114–59.

Goode, Mike. *Sentimental Masculinity and the Rise of History, 1790–1890.* Cambridge: Cambridge University Press, 2009.

Goodfriend, Joyce D. *Before the Melting Pot: Society and Culture in Colonial New York City, 1664–1730.* Princeton, NJ: Princeton University Press, 1992.

———, ed. *Revisiting New Netherland: Perspectives on Early Dutch America.* Leiden: Brill, 2005.

Goodrich, Samuel Griswold. *Peter Parley's Common School History.* Boston: American Stationers', 1838.

———. *Peter Parley's Universal History, on the Basis of Geography: For the Use of Families.* Vol. 2. Boston: American Stationers', 1837.

Gootenberg, Paul. *Imagining Development: Economic Ideas in Peru's "Fictitious Prosperity" of Guano, 1840–1880.* Berkeley: University of California Press, 1993.

Gould, Edward Sherman [Cassio, pseud.]. "The Man in the Claret-Coloured Coat to His Countrymen." In *James Fenimore Cooper Society Website*, edited by Hugh C. MacDougall. http://external.oneonta.edu/cooper/writings/1834-claret.html (accessed November 3, 2006).

Griffin, Susan M. *Anti-Catholicism and Nineteenth-Century Fiction.* Cambridge: Cambridge University Press, 2004.

Grossman, James. *James Fenimore Cooper.* Stanford, CA: Stanford University Press, 1967.

Gruesz, Kirsten Silva. *Ambassadors of Culture: The Transamerican Origins of Latino Writing.* Princeton, NJ: Princeton University Press, 2002.

———. "*El Gran Poeta* Longfellow and a Psalm of Exile." *American Literary History* 10.3 (1998): 395–427.

Guarneri, Carl. *The Utopian Alternative: Fourierism in Nineteenth-Century America.* Ithaca, NY: Cornell University Press, 1991.

Guberman, J. *The Life of John Lothrop Motley.* The Hague: Martinus Nijhoff, 1973.

Habermas, Jürgen. *The Postnational Constellation.* Cambridge, MA: MIT Press, 2001.

Hagensick, Donna. "Irving: A Littérateur in Politics." In *Critical Essays on Washington Irving*, edited by Ralph M. Aderman, 178–91. Boston: G. K. Hall, 1990.

Harvey, Bruce. *American Geographics: U.S. National Narratives and the Representation of the Non-European World, 1830–1865.* Stanford, CA: Stanford University Press, 2001.

Hawthorne, Nathaniel. *The Blithedale Romance.* Edited by William E. Cain. Boston: Bedford Books of St. Martin's Press, 1996.

Hazewell, C. C. "Agrarianism as a Term of Reproach." In *Agrarianism in American History*, edited by Louis H. Douglas, 24–28. Lexington, MA: D. C. Heath, 1969.

Headley, Janet. "Anne Whitney's *Leif Eriksson*: A Brahmin Response to Christopher Columbus." *American Art* 17.2 (2003): 40–59.

Hecht, Roger. "Nature's 'Cunning Alphabet': Pastoral Landscape and Politics in Nineteenth-Century American Literature." PhD diss., Syracuse University, 2002.

Hedges, William L. "*The Knickerbocker History* as Knickerbocker's 'History.'" In *The Old and New World Romanticism of Washington Irving*, edited by Stanley Brodwin, 153–66. New York: Greenwood, 1986.

———. *Washington Irving: An American Study, 1802–1832*. Baltimore: Johns Hopkins University Press, 1965.

Higby, Chester Penn, and B. T. Schantz. Introduction to *John Lothrop Motley: Representative Selections*, by John Lothrop Motley, xi–cxxxi. New York: American Book, 1939.

Hilen, Andrew. *Longfellow and Scandinavia: A Study of the Poet's Relationship with the Northern Languages and Literatures*. New Haven, CT: Yale University Press, 1947.

Hirsh, John C., and John Lothrop Motley. "John Lothrop Motley on the American Republic, 1846: A Document." *Journal of the Early Republic* 6.1 (1986): 59–65.

Hobsbawm, E. J. *The Age of Revolution: Europe, 1789–1848*. New York: Praeger, 1969.

Hollander, John, ed. *American Poetry: The Nineteenth Century*. New York: Library of America, 1993.

Howe, Daniel Walker. *The Political Culture of the American Whigs*. Chicago: University of Chicago Press, 1979.

———. *The Unitarian Conscience: Harvard Moral Philosophy, 1805–1861*. Middletown, CT: Wesleyan University Press, 1988.

Howitt, William. "Longfellow's *Hiawatha*." *Athenaeum*, November 17, 1855, 1337.

Huang, Yunte. *Transpacific Imaginations: History, Literature, Counterpoetics*. Cambridge, MA: Harvard University Press, 2008.

Huston, James. *Calculating the Value of the Union: Slavery, Property Rights, and the Economic Origins of the Civil War*. Chapel Hill: University of North Carolina Press, 2003.

Insko, Jeffrey. "Diedrich Knickerbocker, Regular Bred Historian." *Early American Literature* 43.3 (2008): 605–41.

Irmscher, Christoph. *Longfellow Redux*. Urbana: University of Illinois Press, 2006.

Irving, Washington. *A History of New York*. Edited by Michael L. Black and Nancy B. Black. Vol. 7 of *The Complete Works of Washington Irving*. Boston: Twayne, 1984.

———. *Miscellaneous Writings, 1803–1859*, vol. 2. Edited by Wayne R. Kime. Vol. 29 of *The Complete Works of Washington Irving*. Boston: Twayne, 1981.

———. *Washington Irving: History, Tales and Sketches*. New York: Library of America, 1983.

Jaksić, Iván. *The Hispanic World and American Intellectual Life, 1820–1880*. New York: Palgrave Macmillan, 2007.

Jay, Gregory. "The End of 'American' Literature: Toward a Multicultural Practice." *College English* 53.3 (1991): 264–81.

Jefferson, Thomas. *The Portable Thomas Jefferson*. Edited by Merrill D. Peterson. New York: Penguin Books, 1975.

Johanssen, Robert. *To the Halls of the Montezumas: The Mexican War in the American Imagination*. New York: Oxford University Press, 1985.

John, Richard. "Eben Norton Horsford, the Northmen, and the Founding of Massachusetts." *Cambridge Historical Society Proceedings* 45 (1980–85): 116–44.

Johnson, James H. *Venice Incognito: Masks in the Serene Republic*. Berkeley: University of California Press, 2011.

Jones, Gavin. *American Hungers: The Problem of Poverty in U.S. Literature, 1840–1945*. Princeton, NJ: Princeton University Press, 2008.

Kadir, Djelal. "Introduction: America and Its Studies." Special issue, *PMLA* 118 (2003): 9–24.

Kagan, Richard. "Prescott's Paradigm: American Historical Scholarship and the Decline of Spain." *American Historical Review* 101.2 (1996): 423–46.

Kalewala, das National-Epos der Finnen, nach der zweiten Ausgabe ins Deutsche übertragen von Anton Schiefner. Helsingfors: J. C. Frenckell & Sohn, 1852.

Kammen, Michael. *Colonial New York: A History*. New York: Scribner's, 1975.

Kaplan, Amy. *The Anarchy of Empire in the Making of U.S. Culture*. Cambridge, MA: Harvard University Press, 2002.

———. "'Left Alone with America': The Absence of Empire in the Study of American Culture." In *Cultures of United States Imperialism*, edited by Amy Kaplan and Donald Pease, 3–21. Durham, NC: Duke University Press, 1993.

Kardux, Joke, and Eduard van de Bilt. *Newcomers in an Old City: The American Pilgrims in Leiden, 1609–1620*. Leiden: Burgersdijk & Niermans, 1998.

Keen, Benjamin. *The Aztec Image in Western Thought*. New Brunswick, NJ: Rutgers University Press, 1971.

Kelly, William P. *Plotting America's Past: Fenimore Cooper and "The Leatherstocking Tales."* Carbondale: Southern Illinois University Press, 1983.

Kennedy, J. Gerald. "Cooper's Europe and His Quarrel with America." In *A Historical Guide to James Fenimore Cooper*, edited by Leland S. Person, 91–122. Oxford: Oxford University Press, 2007.

Kenney, Alice P. *Stubborn for Liberty: The Dutch in New York*. Syracuse, NY: Syracuse University Press, 1975.

Knobel, Dale T. *Paddy and the Republic: Ethnicity and Nationality in Antebellum America*. Middletown, CT: Wesleyan University Press, 1986.

Kolodny, Annette. *In Search of First Contact: The Vikings of Vinland, the Peoples of the Dawnland, and the Anglo-American Anxiety of Discovery*. Durham, NC: Duke University Press, 2012.

Kraus, Michael. *The Writing of American History*. Norman: University of Oklahoma Press, 1953.

Kupperman, Karen Ordahl. "International at the Creation: Early Modern American History." In *Rethinking American History in a Global Age*, edited by Thomas Bender, 103–22. Berkeley: University of California Press, 2002.

Lang, Amy. *The Syntax of Class: Writing Inequality in Nineteenth-Century America*. Princeton, NJ: Princeton University Press, 2003.

Lause, Mark. *Young America: Land, Labor, and the Republican Community*. Urbana: University of Illinois Press, 2005.

Laven, David. *Venice and Venetia under the Habsburgs, 1815–1835*. Oxford: Oxford University Press, 2002.

Leask, Nigel. "'The Ghost in Chapultepec': Fanny Calderón de la Barca, William Prescott and Nineteenth-Century Mexican Travel Accounts." In *Voyages and Visions: Towards a Cultural History of Travel*, edited by Jaś Elsner and Joan-Pau Rubiés, 184–209. London: Reaktion Books, 1999.

LeMenager, Stephanie. "Trading Stories: Washington Irving and the Global West." *American Literary History* 15.4 (2003): 683–708.

Levander, Caroline F., and Robert S. Levine. *Hemispheric American Studies*. New Brunswick, NJ: Rutgers University Press, 2008.

Levin, David. *History as Romantic Art: Bancroft, Prescott, Motley and Parkman*. Stanford, CA: Stanford University Press, 1959.

Levine, Robert. *Conspiracy and Romance: Studies in Brockden Brown, Cooper, Hawthorne, and Melville*. Cambridge: Cambridge University Press, 1989.

Lewis, R. W. B. *The American Adam: Innocence, Tragedy, and Tradition in the Nineteenth Century*. Chicago: University of Chicago Press, 1955.

Long, Orie. *Literary Pioneers: Early American Explorers of European Cultures*. Cambridge, MA: Harvard University Press, 1935.

Longfellow, Henry Wadsworth. *The Letters of Henry Wadsworth Longfellow*. 6 vols. Edited by Andrew Hilen. Cambridge, MA: Harvard University Press, 1967–82.

———. *The Poetical Works of Longfellow, Cambridge Edition*. Edited by George Monteiro. Boston: Houghton Mifflin, 1975.

———. *The Song of Hiawatha*. Edited by Daniel Aaron. London: Everyman Library, 1992.

———. "Tegnér's *Frithiof's Saga*." *North American Review*, July 1837, 149–85.

"Longfellow's *Song of Hiawatha*." Review of *The Song of Hiawatha*, by Henry Wadsworth Longfellow. *Putnam's Monthly Magazine*, December 1855, 578–87.

Lowenthal, David. *The Past Is a Foreign Country*. Cambridge: Cambridge University Press, 1985.

Maddox, Lucy. *Removals: Nineteenth-Century American Literature and the Politics of Indian Affairs*. New York: Oxford University Press, 1991.

Manca, Joseph. "Erasing the Dutch: The Critical Reception of Hudson Valley Dutch Architecture, 1670–1840." In *Going Dutch: The Dutch Presence in America, 1609–2009*, edited by Joyce D. Goodfriend, Benjamin Schmidt, and Annette Stott, 59–84. Leiden: Brill, 2008.

Manthorne, Katherine. *Tropical Renaissance: North American Artists Exploring Latin America, 1839–1879*. Washington, DC: Smithsonian Institution Press, 1989.

Martin, Robert K., and Leland S. Person, eds. *Roman Holidays: American Writers and Artists in Nineteenth-Century Italy*. Iowa City: University of Iowa Press, 2002.

Matthews, J. V. "'Whig History': The New England Whigs and a Usable Past." *New England Quarterly* 51.2 (1978): 193–208.

Matthiessen, F. O. *American Renaissance: Art and Expression in the Age of Emerson and Whitman*. London: Oxford University Press, 1941.

McCarthy, Kathleen. *American Creed: Philanthropy and the Rise of Civil Society, 1700–1865*. Chicago: University of Chicago Press, 2003.

McGill, Meredith L. *American Literature and the Culture of Reprinting, 1834–1853*. Philadelphia: University of Pennsylvania Press, 2003.

———. "Poe, Literary Nationalism, and Authorial Identity." In *The American Face of Edgar Allan Poe*, edited by Shawn Rosenheim and Stephen Rachman, 289–98. Baltimore: Johns Hopkins University Press, 1995.

McLamore, Richard V. "The Dutchman in the Attic: Claiming an Inheritance in *The Sketchbook of Geoffrey Crayon*." *American Literature* 72.1 (2000): 31–57.

McWilliams, John. "Fictions of Merry Mount." *American Quarterly* 29.1 (1977): 3–30.

———. *New England's Crises and Cultural Memory: Literature, Politics, History, Religion, 1620–1860*. Cambridge: Cambridge University Press, 2004.

M.D.C. [Moncure Daniel Conway]. "*Hiawatha* and *Kalewala*." *Daily National Intelligencer*, November 29, 1855.

———. "*The Song of Hiawatha*." *Daily National Intelligencer*, November 23, 1855.

Merriman, T. M. *The Trail of History; or, History of Religion and Empire in Parallel.* Johnson, VT: the Author, 1860.

Messmer, Marietta. "Toward a Declaration of Interdependence; or, Interrogating the Boundaries in Twentieth-Century Histories of North American Literature." Special issue, *PMLA* 118 (2003): 41–55.

Meyers, Marvin. *The Jacksonian Persuasion.* Stanford, CA: Stanford University Press, 1960.

Miller, Angela. *The Empire of the Eye: Landscape Representations and American Cultural Politics, 1825–1875.* Ithaca, NY: Cornell University Press, 1993.

———. "Thomas Cole and Jacksonian America: The *Course of Empire* as Political Allegory." *Prospects* 14 (1989): 65–92.

Miller, Perry. *The Raven and the Whale: The War of Words and Wits in the Era of Poe and Melville.* New York: Harcourt, Brace & World, 1956.

Morse, Jedidiah. *The American Geography; or, A View of the Present Situation of the United States of America.* Elizabethtown, NJ: Shepard Kollock, 1789.

Motley, John Lothrop. *The Correspondence of John Lothrop Motley.* 2 vols. Edited by George William Curtis. New York: Harper & Brothers, 1889.

———. *John Lothrop Motley and His Family: Further Letters and Records.* Edited by Susan St. John Mildmay. London: John Lane, 1910.

———. *The Rise of the Dutch Republic: A History.* 3 vols. New York: Harper & Brothers, 1862.

"Motley's *Dutch Republic.*" Review of *The Rise of the Dutch Republic,* by John Lothrop Motley. *Littell's Living Age,* June 26, 1858, 1018–22.

"Motley's *Dutch Republic.*" Review of *The Rise of the Dutch Republic,* by John Lothrop Motley. *Putnam's Monthly Magazine,* May 1856, 552.

"Motley's *Dutch Republic.*" Review of *The Rise of the Dutch Republic,* by John Lothrop Motley. *Southern Quarterly Review,* February 1857, 427–55.

"Motley's History of the Dutch Republic." Review of *The Rise of the Dutch Republic,* by John Lothrop Motley. *Littell's Living Age,* April 19, 1856, 175–78.

"Motley's *Rise of the Dutch Republic.*" Review of *The Rise of the Dutch Republic,* by John Lothrop Motley. *Littell's Living Age,* June 14, 1856, 692–94.

"Motley's *Rise of the Dutch Republic.*" Review of *The Rise of the Dutch Republic,* by John Lothrop Motley. *North American Review,* July 1856, 182–217.

Moyne, Earnest J. *"Hiawatha" and "Kalevala": A Study of the Relationship between Longfellow's "Indian Edda" and the Finnish Epic.* Helsinki: Suomalainen Tiedeakatemia, 1963.

Moyne, Ernest. "Parodies of Longfellow's *Song of Hiawatha.*" *Delaware Notes* 30 (1957): 93–108.

Mulkern, John R. *The Know-Nothing Party in Massachusetts: The Rise and Fall of a People's Movement.* Boston: Northeastern University Press, 1990.

Murphy, Cullen. *Are We Rome? The Fall of an Empire and the Fate of America.* Boston: Houghton Mifflin, 2007.

Murphy, Gretchen. *Hemispheric Imaginings: The Monroe Doctrine and Narratives of U.S. Empire.* Durham, NC: Duke University Press, 2005.

Murray, David. *Forked Tongues: Speech, Writing and Representation in North American Indian Texts.* Bloomington: Indiana University Press, 1991.

Murrin, John M. "English Rights as Ethnic Aggression: The English Conquest, the Charter of Liberties of 1683, and Leisler's Rebellion in New York." In *Authority and Resistance in Early New York,* edited by William Pencak and Conrad Edick Wright, 56–94. New York: New York Historical Society, 1988.

Narrett, David E. "Dutch Customs of Inheritance, Women, and the Law in Colonial New

York City." In *Authority and Resistance in Early New York*, edited by William Pencak and Conrad Edick Wright, 27–55. New York: New York Historical Society, 1988.

Nattermann, Udo. "Ahistorical Histories: Ideological Persuasion in Cooper's European Novels." *Modern Age* 42.3 (2000): 274–80.

Ngai, Mae M. "Transnationalism and the Transformation of the 'Other': Response to the Presidential Address." *American Quarterly* 57.1 (2005): 59–65.

Noble, Louis. *The Life and Works of Thomas Cole*. Cambridge, MA: Harvard University Press, 1964.

Norkunas, Martha. *Monuments and Memory: History and Representation in Lowell, Massachusetts*. Washington, DC: Smithsonian Institution Press, 2002.

Novick, Peter. *That Noble Dream: The "Objectivity Question" and the American Historical Profession*. Cambridge: Cambridge University Press, 1988.

Nyland, Waino. "*Kalevala* as a Reputed Source of Longfellow's *Song of Hiawatha*." *American Literature* 22.1 (1950): 1–20.

O'Connor, Thomas H. *The Athens of America: Boston, 1825–1845*. Amherst: University of Massachusetts Press, 2006.

Ogden, Rollo. *William Hickling Prescott*. Boston: Houghton Mifflin, 1904.

Osborn, Chase S., and Stellanova Osborn. *Schoolcraft, Longfellow, Hiawatha*. Lancaster, PA: Jacques Castell, 1942.

Outland, Ethel R. *The "Effingham" Libels on Cooper: A Documentary History of the Libel Suits of James Fenimore Cooper Centering around the Three Mile Point Controversy and the Novel "Home as Found," 1837–1845*. University of Wisconsin Studies in Language and Literature 28. Madison: Antes, 1929.

Padgett, Tim. "*Apocalypto* Now." *Time Magazine*, March 27, 2006.

Parkman, Francis. *France and England in North America*. 2 vols. New York: Library of America, 1983.

Parrington, Vernon. *Main Currents in American Thought: An Interpretation of American Literature from the Beginnings to 1920*. 3 vols. New York: Harcourt, Brace, 1930.

Payne, John. *An Epitome of History; or, A Concise View of the Most Important Revolutions, and Events, Which Are Recorded in the Histories of the Principal Empires, Kingdoms, States, and Republics, Now Subsisting in the World*. London: J. Johnson; New York: Berry, Rogers & Berry, 1794.

Peabody, Elizabeth Palmer. *First Steps to the Study of History: Being Part First of a Key to History*. Boston: Hilliard, Gray, 1832.

———. *The Polish-American System of Chronology, Reproduced, with Some Modifications, from General Bem's Franco-Polish Method*. Boston: 13 West Street; New York: Putnam, 1850.

Pearce, Colin. "Prescott's Conquests: Anthropophagy, Auto-da-Fe and Eternal Return." *Interpretation* 24.3 (1997): 339–61.

Pease, Donald. "The Extraterritoriality of the Literature for Our Planet." *ESQ* 50.1–3 (2004): 177–221.

Peck, Harry Thurston. *William Hickling Prescott*. 1905. Reprint, New York: Greenwood, 1969.

Pfitzer, Gregory. *Picturing the Past: Illustrated Histories and the American Imagination, 1840–1900*. Washington, DC: Smithsonian Institution Press, 2002.

———. *Popular History and the Literary Marketplace, 1840–1920*. Amherst: University of Massachusetts Press, 2008.

Philbrick, Thomas. *James Fenimore Cooper and the Development of American Sea Fiction*. Cambridge, MA: Harvard University Press, 1961.

Philbrick, Thomas, and Marianne Philbrick. "Historical Introduction." In *The Water-Witch; or, Skimmer of the Seas*, by James Fenimore Cooper, xi–xxxi. New York: AMS, 2010.

"Philip II. and His Times." Review of *History of the Reign of Philip the Second, King of Spain*, by William Hickling Prescott, and *The Rise of the Dutch Republic*, by John Lothrop Motley. *Littell's Living Age*, March 7, 1857, 577–602.

Pike, Robert. *Intellectual Chronology*. Montrose, PA: "Spectator" Office, 1837.

Pocock, J. G. A. *The Machiavellian Moment: Florentine Political Thought and the Atlantic Republican Tradition*. Princeton, NJ: Princeton University Press, 1975.

Poole, Deborah. "Landscape and the Imperial Subject: U.S. Images of the Andes, 1859–1930." In *Close Encounters of Empire: Writing the Cultural History of U.S.-Latin American Relations*, edited by Gilbert M. Joseph, Catherine C. LeGrand, and Ricardo D. Salvatore, 106–38. Durham, NC: Duke University Press, 1998.

Pratt, Mary Louise. *Imperial Eyes: Travel Writing and Transculturation*. 2nd ed. London: Routledge, 2008.

Prescott, William Hickling. *The Correspondence of William Hickling Prescott, 1833–1847*. Edited by Roger Wolcott. Boston: Houghton Mifflin, 1925.

———. *History of the Conquest of Mexico; and History of the Conquest of Peru*. New York: Cooper Square, 2000.

———. *History of the Reign of Philip the Second, King of Spain*. Vol. 1. Boston: Phillips, Samson, 1855.

———. *The Literary Memoranda of William Hickling Prescott*. 2 vols. Edited by C. Harvey Gardiner. Norman: University of Oklahoma Press, 1961.

———. "Transcribed Correspondence, 1834–1850." Edited by Roger Wolcott, box 11. William Hickling Prescott Papers, Massachusetts Historical Society, Boston.

———. *Unpublished Letters to Gayangos in the Library of the Hispanic Society of America*. Edited by Clara Louisa Penney. New York: Hispanic Society of America, 1927.

Pritzker, Barry. *A Native American Encyclopedia: History, Culture, and Peoples*. Oxford, New York: Oxford University Press, 2000.

Purvis, Thomas L. "The European Ancestry of the United States Population, 1790: A Symposium." *William and Mary Quarterly* 41 (1984): 85–101.

Putnam, George. *The World's Progress: A Dictionary of Dates*. New York: Putnam, 1851.

Radway, Janice. "What's in a Name? Presidential Address to the American Studies Association, 20 November, 1998." *American Quarterly* 51.1 (1999): 1–32.

Ramírez, Susan. *Provincial Patriarchs: Land Tenure and the Economics of Power in Colonial Peru*. Albuquerque: University of New Mexico Press, 1986.

Ramsay, David. *Universal History Americanised; or, An Historical View of the World from the Earliest Records to the Year 1808. With a Particular Reference to the State of Society, Literature, Religion, and Form of Government, in the United States of America*. 9 vols. Philadelphia: M. Carey & Son, 1819.

Reinhold, Meyer. *Classica Americana: The Greek and Roman Heritage in the United States*. Detroit: Wayne State University Press, 1984.

"Revolt of the Netherlands." Partial reprint of *The Rise of the Dutch Republic*, by John Lothrop Motley. *Ladies Repository*, August 1856, 467–72.

Richards, Jeffrey H. Headnote to *The Gladiator*, by Robert Montgomery Bird. In *Early American Drama*, edited by Jeffrey H. Richards, 166–70. New York: Penguin Classics, 1997.

Ringe, Donald A. "*The Bravo*: Social Criticism in the Gothic Mode." *James Fenimore Cooper: His Country and His Art* 8 (1991): 124–34.

———. "New York and New England: Irving's Criticism of American Society." *American Literature* 38.4 (1967): 455–67.

Rink, Oliver. *Holland on the Hudson: An Economic and Social History of Dutch New York.* Ithaca, NY: Cornell University Press, 1986.

"*The Rise of the Dutch Republic.*" Review of *The Rise of the Dutch Republic*, by John Lothrop Motley. *Democratic Review*, August 1856, 71–79.

"*The Rise of the Dutch Republic.*" Review of *The Rise of the Dutch Republic*, by John Lothrop Motley. *Harper's New Monthly Magazine*, April 1856, 693–95.

"*The Rise of the Dutch Republic.*" Review of *The Rise of the Dutch Republic*, by John Lothrop Motley. *Harper's New Monthly Magazine*, May 1856, 769–79.

"*The Rise of the Dutch Republic.*" Review of *The Rise of the Dutch Republic*, by John Lothrop Motley. *Harper's New Monthly Magazine*, June 1856, 83–96.

"*The Rise of the Dutch Republic.*" Review of *The Rise of the Dutch Republic*, by John Lothrop Motley. *Littell's Living Age*, May 24, 1856, 449–64.

"*The Rise of the Dutch Republic.*" Review of *The Rise of the Dutch Republic*, by John Lothrop Motley. *Putnam's Monthly Magazine*, June 1856, 592–99.

Robbins, Royal. *The World Displayed.* New York: W. W. Reed, 1830.

Rostworowski de Diez Canseco, María. *History of the Inca Realm.* Translated by Harry B. Iceland. Cambridge: Cambridge University Press, 1999.

Roth, Martin. *Comedy and America: The Lost World of Washington Irving.* Port Washington, NY: Kennikat, 1976.

Rothman, David. *The Discovery of the Asylum: Social Order and Disorder in the New Republic.* Boston: Little, Brown, 1990.

Rowe, John Carlos. *Literary Culture and U.S. Imperialism: From the Revolution to World War II.* New York: Oxford University Press, 2000.

———. *The New American Studies.* Minneapolis: University of Minnesota Press, 2002.

———. "Nineteenth-Century United States Literary Culture and Transnationality." Special issue, *PMLA* 118 (2003): 78–89.

Rowson, Susanna. *Exercises in History, Chronology, and Biography, in Question and Answer. For Use of School. Comprising, Ancient History, Greece, Rome, &c. Modern History, England, France, Spain, Portugal, &c. The Discovery of America, Rise, Progress and Final Independence of the United States.* Boston: Richardson & Lord, 1822.

Rubin-Dorsky, Jeffrey. *Adrift in the Old World: The Psychological Pilgrimage of Washington Irving.* Chicago: University of Chicago Press, 1988.

Ryan, Susan M. *The Grammar of Good Intentions: Race and the Antebellum Culture of Benevolence.* Ithaca, NY: Cornell University Press, 2003.

Saldívar, José David. *The Dialectics of Our America: Genealogy, Cultural Critique, and Literary History.* Durham, NC: Duke University Press, 1991.

Sargent, Mark L. "The Conservative Covenant: The Rise of the Mayflower Compact in American Myth." *New England Quarterly* 61.2 (1988): 233–51.

Schachterle, Lance. "A Long False Start: The Rejected Chapters of Cooper's *The Bravo* (1831)." *Proceedings of the American Antiquarian Society* 115.1 (2006): 81–126.

Schoolcraft, Henry Rowe. *Inquiries Respecting the History, Present Condition, and Future Prospects of the Indian Tribes of the United States.* Philadelphia: Lippincott, Grambo, 1851.

Schoone-Jongen, Terence G. *The Dutch American Identity: Staging Memory and Ethnicity in Community Celebrations.* Amherst, NY: Cambia, 2008.

Schramm, Wilbur. "*Hiawatha* and Its Predecessors." *Philological Quarterly* 11.4 (1932): 321–43.

Schueller, Malini Johar. *U.S. Orientalisms: Race, Nation, and Gender in Literature, 1790–1890*. Ann Arbor: University of Michigan Press, 1998.

Scott, William B. *In Pursuit of Happiness: American Conceptions of Property from the Seventeenth to the Twentieth Century*. Bloomington: Indiana University Press, 1977.

Secor, Robert. "Ethnic Humor in Early American Jest Books." In *A Mixed Race: Ethnicity in Early America*, edited by Frank Shuffelton, 163–93. New York: Oxford University Press, 1993.

Sharp, James Roger. *American Politics in the Early Republic: The New Nation in Crisis*. New Haven, CT: Yale University Press, 1993.

Shell, Marc. *Art and Money*. Chicago: University of Chicago Press, 1995.

———. *Money, Language and Thought: Literary and Philosophical Economies from the Medieval to the Modern Era*. Berkeley: University of California Press, 1982.

Shepard, Elizabeth. *A Guide-book to Norumbega and Vineland; or, The Archaeological Treasures along Charles River*. Boston: Damrell & Upham, 1893.

Shields, John C. *American Aeneas: Classical Origins of the American Self*. Knoxville: University of Tennessee Press, 2001.

Sigourney, Mrs. L. H. [Lydia Huntley]. *Pocahontas and Other Poems*. New York: Harper, 1841.

Skaggs, Jimmy. *The Great Guano Rush: Entrepreneurs and American Overseas Expansion*. New York: St. Martin's, 1994.

Smith, Joshua Toulmin. *The Northmen of New England*. Boston: n.p., 1839.

Sollors, Werner. *Beyond Ethnicity: Consent and Descent in American Culture*. New York: Oxford University Press, 1986.

"*The Song of Hiawatha*." Review of *The Song of Hiawatha*, by Henry Wadsworth Longfellow. *North American Review*, January 1856, 272–75.

Spiller, Robert E. *Fenimore Cooper: Critic of His Times*. New York: Milton, Balch, 1931.

Spivak, Gayatri. *Death of a Discipline*. New York: Columbia University Press, 2003.

Sprunger, Keith. *Dutch Puritanism: A History of English and Scottish Churches of the Netherlands in the Sixteenth and Seventeenth Centuries*. Leiden: Brill, 1982.

St. John de Crèvecoeur, J. Hector. *Letters from an American Farmer and Sketches of Eighteenth-Century America*. Edited by Albert E. Stone. New York: Penguin Books, 1981.

Stott, Annette. *Holland Mania: The Unknown Dutch Period in American Art and Culture*. Woodstock, NY: Overlook, 1998.

———. "Inventing Memory: Picturing New Netherland in the Nineteenth Century." In *Revisiting New Netherland: Perspectives on Early Dutch America*, edited by Joyce D. Goodfriend, 13–39. Leiden: Brill, 2005.

Sundquist, Eric J. *Empire and Slavery in American Literature, 1820–1865*. Jackson: University Press of Mississippi, 2006.

Swierenga, Robert P. Introduction to *The Dutch in America: Immigration, Settlement and Cultural Change*, edited by Robert P. Swierenga, 1–11. New Brunswick, NJ: Rutgers University Press, 1985.

Taft, Kendall B. *Minor Knickerbockers: Representative Selections*. New York: American Book, 1947.

T.C.P. [Thomas Conrad Porter]. "To the Editors." *Daily National Intelligencer*, November 26, 1855.

Templin, Mary. "'Dedicated to Works of Beneficence': Charity as Model for a Domesticated Economy in Antebellum Women's Panic Fiction." In *Our Sisters' Keepers: Nineteenth-Century Benevolence Literature by American Women*, edited by Jill Bergman and Debra Bernardi, 80–104. Tuscaloosa: University of Alabama Press, 2005.

———. "Panic Fiction: Women's Responses to Antebellum Economic Crisis." *Legacy* 21.1 (2004): 1–16.

Thurin, Erik Ingvar. *The American Discovery of the Norse: An Episode in Nineteenth-Century American Literature*. Lewisburg, PA: Bucknell University Press, 1999.

Ticknor, George. *Life of William Hickling Prescott*. 1864. Reprint, Philadelphia: J. B. Lippincott, 1875.

Tilton, Eleanor M. "Holmes and His Critic Motley." *American Literature* 36.4 (1965): 463–74.

Trachtenberg, Alan. *Shades of Hiawatha: Staging Indians, Making Americans, 1880–1930*. New York: Hill & Wang, 2004.

Trafton, Scott. *Egypt Land: Race and Nineteenth-Century American Egyptomania*. Durham, NC: Duke University Press, 2004.

Trent, William, ed. *The Cambridge History of American Literature*. New York: G. P. Putnam's Sons, 1918.

Tuveson, Ernest Lee. *Redeemer Nation: The Idea of America's Millennial Role*. Chicago: University of Chicago Press, 1968.

"US Is Like Doomed Mayans: Gibson." *Australian*, September 27, 2006, 10.

Van Tassel, David D. *Recording America's Past: An Interpretation of the Development of Historical Studies in America, 1607–1884*. Chicago: University of Chicago Press, 1960.

Voss-Hubbard, Mark. *Beyond Party: Cultures of Antipartisanship in Northern Politics before the Civil War*. Baltimore: Johns Hopkins University Press, 2002.

Wallach, Alan. "Thomas Cole: Landscape and the Course of American Empire." In *Thomas Cole: Landscape into History*, edited by William H. Truettner and Alan Wallach, 23–111. New Haven, CT: Yale University Press, 1994.

Wallerstein, Immanuel Maurice. *Capitalist Agriculture and the Origins of the European World-Economy in the Sixteenth Century*. New York: Academic Press, 1974.

———. *Mercantilism and the Consolidation of the European World-Economy, 1600–1750*. New York: Academic Press, 1980.

Waples, Dorothy. *The Whig Myth of James Fenimore Cooper*. Yale Studies in English 88. [Hamden, CT]: Archon Books, 1968.

Wasserman, Renata R. Mautner. *Exotic Nations: Literature and Cultural Identity in the United States and Brazil, 1830–1930*. Ithaca, NY: Cornell University Press, 1994.

Webster, Clarence M. "Irving's Expurgation of the 1809 History of New York." *American Literature* 4.3 (1932): 293–95.

Wermuth, Thomas S. *Rip Van Winkle's Neighbors: The Transformation of Rural Society in the Hudson River Valley, 1720–1850*. Albany: State University of New York Press, 2001.

Wertheimer, Eric. *Imagined Empires: Incas, Aztecs, and the New World of American Literature, 1771–1876*. Cambridge: Cambridge University Press, 1999.

Wheaton, Robert. "Motley and the Dutch Historians." *New England Quarterly* 35.3 (1962): 318–36.

Whelpley, Samuel. *Compend of History*. Boston: Richardson & Lord, 1825.

———. *Historical Compend*. 2 vols. Morris-town, [NJ]: Henry P. Russell, 1806–7.

[Whipple, E. P.] Review of *History of the Conquest of Peru*, by William Hickling Prescott. *Methodist Quarterly Review* 30 (1848): 268–82.

White, Ed. "History as Literature." In *Oxford Handbook of Early American Literature*, edited by Kevin J. Hayes, 569–91. Oxford: Oxford University Press, 2008.

Whitman, Walt. "*The Gladiator*—Mr. Forrest—Acting." In *The American Theatre as Seen by Its Critics*, edited by Montrose J. Moses and John Mason Brown, 69–70. New York: Norton, 1934.

Widmer, Edward L. *Young America: The Flowering of Democracy in New York City*. New York: Oxford University Press, 1999.

Willard, Emma. *Universal History in Perspective: Divided Into Three Parts, Ancient, Middle, and Modern; Illustrated by a Series of Maps and Engravings, a Chronological Table, and Map of Time*. New York: A. S. Barnes, 1857.

———. *Willard's Historic Guide: Guide to the Temple of Time; and Universal History, for Schools*. New York: A. S. Barnes; Cincinnati: H. W. Derby, 1849.

Williams, Mentor. *Schoolcraft's Indian Legends*. East Lansing: Michigan State University Press, 1956.

Williams, Stanley T. *The Life of Washington Irving*. 2 vols. New York: Oxford University Press, 1935.

———. *The Spanish Background of American Literature*. 1955. Reprint, Hamden, CT: Archon Books, 1968.

Williams, Stephen. *Fantastic Archaeology: The Wild Side of North American Prehistory*. Philadelphia: University of Pennsylvania Press, 1991.

Wilson, Charles. *Queen Elizabeth and the Revolt of the Netherlands*. London: Macmillan, 1970.

Winterer, Caroline. *The Culture of Classicism: Ancient Greece and Rome in American Intellectual Life, 1780–1910*. Baltimore: Johns Hopkins University Press, 2002.

———. *The Mirror of Antiquity: American Women and the Classical Tradition, 1750–1900*. Ithaca, NY: Cornell University Press, 2007.

Winters, Yvor. "Fenimore Cooper or the Ruins of Time." In *James Fenimore Cooper: A Collection of Critical Essays*, edited by Wayne Fields, 16–36. Englewood Cliffs, NJ: Prentice-Hall, 1979.

Wish, Harvey. *The American Historian: A Social-Intellectual History of the Writing of the American Past*. New York: Oxford University Press, 1960.

Wood, Gordon S. *The Creation of the American Republic, 1776–1787*. Chapel Hill: University of North Carolina Press for Institute of Early American History and Culture, 1969.

Worcester, Joseph Emerson. *Elements of History*. Boston: Cummins, Hilliard, 1826.

Wright, Conrad Edick, ed. *American Unitarianism, 1805–1865*. Boston: Massachusetts Historical Society and Northeastern University Press, 1989.

Wright, Julia. *Ireland, India, and Nationalism in Nineteenth-Century Literature*. Cambridge: Cambridge University Press, 2007.

Index

References to people from a particular country of origin are indexed under the country's name (e.g., "the English" under "England" and "the Spanish" under "Spain"). Dutch people from the Netherlands, including those settled in the New Netherland colony, are indexed under "Netherlands, the," but the ethnic Dutch living in New York and New Jersey are indexed under "Dutch Americans." Languages (e.g., "Spanish," "Dutch") are indexed under "Language" and are broken out into specific subheadings.

Aaron, Daniel, 119, 138
Adams, John, 103
Adams, John Quincy, 66
Alexander, Gregory, 61
Alhalla (Schoolcraft), 145
Almagro, Diego de, 58
Alva, Duke of, 78, 80, 85, 94
American Adam, The (Lewis), 16
American Geography (Morse), 118
Americas (also "New World"), 10, 17, 18, 21, 26, 32, 45, 52, 58, 64, 82, 96, 120–24, 126, 129, 130, 136, 153, 156
Antelyes, Peter, 108
Antiquitates Americanae (Rafn), 123, 129
Apocalypto (Gibson), 19, 152–61
As You Like It (Shakespeare), 25–26
Athenaeum (London), 140, 142, 144
Athens of America, The (O'Connor), 16
Austria, 24, 37

Ballads and Other Poems (Longfellow). *See* Longfellow, Henry Wadsworth, works of
Bancroft, George, 12
Barnes, Geraldine, 130, 131
Baym, Nina, 13
Belgium, 92
Belknap, Jeremy, 100
Bell, Michael Davitt, 84
Bender, Thomas, 6
Bergland, Renée, 130
Bewley, Marius, 38
Bible, 86, 155
Billington, Ray, 88
Bird, Robert Montgomery, 4–5, 9, 16
Bradford, William, 82–83
Bradley, Elizabeth, 106
Bravo, The (Cooper). *See* Cooper, James Fenimore, works of
Brazil, 19
"Bridge, The" (Longfellow). *See* Longfellow, Henry Wadsworth, works of
Britain, 8, 10, 18, 19, 26, 30, 96–97, 100–102, 104, 105, 112, 136, 148–49. *See also* England
Brooks, Van Wyck, 76
Bruins, Elton, 104
Buell, Lawrence, 119
Bull, Ole, 123
Bush, George, 160

Caesar, Julius, 78
Callcott, George, 3, 11
Canada: Newfoundland, 149; Nova Scotia (Acadia), 132; Québec, 133
Caribbean, the (West Indies), 48, 126
Casey, Marion, 110
Charles I (of England), 82
Charles V (Holy Roman Emperor), 74, 75, 78, 89
Charlotte Temple (Rowson), 14

Charvat, William, 50, 66–67
"Children of the Last Supper, The" (Longfellow). *See* Longfellow, Henry Wadsworth, works of
China, 19, 42
Christian Intelligencer, 110
Choate, Rufus, 4
Civilis, Claudius (Gaius Julius), 78
Civil War, U.S., 47, 66, 67, 72, 86, 138, 148, 150
Class, 5, 15, 55–56, 160; aristocracy (Venetian and U.S.), 18, 21, 31, 32–35, 37–44; middle-class identity, 55; mobs as classed phenomenon, 31, 35, 37, 41, 43, 86, 88, 102, 150; the poor, 30, 46, 49–51, 53–54, 56, 58, 160; propertied classes, 52–54; working classes, 53, 54, 72. *See also* Cooper, James Fenimore; Prescott, William Hickling
Cohen, David, 110
Cole, Thomas, 31
Columbus, Christopher, 17, 120, 126, 128, 131, 154–56, 158–60
Communist Manifesto, The (Marx and Engels), 53
Complete History of Connecticut (Trumbull), 100
Condorcet, Marquis de, 25
Connecticut, 86, 100
Contact zone (esp. spatiotemporal form), 6–7, 9, 12, 16–17, 22, 39, 48, 57, 75–76, 85, 103, 125–26, 128, 147, 151–52
Conway, Moncure Daniel, 140–42, 144
Cooper, James Fenimore, 1, 11, 16, 17, 50, 52, 75, 112, 156, 160; America, imperial ascendance of, 18, 20–21, 23–25, 28–29, 30; cyclical history, 20–21, 25–26, 29–34; European travels, 6, 20, 23, 27, 43; Italy, imperial decline of, 18, 20–21, 23–31, 33, 36–37, 45; political views, 12, 15, 18, 21, 23, 37–44; republicanism, 32–35; socioeconomic attitudes, 15, 18, 21, 40–44, 47; theory of principles versus things, 21, 22–23, 39–41, 44; Whig attacks on, 39–43; Whig oligarchy, fears of, 18, 21, 23, 37–39
Cooper, James Fenimore, works of: *The Bravo*, 11, 18, 20–26, 30–45, 50; Effingham novels, 43; *The Headsman*, 22; *The Heidenmauer*, 22; Leatherstocking Tales, 22, 30; *A Letter to His Countrymen*, 21, 22–23, 37–43; *Precaution*, 39; *The Water-Witch*, 18, 20–31, 36, 43–44, 75, 112
Course of Empire, The (Cole), 31
Daily National Intelligencer, 140–41
Damrosch, David, 6, 7, 8
DeGuzmán, María, 10
Delabarre, Edmund, 130
Delaware, 100
Democratic Party (incl. Democratic-Republicans), 12, 15, 16, 21, 38, 39, 42, 63, 84–87, 102, 117
Democratic Review, 16, 84–87, 94–95
Denmark, 112, 121, 123
Dimock, Wai Chee, 7, 99, 122
Durant, Will, 152
Dutch Americans, 19, 97–99, 103–19, 138, 152
Dutch revolt from Spain, 10, 18, 74–83, 90, 94. *See also* William I

Edda, 140, 141, 143, 144
Edwards, O. D. [Owen Dudley], 91
Effingham novels (Cooper). *See* Cooper, James Fenimore, works of
Egypt, 42. *See* History, ancient history
England, 39, 40, 42, 75, 77–78, 81–83, 92, 93, 96, 100, 104, 109, 112, 142, 148–51; London (incl. Cheapside), 43, 140, 142. *See also* Britain
Eriksson, Leif, 120, 122–28, 131, 143
Esquisse d'un tableau historique des progrès de l'esprit humain (Condorcet), 25
Ethnicity. *See* Irving, Washington
Europe, 18, 19, 22–23, 26, 28, 29, 34, 40, 41, 43, 45, 49, 52, 56–57, 74, 91, 108, 119–121, 123, 124, 126, 128, 129, 131, 135–38, 140, 142–43, 147, 153, 154, 156–60. See also *individual countries*
Evangeline (Longfellow). *See* Longfellow, Henry Wadsworth, works of

Fabend, Firth, 104, 110, 114
Farmer, Jared, 138
Farnese, Alexander, 90
Federalists, 15, 32, 102, 117
Ferdinand II (of Aragon, the Catholic), 74
Ferguson, Robert, 103
Fillmore, Millard, 86
Finland, 19, 120, 121, 139–45
First Steps to the Study of History (Peabody), 14
Forrest, Edwin, 4

Fourier, Charles, 54
France, 1, 8, 10, 18, 19, 38, 42, 89, 92, 112, 133, 135–36, 139, 146–51; Paris, 30, 149. *See also* Gaul; New France
France and England in North America (Parkman), 148
Freiligrath, Ferdinand, 144
French and Indian War (Seven Years' War), 136, 148, 150

Gaul, 78, 90, 91
Gayangos, Pascual de, 52, 54, 56, 68
George III (of Great Britain), 77, 113, 150
Germany, 83, 85, 92, 110
Gibbon, Edward, 25, 101
Gibson, Mel, 19, 152–55, 160–61
Giles, Paul, 108
Gladiator, The (Bird), 4–5, 9
Goethe, Johann Wolfgang von, 140, 143, 144
Goodfriend, Joyce, 104
Gould, Edward Sherman, 41–43
Greece, ancient empire. *See* History, ancient history
Griffin, Susan, 88–89
Groen van Prinsterer, Guillaume, 78
Grossman, James, 29
Guarneri, Carl, 54–55, 56

Half-Century of Conflict, A (Parkman), 148
Hallam, Henry, 56
Harbinger, 54
Haroun Al Raschid (Harun al-Rashid), 140
Hawthorne, Nathaniel, 14, 16, 17, 54
Headley, Janet, 128
Headsman, The (Cooper). *See* Cooper, James Fenimore, works of
Heidenmauer, The (Cooper). *See* Cooper, James Fenimore, works of
Henry VI, Part 2 (Shakespeare), 43, 88
Hilen, Andrew, 132
Historiography: history as discipline in nineteenth century, 11–12, 91–93, 148; international audience for, 8, 77; popular audience for, 3, 13, 17, 47, 77, 93, 97, 134, 142, 153; regional differences in, 15–16, 100; research (esp. archival), 2, 6, 8–9, 11–13, 15, 52, 57–58, 77, 88, 89, 92, 115, 134, 152, 153; Romantic historians, 12, 51, 91, 148; women history writers, 13–15
History (major eras and frameworks for understanding): ancient history, 4–5, 9, 11, 25, 32–33, 78, 90, 91, 101, 111, 115; early modern history/domino pattern, 2–3, 9–11, 17–18, 19, 32–34, 45, 47, 74, 76–77, 96, 148, 150, 152; exceptionalism, belief in American, 3, 10, 25, 31–34, 38–39, 56, 78, 103, 148, 150–51; proto-national, colonial period treated as, 8, 82, 97, 99–100, 138; rise and fall of empires trope, 1, 3, 9–11, 15, 18, 20–21, 25, 31, 74, 97, 98, 101–2, 118, 135, 150; world history, definition of, 7; world history, importance of, 1, 3–4, 14, 52, 81, 151–52. *See also* Cooper, James Fenimore, cyclical history
History as Romantic Art (Levin), 12
History of New Hampshire (Belknap), 100
History of New York, A (Irving). *See* Irving, Washington, works of
History of the Conquest of Mexico (Prescott). *See* Prescott, William Hickling, works of
History of the Conquest of Peru (Prescott). *See* Prescott, William Hickling, works of
History of the Decline and Fall of the Roman Empire, The (Gibbon), 25, 101
History of the Reign of Ferdinand and Isabella, the Catholic (Prescott). *See* Prescott, William Hickling, works of
History of the Reign of Philip the Second, King of Spain (Prescott). *See* Prescott, William Hickling, works of
History of the United States (Bancroft), 12
Hobsbawm, Eric, 55
Horsford, Eben Norton, 123, 125, 127
Howe, Daniel Walker, 71, 93
Huston, James, 66
Hutchinson, Anne, 83

Iceland, 120, 121, 123, 125, 131, 139
India, 19, 26
Insko, Jeffrey, 100
Ireland, 85, 87, 91
Irmscher, Christoph, 133, 134, 145
Irving, Washington, 1, 11, 12, 16, 17, 18, 92, 119, 161; assimilation (esp. Anglicization), 97–98, 103–6, 111, 112, 114, 117–18; assimilation,

resistance to (esp. Batavianization), 97–98, 103, 105, 110–18; ethnicity as alienation, 19, 98, 103, 107–9, 111, 113–14, 116, 118; ethnicity as anachronism, 19, 98, 114–18; as Federalist, 102–3, 117; homogeneity/melting pot idea, 98, 112, 116; humor, function of, 99, 103, 110, 112, 115–16; New Netherland as foreign land, 8, 19, 97–101, 103, 107–9; urbanism versus ruralism, 98, 104, 105–6, 109–12, 117–18; vanishing as racist trope, 98, 108–10, 118, 119
Irving, Washington, works of: *A History of New York* (1809), 96–119, 138; *A History of New York* (1848), 102, 116; "The Legend of Sleepy Hollow," 97, 99; "Rip Van Winkle," 97, 113; *The Sketch Book of Geoffrey Crayon, Gent.*, 97
Isabella I (of Castile, the Catholic), 74
Italy, 6, 10, 20–21, 23–30, 33–36, 44, 94, 128; Florence, 20, 25; Naples, 24, 27–30; Rome, 20, 25; Sorrento, 27; Tuscany, 26; Venice, 1, 2, 3, 11, 17, 18, 20–27, 31, 33–40, 44, 45, 52, 75, 151–52, 156, 160. *See also* Cooper, James Fenimore

James I (of England), 82
Jackson, Andrew, 31, 38, 63
Jefferson, Thomas, 98, 102–3, 117
John, Richard, 125, 126

Kagan, Richard, 50
Kalevala, 19, 120, 121, 139–45, 147
Karlsefni, Thorfinn, 124, 125
Kieft, Wilhelmus, 100, 102, 107
Knickerbocker Magazine, 122
Kraus, Michael, 67
Kupperman, Karen Ordahl, 99

La Gasca, Pedro de, 67–69, 71
Language, 104; Algonquin, 129; Aramaic, 153; Dutch, 100, 104–6, 110–14; English, 8, 104, 110, 118, 133–35, 138, 146; Finnish, 19, 120, 139, 140, 142, 144, 145; French, 34, 41, 133–35, 138, 146; German, 134, 139, 140, 144, 145; Greek, 155; Hebrew, 153; Latin, 89, 90, 153; Ojibwan, 134–35, 138, 146; Swedish, 132, 146; Yucatec Maya, 153. *See also* Longfellow, Henry Wadsworth, translation and polyglot poetics
Las Casas, Bartholomé de, 64–69, 71
Laud, William, 82
Leatherstocking Tales (Cooper). *See* Cooper, James Fenimore, works of
"Legend of Sleepy Hollow" (Irving). *See* Irving, Washington, works of
Lenapehoking, 100
Letter to His Countrymen, A (Cooper). *See* Cooper, James Fenimore, works of
Levin, David, 12, 51, 89, 91
Levine, Robert, 38
Lewis, R. W. B., 16–17
Literary World, 16
Longfellow, Henry Wadsworth, 1, 11, 12, 17, 18, 83, 97, 152, 153, 157, 161; "discovery" of New World by Europeans as racist narrative, 120, 131; *Kalevala* plagiarism controversy, 19, 120–21, 139–45; land, competing claims on, 8, 19, 121, 132–33, 135–39, 146–47; landscape architecture, 121, 125–26, 127–28, 146–47; sectionalism, fears of, 138; translation and polyglot poetics, 6, 121, 132, 133–35, 138, 146, 147, 153; vanishing Indian trope, Longfellow's complicity with and resistance to, 19, 110, 119–22, 130–31, 137, 138, 144–47; Vinland theory, 19, 120, 122–31, 139, 143, 144, 147
Longfellow, Henry Wadsworth, works of: *Ballads and Other Poems*, 122; "The Bridge," 127; "The Children of the Last Supper," 132; *Evangeline*, 132; "The Skeleton in Armor," 122–23, 128–29, 130–31, 143; *The Song of Hiawatha*, 97, 110, 119–22, 129, 130, 131–47, 152, 153, 157; "Tegnér's *Frithiof's Saga*," 132, 146
Lönnrot, Elias, 139
Lowenthal, David, 9
Loyola, (Saint) Ignatius, 89
Luther, Martin, 79, 89

"Man in the Claret-Coloured Coat to His Countrymen, The" (Gould), 41–43
Manthorne, Katherine, 47
Marquette, Jacques, 135–36, 148
Marx, Karl, 53
Massachusetts, 4, 71, 81–82, 86, 88, 91, 124, 126; Boston, 16, 45, 50, 54, 74, 85, 123, 126, 127, 128, 148; Cambridge, 122, 123–124,

126, 127; Charlestown, 86; Concord, 78; Fall River, 122, 123, 129, 130; Lexington, 78; Plymouth, 82–83, 99; Salem, 83; Taunton, 130; Watertown, 123, 126
Matthiessen, F. O., 54
McWilliams, John, 83
Melville, Herman, 16, 17
Merry-Mount (Motley). *See* Motley, John Lothrop, works of
Meyers, Marvin, 56
Mexico, 6, 11, 48, 57, 69, 74; U.S. war with, 47–48, 69–70
Michigan, 133, 135, 146–47; Grand Marais, 133; Munising, 133; Sault Sainte Marie, 135
Miller, Angela, 128
Minnesota, 136, 137; Pipestone, 136
Missouri, 70
Montana, 137
Montcalm and Wolfe (Parkman), 148–51
Morse, Jedidiah, 117–18
Morton, Thomas, 83
Motley, John Lothrop, 1, 2, 6, 17, 18, 20, 96, 111, 148, 161; Anglo-Saxonism, 77–79, 81–82; anti-Catholicism, 18, 76, 80, 83, 85–91, 93–95; as historiographer, 11, 12, 77, 88–89, 91–93; Inquisition, 18, 74, 76, 78–81, 83, 85, 86, 88–89, 94–95; Know-Nothings, 18, 85–88, 94–95; Puritans, 76, 81–85, 88; religious tolerance, 18, 76–77, 79–85, 87–88, 90–91, 93–95; Revolutionary War, U.S., 76–79, 81–82, 94; Spanish imperial decline, 74–75, 78, 87, 95; as Unitarian, 83–84, 93–94
Motley, John Lothrop, works of: *Merry-Mount*, 83; *Rise of the Dutch Republic*, 18, 20, 74–96, 111; *Rise of the Dutch Republic*, reviews of, 84–88, 90–96
Mulkern, John R., 86
Murray, David, 110

Narrative of imperial eclipse: standard form of, 1–3, 8–9, 12, 17, 21, 24, 44, 45, 46, 48, 62, 84, 95, 102–3, 138, 148, 150–54; variations on, 20, 31, 75–76, 98–99, 103, 115–16, 119–20, 122, 125
Native Americans, 10, 17, 19, 22, 45, 74, 98, 109–10, 119–22, 128–32, 135–47, 150, 153; Aztec, 10, 47, 57; Blackfeet, 136–37; Crow, 136–37; Dakotah (Dakota), 133, 136–38, 161; Fox, 136–37; Lenape, 100; Maya, 19, 152–61; Mohegan, 132; Narragansett, 129, 132; Ojibway (Anishinaabe), 1, 2, 8, 10, 11, 18, 19, 120–22, 132–38, 146–48, 151–52, 161; Pequot, 132; Peru, indigenous peoples of (incl. Incas), 10, 18, 45–46, 48–52, 53–54, 57–65, 67–70, 73, 151–52
"Nattvardsbarnen" (Tegnér), 132
Nero, 78
Netherlands, the, 1, 2, 6, 8, 10, 11, 17, 18, 29, 43–44, 74–83, 85, 87–88, 90, 92, 93, 96–100, 102–4, 106, 108, 110–16, 118, 149, 150, 151, 161; Amsterdam, 83, 104; Antwerp (as part of Low Countries), 89; Friesland/Frisia, 78, 81; Leyden, 83; Walloon-dominated areas, 78, 90; Zealand, 78. *See also* Dutch Americans; Dutch revolt from Spain; Irving, Washington; Motley, John Lothrop; New Netherland; William I
New England, 8, 19, 84, 94, 99, 100, 103, 108, 109, 120–31, 144; declining importance of in nineteenth century, 123; literary culture of, 16, 54; Puritans, 76, 82–85, 88, 99, 126; racial tensions in, 128. See also *individual states*
New France, 11, 99, 135, 148, 150; Louisiana, 99
New Hampshire, 100
New Jersey, 19, 98, 104, 110–12, 114, 118; Jersey City (Communipaw), 111–15
New Netherland, 10, 11, 19, 96–108, 110, 113–16, 151–52, 161; New Amsterdam, 17–18, 96, 100, 102, 103, 113. *See also* New York
New York, and places in, 1, 4, 8, 16, 18, 19, 24, 27–30, 43–44, 71, 85–87, 93, 97–101, 103–4, 107–10, 112–13, 118; Albany, 109; Hudson River Valley, 31, 109; Long Island, 113; Manhattan, 28, 101, 107, 108, 109; Mohawk Valley, 114; New York City, 16, 20, 24, 105–6, 107, 109, 112; Tarrytown, 99
New York, topics regarding: increasing importance of in nineteenth century, 20, 24, 27–29; land ownership reforms in, 43–44, 71, 86; literary culture, 16; New England, rivalry with, 16, 100, 103, 108–9; New Netherland, relationship to, 8, 19, 97, 99–101
Nicholas (Saint), 105
North America, 19, 97, 99, 119, 139, 140, 142, 147, 148–49
North American Review, 83, 143

North, the (northern U.S. states), 69, 71, 72, 133, 138, 139, 152
North Dakota, 137
Northmen in New England, The (Smith), 130
Norway, 112, 120, 121, 123
Notes on the State of Virginia (Jefferson), 117
Núñez Vela, Blasco, 65, 69

Of Plymouth Plantation (Bradford), 82–83
Ojibway. *See* Native Americans
Owen, Robert, 54

Parkman, Francis, 11, 12, 18, 19, 148–51
Passion of the Christ, The (Gibson), 153
Peabody, Elizabeth Palmer, 14
Pennsylvania, 86, 110; Philadelphia, 16, 85
Peru, 1, 2, 10, 11, 17, 18, 45–53, 57–65, 67, 69–70, 73, 74, 151, 160; Lima, 59; Quito (as Incan conquest), 54; versus Mexico, 47–48. *See also* Prescott, William Hickling
Petrarch, Francesco, 141
Philbrick, Thomas, 29
Philip II (of Spain), 18, 74–78, 80, 81, 82, 84, 85, 87, 89, 93, 94
Pizarro, Francisco, 58–61
Pizarro, Gonzalo, 58, 59
Poe, Edgar Allan, 140
Politics, nineteenth-century U.S.: Congress, 18, 37–38, 66, 160; Free Soil Party, 71; Republican Party, 86. *See also* Democratic Party; Federalists; Motley, John Lothrop, Know-Nothings; Whigs
Porter, Thomas Conrad, 140–42, 146
Portugal, 130
Pratt, Mary Louise, 6
Precaution (Cooper). *See* Cooper, James Fenimore, works of
Prescott, William Hickling, 1, 6, 11, 12, 16–17, 18, 74, 77, 83, 92, 93, 148, 153, 160; abolition, 46–47, 48, 63–73, 79; communist movements in nineteenth-century United States, 46, 48, 52–57, 62, 66, 71–73; conquistadorial Peru, 46–48, 58–65, 67–70, 73; Incan Peru, 45–46, 48–54, 57–63, 70, 73; laissez-faire capitalism, 45–46, 50–51, 55–63, 70; Panic of 1837, 55–57, 63; on property, 18, 46–50, 52–54, 56–58, 61–67, 70–73; wealth and related social attitudes, 46, 50–51, 53, 55, 61–63, 67, 72; as Whig, 46–47, 56, 60–61, 63, 66, 69–72
Prescott, William Hickling, works of: *History of the Conquest of Mexico*, 45, 47, 65–66, 68–69, 74; *History of the Conquest of Peru*, 18, 45–54, 56–65, 67–70, 72–74; *History of the Reign of Ferdinand and Isabella, the Catholic*, 55, 74; *History of the Reign of Philip the Second, King of Spain*, 74
Putnam's Monthly Magazine, 142–43

Race, 4, 5, 64, 116; Anglo-Saxonism, 51, 77–79, 81–82, 120, 130. *See also* Irving, Washington, vanishing as racist trope; Longfellow, Henry Wadsworth; Native Americans; New England, racial tensions in
Rafn, Carl, 123, 129
Ramsay, David, 8, 12
Ranke, Leopold von, 92
Religion: Dutch Reformed Church, 104–5, 110–11; Puritans (incl. "Pilgrims"), 76, 81–85, 88, 99, 126; Quakers, 83; Roman Catholic Church (incl. Jesuits), 76, 79–80, 83, 85–86, 88–94, 128, 135–36, 139, 147; Protestants (esp. versus Catholics), 51, 76, 79–80, 82, 83, 85–86, 89–93, 136, 138; Unitarians, 83–84, 93–94. *See also* Motley, John Lothrop
Revolutionary War, U.S., 10, 30, 76–79, 81–82, 94, 105, 113–14, 149, 150
Rhode Island, 84, 126; Newport, 122, 124
"Rip Van Winkle" (Irving). *See* Irving, Washington, works of
Rise of the Dutch Republic, The (Motley). *See* Motley, John Lothrop, works of
Rome, ancient empire. *See* History, ancient history; Italy; Religion
Roth, Martin, 102, 108
Rowe, John Carlos, 6
Rowson, Susanna, 14–15
Ruines, Les (Volney), 25
Russia, 19, 42, 121

Safinia, Farhad, 154, 155, 160
Saint-Simon, Henri de, 54
Santayana, George, 4
Scandinavia, 19, 120–22, 123, 128, 131, 132,

139–43, 147; as a region, 121; Vikings, 19, 120–31, 143, 147, 152. See also *individual countries*
Schiefner, Anton, 139, 144, 145
Schoolcraft, Henry Rowe, 129, 144, 145
Schramm, Wilbur, 145
Scott, Walter, 42
Scott, William, 70, 72
Secor, Robert, 110, 112
Shakespeare, William, 25–26, 43, 88
"Skeleton in Armor, The" (Longfellow). *See* Longfellow, Henry Wadsworth, works of
Sketch Book of Geoffrey Crayon, Gent., The (Irving). *See* Irving, Washington, works of
Slavery, 86, 138; abolitionism, 17, 18, 46–48, 64–73, 79; encomienda system in Spanish Americas, 64–67; slave revolt, danger of, 4–5. *See also* Prescott, William Hickling
Smith, Joshua Toulmin, 130
Spain, 1, 2, 3, 6, 10, 11, 17, 18, 19, 45–48, 52, 58–65, 67, 70, 74–78, 81, 83, 86, 94–95, 96, 112, 149, 150, 152–61; Alta California (New Spain), 99; Castile, 58. *See also* Dutch revolt from Spain; Motley, John Lothrop; Philip II; Prescott, William Hickling; Slavery
Sollors, Werner, 114
Song of Hiawatha, The (Longfellow). *See* Longfellow, Henry Wadsworth, works of
Southern Literary Messenger, 91–92
Southern Quarterly Review, 87–88, 90–91, 94
South, the (southern U.S.), 66, 70–71, 133, 138, 139, 152
Stuyvesant, Peter, 100, 103, 105, 117
Sumner, Charles, 144
Sweden, 6, 100, 112, 120, 121, 132, 143, 144; New Sweden, 100
Switzerland, 83

Tasso, Torquato, 27–28
Tawney, R. H., 51
Tegnér, Esaias, 132, 146
"Tegnér's *Frithiof's Saga*" (Longfellow). *See* Longfellow, Henry Wadsworth, works of
Textbooks, 1, 3, 11, 13–15, 101, 117–18, 151
Tiberius, 78
Time Magazine, 160
Titelmann, Peter, 80–81
Trumbull, Benjamin, 100
Turkey, 42
Turner, Nat, 4
Twiller, Wouter Van, 100, 103, 107

Universal History Americanised (Ramsay), 8, 12
Universal History in Perspective (Willard), 1

Velasco, Juan de, 54
Venice. *See* Italy
Vermont, 71
Vikings. *See* Scandinavia
Virginia, 4, 8
Volney, Constantin-François, 25

Wallach, Alan, 31
Waples, Dorothy, 42
War of 1812, 136
Washington, DC, 42
Washington, George, 76, 77, 79, 81, 94, 113
Water-Witch, The (Cooper). *See* Cooper, James Fenimore, works of
Weber, Max, 51
Webster, Daniel, 71–72, 103
Western Hemisphere. *See* Americas
West River Bridge Company v. Dix, 71–72
West, the (western United States), 25–26, 53, 56, 63, 71, 109, 119, 136–37; Midwest, 8, 99, 123, 131
Whelpley, Samuel, 3
Whigs, 4, 15, 16, 18, 21, 37–42, 46–47, 52, 56, 60–61, 63, 66, 69–72, 79, 103, 152
White, Ed, 100
Whitman, Walt, 16, 17
Widmer, Edward, 16
Willard, Emma, 1, 3, 9–10, 14, 25
William I (of Orange, the Silent), 75–85, 87, 90, 91, 93, 94, 102
William III (of England), 75
Williams, Roger, 83, 84
Williams, Stephen, 130
Winthrop, John, 88
Wisconsin, 136, 137
Wood, Gordon, 32–33
World history. *See* History

Young America (Widmer), 16